TAKE STOCK

A ROADMAP TO PROFITING FROM

YOUR FIRST WALK DOWN WALL STREET

ELLIS TRAUB

DEARBORN™
TRADE

A **Kaplan Professional** Company

This publication is designed to provide accurate and authoritative information in regard to the subject matter covered. It is sold with the understanding that the publisher is not engaged in rendering legal, accounting, or other professional service. If legal advice or other expert assistance is required, the services of a competent professional person should be sought.

Vice President and Publisher: Cynthia A. Zigmund
Senior Managing Editor: Jack Kiburz
Interior Design: Lucy Jenkins
Cover Design: KTK Design Associates
Typesetting: Elizabeth Pitts

Library of Congress Cataloging-in-Publication Data

Traub, Ellis.
    Take stock! : a roadmap to profiting from your first walk down Wall
Street / by Ellis Traub.
        p.   cm.
    ISBN 0-7931-4149-4
    1. Investments. 2. Stocks. 3. Portfolio management.   I. Title.
    HG4521   .T683 2001
    332.63'22—dc21
                                                                00-010601

Dearborn Trade books are available at special quantity discounts to use as premiums and sales promotions, or for use in corporate training programs. For more information, please call the Special Sales Manager at 800-621-9621, ext. 4514, or write to Dearborn Financial Publishing, Inc., 155 North Wacker Drive, Chicago, IL 60606-1719.

DEDICATION

To Dianne, who told me I could; and to David, who told me I should.

CONTENTS

ACKNOWLEDGMENTS

In addition to those close to me to whom this book is dedicated, many people had a part to play in making this book happen.

Certainly George Nicholson and Tom O'Hara deserve the credit for devising a simple and successful investment methodology and having the vision and selfless determination to build an organization to share it with the rest of the world—the National Association of Investors Corporation (NAIC). Ken Janke must surely be recognized for his steady stewardship of that organization for more than three decades.

I want to express my deep gratitude to Phil Keating, constant friend and mentor, for introducing me to NAIC and shepherding me through my latter-day education.

My thanks also go to Don Danko, longtime editor in chief of *Better Investing* magazine, and his worthy colleague, Mark Robertson, both of whom have inspired and encouraged me to stay focused on the purity of the mission—to empower everyman to invest successfully—as they have so faithfully.

I'd like to also single out Ralph Seger, Peggy Schmeltz, Betty Taylor, and Herb Barnett, who, along with those above, thoughtfully responded to my request to share their approach toward making some of the more critical judgment decisions that arise in the course of studying a stock. While we are saving their written responses for another purpose, their views certainly contributed to this offering.

Nancy Isaacs and scores of others on NAIC's I-Club list were delightful motivators—insisting that this book was high on their wish list. Late in the game, acting as the consummate surrogate for my intended readership, Nancy became an invaluable contributor.

My thanks to Doug Gerlach for willingly sharing his experience and contacts as a published author with me. And I'm especially grateful to Nikki Ross, who sought some help from me when she began her project and who returned that help in spades when I started mine. It's a privilege to share ideas, publishers, and editors with her.

Of course, I must thank Cynthia Zigmund for her help, encouragement, and the normal hand-holding that I presume editors must do.

I want to express my appreciation for the many and varied contributions that the team at Inve\$tWare has made to this offering. In producing the software within such a limited time, David Traub again did the impossible—at no small cost to his and Mary's quality of life. I must also highlight Bryan Wilson's and Josh Prager's contributions to producing that miracle. Shirley Knudsen and Irving Roth have been great contributors from their depth of NAIC experience. Richard Bennett, Kurt Hagerbaumer, and Mirna Alfaro, also added much in a wide variety of significant ways.

And my wife, Dianne, turned out to be not only my main supplier of moral support but a very capable and relentless resident editor as well, for which I must add my gratitude.

Why You Need This Book

What makes this book better than—or even different from—any other investment book? After all, there are thousands of them out there competing for your attention.

First of all, it's about something you've likely never heard of—*technamental investing*. Actually, the only thing new about this discipline is its name. Its roots are embedded in a methodology that's been practiced with enormous success by more than 5 million investors for nearly a half century. First taught by the original founders of the National Association of Investors Corporation (NAIC), George A. Nicholson Jr., Thomas E. O'Hara, Frederick C. Russell, and a few others, it's been spread across the nation—around the world, in fact—by a zealous corps of volunteers.

Technamental investing has been referred to at various times as "growth/value," "long-term," "fundamental," "buy and hold," or simply "NAIC-type" investing; even NAIC has not put a name to it. But each of the above terms describes a facet of technamental investing. I've coined that term because, in my opinion, it captures the essence of what we do. And what we do needs a name.

The investment community likes to make a sharp distinction between fundamental analysis and technical analysis, as well it should, because they are as far apart in practice as heaven and hell. Technical analysis involves graphing and visually analyzing the movement and volume of the overall market and the prices of its individual stocks. Over the years, scores of hopeful amateurs and erudite academics have sought—and have even named—repetitive price and volume patterns in an effort to find some consistent relationship between the historical movement of stock prices and their future movement. They've had little success.

Fundamental analysis is the study of the fundamentals of companies—their actual operation and financial condition. Without question, the changes in a company's fundamentals—its revenues, earnings, profit margins, and other data that address the lifeblood of a company—can have an enormous impact on the future performance of a stock. Patterns here can easily be seen, are not at all hard to interpret, and have a great deal of predictive value.

The "technical" component of technamental investing is the use of charts and visual analysis. It capitalizes on the belief that pictures are indeed worth thousands of words—and volumes of numbers. It puts the fun back into fundamental analysis, which seems to have become unnecessarily sophisticated and too mysterious for the average person.

My challenge is to cut the fundamentals down to size and make them simple enough for a grade-school kid or his grandma to understand. By explaining technamental analysis, which converts much of the mysterious stuff into pictures, hopefully I've met that challenge here.

The second reason this book is a must is that it is virtually the only book on the shelves that presents a demonstrably successful and elegantly simple investment discipline—*simply.*

The third reason is that investing—making money in the stock market—should be neither dangerous, tedious, nor time consuming. It should be fun! This book should entertain you as you learn how to become financially successful.

NAIC, a nonprofit organization, was launched in 1951. Perhaps one of the better-kept national secrets, the association has always been a bit bashful about blowing its own horn. (I think it's time to do a little crowing on its behalf!)

Its wonderful volunteers, in more than 110 chapters across the country, put on more than 10,000 events annually. The events' sole purpose is to convince people who are afraid of the stock market that they don't need to be—to empower people to make their own decisions about what stocks to buy and how long to hold on to them.

Small wonder that the financial press seems to pretend that this evangelical movement isn't there. It's understandable that publicity is rare concerning an organization whose approach and mission would deprive so many professionals of their fees.

Only when a maverick like Peter Lynch comes along and devotes a chapter of a bestseller like *Beating the Street* to extolling NAIC's virtues, or when the Beardstown Ladies make a splash, do the phones ring off the walls at NAIC's headquarters in Madison Heights, Michigan. Otherwise, it's hard to even find mention in the regular press about the monthly events that NAIC chapters sponsor at low cost or free of charge.

While I give full credit to NAIC for introducing me to the philosophy behind technamental investing, I make no claim that the organization approves, endorses, or even agrees with my interpretation of its methods or with my approach. NAIC did commission my company to develop its official software to electronically implement its methods; and I suppose that might entitle us to some such credential. But I seek neither NAIC's approval nor its endorsement.

I am sincerely grateful to NAIC for having made a huge difference in my life, and I am hopeful that this book will do all that is possible to stimulate public interest in that organization and to attract members and volunteers to its ranks. Being a part of NAIC is the best way I know for you to learn the ropes and to follow up on what you will learn from this book. The organization offers countless resources to those who want to acquire wealth on their own.

I don't expect you to take anything on faith. NAIC members who have followed their organization's methods diligently have been able to pick four out of five winners and have been able to double their money every five years. This is an established fact and is part of NAIC lore.

However, I challenge you to weigh what you're about to read on the scales of logic and common sense. Ask yourself whether what you are reading makes sense to you. If it does, then look for the flaws. Only after you find that you can't poke holes in the logic should you put the principles to work for yourself and "put your money where *our* mouth is."

What you are about to read should both inspire and educate you. In Chapter 1 I'll tell you just why a college dropout like me, with no education in finance, is the logical person to write this book.

Then in Chapter 2 I'll go to work. I'll tell you that common stocks are the most lucrative investment you can make, and I'll explain why.

In Chapter 3 I'll convince you that you can do it, that technamental investing is not beyond you or over your head, and in Chapter 4 I'll prove my point by introducing you to the only ten terms you need to know.

Chapter 5 builds on the terms you have learned and introduces you to the concept of growth, which is central to technamental investing.

In Chapter 6 I'll tell you where to find candidates for consideration and how to select them—what you should look for, what you should avoid.

Chapters 7 and 8 apply what you learned about growth to help you decide if a company is of good enough quality for you to consider buying its stock.

Chapter 9 deals with management's "report card," which enables you to assess management's ability to maintain the company's winning track record.

Assessing the quality of your prospective investment is the most important task; however, a good stock at a price that is too high is not a good investment. Chapter 10 leads you through the steps required to analyze the potential reward of buying a particular stock, to assess the risk involved, and to determine what a fair price would be.

In Chapter 11 I'll tell you how to compare companies that you're interested in to find out which would be the best stock to add to your portfolio.

Chapter 12 covers portfolio management. With these easily employed defensive and offensive technamental strategies, you can ensure that your entire portfolio doesn't suffer from the misfortunes that can befall any specific stock you own, and you can achieve the highest return possible.

Finally, Chapter 13, "Finer Points and 'Fudge Factors,'" deals with the things that I left out of the basic explanation because they aren't necessary and can be confusing or misleading. The chapter includes some of the strategies that you might later use to fine-tune your investing process, and it does so with the warning that you should use them with great care.

Most readers have a computer of their own or have one available. I want to stress, however, that this book does not exclude people who don't have access to a computer. These methods are just as valid for people who are equipped with only a pencil, a ruler, and a financial calculator. Technamental investing is a little easier for those with computers because computers are faster and more accurate. However, in Appendix A I have provided all of the instructions necessary for the pencil-and-paper investor to do the things that computer users do. You'll find a roadmap to the data, a clear description of the arithmetic (it's not even math), and a guide to the printed forms that make it easy for you to accomplish the tasks involved.

I conclude with notes on the software that is available to implement technamental investing (Appendix B), and I recommend some books to supplement your learning.

I hope that this introduction to technamental investing will be an enjoyable and profitable adventure for you, and I wish you well on your journey.

CHAPTER 1

Look Who's Talking!

First, let me tell you why I think I'm qualified to write this book and why I'm presumptuous enough to offer you advice about investing.

Right off the bat, I'll tell you what I'm not. I am not an MBA, a CFA, or a CFP. My letterhead doesn't include a wake of alphabet soup trailing after my name. I'm not a professional money manager, a securities analyst, a college professor, or a stockbroker. In fact, I don't even have a degree! I did attend college, but I dropped out of Harvard when the Korean War broke out in 1951.

Determined to postpone my education until I could figure out what I really wanted to do for a living, I applied for both the Air Force and the Navy pilot training programs and opted to train with the Navy. Later I took my commission in the U.S. Marine Corps, with which I served in the Korean theater as an all-weather fighter pilot. Fortunately for me, the war ended before I saw any serious action.

I returned to school in 1956, this time to Cornell University, where I studied hotel administration. Again my interests changed, and although I was on the dean's list, I left to fly for Eastern Airlines, embarking on a career that spanned the next 31 years. I also became a spokesman for the Air Line Pilots Association

(ALPA) and handled public relations for that organization in South Florida for 14 years.

Frustrated by the responses that I received from management when I tried to suggest ideas to improve the company's operations, I started a movement to infuse participative management into Eastern's corporate culture. When Frank Borman, then Eastern's chairman and CEO, later made the effort to effect such a cultural change, I worked actively with Eastern's consultants, picking up yet another set of skills.

Eventually disheartened by the continuing impasse between labor and management, and dismayed at the direction that my cherished profession had taken, I retired from Eastern in 1988, three years before my age would have forced me to. Armed with glowing testimonials from both Borman and his adversary, Charles Bryan, the head of the combative machinists' union, I hung out my shingle as a management consultant in labor relations, community relations, and conflict management.

It was at that point that I again made a midcourse correction in my eclectic career and discovered the investment philosophy that changed my life forever.

My past investing experience had been nothing short of a disaster. Years earlier, in 1972, with four sons nearing college age, I had realized that my savings were inadequate to finance their education. I had neither put aside enough money to provide for it, nor properly managed the money I had saved.

Nineteen seventy-two was an election year, and I had become actively interested in the presidential campaign. One of the campaign workers I met was a stockbroker for a major firm. Thinking that he might be able to help with my financial predicament, I asked my new friend for some guidance.

His advice was this: "Since it's an election year, you should invest your savings in a hot stock and hold it until about two weeks before the election. The incumbents will do everything in their power to keep the economy strong as long as possible, so you can't go wrong. Sell your stock just before the election, and you'll be in clover!"

I not only invested all of my savings in a rapidly rising stock, I borrowed on those holdings to buy more, and then borrowed more money on my signature to put into my prize investment. What did I know?

Of course I had gambled and I lost. When shortly before the election I finally sold my holdings, I, along with half of Wall Street, found that I had taken a bath. All I had left was my considerable debt, my house, and, fortunately, a good job. Worst of all, the experience scared me out of the stock market for the next 15 years.

Fortunately, I didn't have access to my retirement fund in 1972, or I might have lost all of that as well. When I left Eastern many years later, most of my pension was intact, and I elected to accept it as a lump sum. Once again, I ventured into the stock market. This time, I was intent on *learning* what I needed to know to be successful. So I formed a committee consisting of two other people and myself. One member was another young, but far more knowledgeable and ethical, stockbroker. The second was my accountant.

The modus operandi was to be that we would make no decision unless it was unanimous. I believed that I could learn something from discussions involving the pros. As it worked out in practice, however, I would receive a call from Bill (the accountant) saying that he thought I should buy a certain stock. I would then call John (the broker) and ask what he thought. John would say, "Sounds like a good idea to me!" So I would buy the stock. Not much of an education there!

After about a year and a half of this process, and with all of my money invested, I sat at my computer to assess my progress and plot the trend. Sadly I discovered that if I continued to invest as I had been, in about nine years I'd be living under a bridge!

This happened on a Saturday. On the following day an article appeared in the paper written by Jim Russell, then the financial editor for the *Miami Herald.* At the end of the article Russell mentioned that on the following Saturday the National Association of Investors Corporation (NAIC) was offering a seminar on how to evaluate common stocks. (NAIC is a nonprofit membership organization whose goal is to empower both investment club members and individual investors to invest successfully in common stocks.)

That next Saturday my life radically changed. I spent four hours listening to Phil Keating, an investment professional and one of the 3,000-plus volunteers across the country who unselfishly donate their time to NAIC, talk about the organization's methodology. Amazed at the method's elegant simplicity and at the cross section of people who attended and learned (there were no rocket scientists there), I sat entranced.

When I returned home that afternoon, I sat at my computer and entered all of the formulas and calculations I had just learned into a spreadsheet. By that night I was able to duplicate the tasks required to analyze a stock for prospective purchase.

From then on I was hooked. I attended workshops, learned the methodology well enough to teach it, and then volunteered to instruct others. My computer spreadsheet became more and more elaborate until it grew into a program called Take $tock, which embraced the NAIC methodology and included a few embellishments of my own. Not long thereafter I was invited to join NAIC's national computer organization, and NAIC asked me to let them sell my software.

Take $tock was so successful that NAIC invited me to develop its own official software product, and the Investor's Toolkit was born. Today about 50,000 investors use the toolkit, and each day another 20 to 30 join their ranks.

I continue to serve NAIC, now a 750,000-member organization, as a volunteer and as a frequent speaker at its events across the country. In 1999 I was privileged to be the closing speaker at both of NAIC's national conventions.

Whereas once I was concerned about how long I might live before my funds ran out, now I could live forever—at least in terms of financial security. And today I chalk it all up to what I learned from NAIC.

My company, Inve$tWare Corporation, now employs nine people. I have written this book hoping that the hundreds of thousands of others who know no more than I did back in 1972 might learn how to "Take $tock" and be successful investors without having to experience the angst that I did.

So that's who I am and why you have this book in your hand. Education, after all, is nothing more than a jump start on experience. It allows us to learn from others' experiences so that we don't have to start from scratch. I hope that what I've written here will serve that purpose for you.

LET'S TAKE STOCK OF
The Mistakes I Made

Remember the kids' puzzle in the Sunday comics: "How many errors can you spot in this picture?" Here are my most significant mistakes, from which you can learn as I did:

- Not starting at an early age to put aside "untouchable" money for the future

- Not properly investing the money I did put aside

- Looking for advice from an unqualified person

- Taking that advice

- Investing all of my savings in a single "hot" stock

- Borrowing on those holdings

- Gambling with my remaining credit

- Selling because of the price of the stock rather than the performance of the company

- Staying away from the stock market after my disastrous first experience

Unfortunately, these are the kinds of mistakes that we don't know are mistakes until it's too late and we suffer for them. Hopefully this book will help you to avoid the same mistakes before you, too, have to suffer. Better yet, perhaps this book will help you to accumulate wealth and become financially secure by taking the right steps before it's too late.

CHAPTER 2

Why Take Stock?

There are gazillions of investments to put your money into, so why should you be interested in stocks?

If my assumption is correct, that you're interested in making money with your money and not simply indulging your ego with ownership—be it a painting or a professional ball team—then owning stocks is where it's at.

There are few things in which you can invest that are alive. Diamonds, though they sparkle, are dead. Paintings, whether of still lifes or live models, are said to have life, if they're well done, but they lie dormant as they increase in value. Most of these "dead" objects increase in price because the dollars that were initially paid for them are the equivalent of more dollars today. In other words, inflation drives up the prices of inanimate objects. In addition to inflation, the relative scarcity of the kind of item you're holding will increase the perception of its value, so the price will increase as the item's perceived value increases. Sad but true, the value of a painting rises nicely when the artist dies.

Even bonds or Treasury bills that pay a fixed amount of interest are reasonably stable in price, except when interest rates fluctuate and the bonds are sold or purchased above or below their original price. Again, interest-rate changes, like inflation, do not add real value to an investment.

WHAT IS MONEY AND HOW IS IT MADE?

To fully understand the significance of investing in something "live," which is central to technamental investing, let's take a quick run through something that you probably know but haven't thought much about. In order to build my case, I'm going to start at a point where everyone is in agreement—as rudimentary as it may be. So here goes.

Meet Oog and Mog. Oog was a fellow who lived in a cave when that lifestyle was the equivalent of living in our modern-day suburbia. Now Oog wasn't the hunter that Mog was. In fact, he couldn't run as fast or jump as high as Mog. If the truth were known, Oog was scared to death of saber-toothed tigers. But he had a special skill. He could make a heck of an arrowhead out of stone. And he learned to wrap it tightly on a pole, creating a mean spear.

Mog, on the other hand, was all thumbs when it came to tapping stones. He couldn't wrap the thongs around the poles; he simply didn't have the patience for it. But he was as brave as he was clumsy, and he was a heck of a hunter.

You already see where I'm going with this. Oog would make the spears for Mog, and Mog would give him meat in return. And this was how the concept of money began—with barter. One person would do something of value for another person, who would give back something of value to the first person.

Years later, Oog's and Mog's descendants began to exchange tokens. These stones or animal teeth were nothing more than a convenient way to barter. Tokens evolved into coins (introduced by the Lydians in the 7th century B.C.), and later into currency, or money (first introduced in China and many centuries later in late 18th-century France). As civilization progressed and goods and services proliferated beyond the point where people could meet at a marketplace and conduct their barter, money made it possible for each person to do what he or she did best when it was most convenient to do it. People could store up credits and use them for goods or services when the time was right.

The concept of currency has taken a beating in recent years as governments have postponed immediate trouble by printing more of it, by borrowing against future confiscation through taxation, and by otherwise cheapening its real value. Still, nothing has really changed since Oog's time. The real value of money, and the way it is made, is timeless. To make money—to really create money and not just pass it around or diminish its value—one has to do one of two things: add value to a resource or provide a service that is of value to someone else.

Adding value. Charlie, a construction worker, goes to work one morning and is told to dig a hole that measures four feet deep by four feet wide by four feet long. He finishes the task by noon.

When he comes back from lunch, his boss tells him that he's sorry, but the morning's work was a mistake. His job for the afternoon is to go get the dirt and sod and to make the hole he has just spent the morning digging disappear.

At the end of the day, when the afternoon's task has been completed, will Charlie have made any money?

Charlie will *earn* money—he certainly deserves to be paid for his sweat and strain—he will not have *made* anything! The wage paid to him for his effort will be a loss because it will add no value to any resource, nor will it provide a service of any value to anyone—not even his boss or his company.

To paraphrase a saying, "It's the output, stupid!" What is worth the money is the value of what is *produced*, not the value of the input it took to produce it. (Wouldn't labor relations take a different direction if all parties thoroughly understood *that* concept!)

Providing a service. Again, the key to the creation of wealth is adding value to a resource, or providing a service that is of value and accumulating the rewards for doing so. Making steel out of ore, machining a part out of steel, building an automobile out of parts, and selling that automobile to the public—all are examples of adding value or providing a service. Manufacturing, information services, transportation, construction—whatever business you are in—must add value or provide a service that entices or induces someone who benefits from that value or service to pay for it.

It's rarely possible to add actual value to collectible objects or to income instruments such as corporate or government bonds. For that reason collectibles and bonds don't have nearly the investment potential that you'll find in a business.

STARTING A BUSINESS

A business, on the other hand, is created for the sole purpose of adding value or performing services of value. Therefore, being in business is the key to the creation of wealth.

An entrepreneur dreams up an idea for something that she thinks will be of value, then follows through on it. Whether she's providing a product or a service, the enterprise involves substantial risk. No one can accurately predict how much demand there will be until the product or service is available, and no one can predict the cost of making it available until that cost has been paid. Nor can anyone predict whether demand for the product or service will last long enough for the entrepreneur to recover her investment.

Taking an idea from its birth in the brain to its tangible realization takes guts, intimacy with the product or service, and usually a whole lot of capital. Unfortunately, according to studies made for the U.S. Department of Commerce, more new companies go belly-up than survive.

That's why those who provide venture capital and start-up money to a new business demand and receive a sizeable chunk of the business and a substantial portion of the reward. And that's why you don't want to put your life's savings into someone else's new business. Even if the reward for picking a winner is fantastic, the chance of picking that winner is slim indeed. So leave the financing of new companies to those who know that business, who deal regularly with the odds, and who can afford the risk.

BUYING A BUSINESS

How about buying a business that's already successful? Maybe that's the ticket. Most of the initial risk is gone and the concept has already been proven. Instead of being 80 percent against you, the odds are somewhat more favorable.

Of course, the cost of buying such a business, now that the initial concerns have been laid to rest, would be much greater since someone has already assumed the greater part of the risk and has done all of the start-up work.

Let's assume for the moment, however, that you have enough money to buy a business outright. You'll then have to think about the management of that business. Will the original founder, owner, or staff stay on? Or will you have to take over the business and manage it? Is it a business you know something about? If the need arose, would you be able to manage it successfully on your own?

What are your skills? Are they in the domain of the product or service that the company provides? Or are they in the area of business management? Personnel management? Marketing? Would you know enough about the results each aspect of the business should achieve to hold the appropriate people's feet to the fire?

Are you prepared to take the risks that still remain? There will be many. Businesses are not static. They and the economic environment that surrounds them can change at the drop of a hat or the utterance of a politician.

Aggressive competition, the loss of a key management person, a marketing misstep, a sustained downswing in the economy, a public relations gaffe, and product obsolescence are but a few of the host of things that can torpedo a business.

The rewards of owning a business are considerable, but there are still plenty of risks, not the least of which are those revolving around liability and litigation—especially in today's world.

Each step you take to decrease risk decreases your reward at the same time. But you're still looking at the real benefits of adding value to create money and wealth, which is what a business does.

Perhaps it would be worthwhile to share the risk and the management responsibility with a partner or partners. Whatever money and skills you don't bring to the table, maybe other individuals could.

If you take on a partner or partners, however, you take on additional risks. Many partnerships just don't work out because too much disagreement develops over management or finance issues, or over the direction the company should take. Besides, taking on partners still doesn't remove the risk of litigation. Don't forget, as a partner you can be sued for everything you own, not just for what you have invested in the company.

If you want to share the business risks *and* eliminate the risk of liability, the answer is the corporation. With a corporation you can own the business or a part of it, share the risks, and limit your liability to just the extent of your ownership. This is by far the safest way to harness the ability of a business to add value and create wealth—your wealth. And owning an already successful corporation will probably swing the odds around to your favor.

Evaluating the Business

So what's your desired corporation worth? You need to figure out a way to determine how much to pay for it.

First of all, you need to hire a competent accountant or analyst to look at the books. You wouldn't want to just take anyone's word that the company's strong. And you would want to make sure that the books have been audited. These things require a professional.

You then need to look at the value of the machinery and property that the business owns, knocking off something for wear and tear and obsolescence. And you want to know whether the business is profitable and to ensure that it doesn't owe more money than it can comfortably afford to pay out of income. All of this comes from the company's financial statements, which you'll find reduced to their simplest terms in Chapter 4.

All of the above notwithstanding, the most important determination you need to make is an assessment of how profitable the business can be for you. The bottom line (quite literally) is an evaluation of how quickly you'll get your investment back and start making money yourself. Whether you put the profit back in your pocket or let the business retain it, you'll start making money only after the business has recovered the cost of your original investment.

Negotiating the Price

You'll need to know how much of a profit the business makes each year, and you'll negotiate a price that is some multiple of that. Depending upon the kind of business, there are rules of thumb that suggest what conventional wisdom considers to be a fair multiple. Some businesses are typically valued at five times their earnings, and others at only three. There's no hard-and-fast rule beyond fair market value: the price at which there is a willing seller and a willing buyer. But whatever the price that is paid for a business, it translates into a multiple of the company's profits.

If you want to buy someone else's business and assume all of the responsibilities for running it as well as its risks and liabilities, multiples of three to five times the annual profit are about par for the course. And you will wind up paying something over and above the sticker price in the form of sweat equity: you will be doing the work and handling the responsibilities yourself.

Let's say that you are willing to pay three times last year's profit for a company that is capable of producing that profit year after year, a somewhat conventional multiple. After three years, you will have recovered your investment, and from then on everything will be gravy.

However, just think of what would happen if the profits were growing each year before your purchase instead of just remaining the same. Certainly the price that you'd expect to pay for the business would be higher because it would be a much more valuable business to start with. You would probably be willing to pay as much as five or six times last year's profit if it would still take you only three years to recover your investment and start making money. Thus, a fair multiple of profits is, in a sense, a measure of time: "How long will it take me to recover my investment?"

When you look at a business that is successful, that is increasingly profitable and is well managed by a team of accomplished professionals, and that will insulate you from the business's risks and liabilities because of its status as a corporation, you must expect—and will be willing—to pay a whole lot more.

To sum up, each of the levels of business participation I've described above represents a reduction in risk; but it also represents an increase in the price of participation. To enjoy the greatest reward with the least risk, you should own a corporation—or a share of one and thus share the risk by sharing ownership with other investors. You would limit your liability to just the value of your investment. Your ownership would be based upon the amount of stock that you hold in the corporation, and you wouldn't have to worry about losing your home if someone sued the business. You would hire or retain the management that's capable of running your company successfully. And you would then reap your share of the profits.

If you could buy such a company, or an interest in it, and recover your investment from its profits within five years, your purchase price wouldn't be too much to pay. As you will see, my goal is to help you not just to recover your money in five years, but to double it. Surprisingly enough, the goal is an achievable one.

OWNING STOCK

A share of *common stock* represents part ownership of a corporation whose stock you have purchased. It entitles you to a "piece of the action." It gives you all of the benefits of outright ownership with few of the risks.

As an owner, you're entitled to a fractional share—a small fraction, to be sure —of the profits of that business, and you own a portion of its assets. Even if the company goes belly-up, you will receive a share of whatever value of the company might remain after its debts have been paid off.

If you own stock in a larger company that isn't growing or is growing only modestly, you will likely receive at least a portion of your profit in dividends. But that's not the most desirable option unless you're past retirement age and want to invest strictly for the income. Even then, there are compelling arguments against investing in such companies. I'll talk a little about the disadvantages later.

If, however, you own stock in a company whose profits grow every year, then you will probably not see any cash because your money will be plowed back into the company, showing up only as increased value. Until you sell your interest in the company, you won't be able to put that portion of its profit in the bank. Nor, by the way, will you have to pay taxes on it.

Only when you sell your interest to someone else will you realize the gain and pay the taxes. And because the company's profits will have grown, the price you can demand and receive for your interest in the company will have grown as well.

As a technamental investor you are going to select only world-class companies that have excellent track records and are still growing. (Chapter 6 goes into detail about the kinds of companies you should look for and how to find them). You'll find these companies listed on the New York Stock Exchange, the American Exchange, or the Nasdaq (National Association of Securities Dealers Automated Quotations), an electronic, "virtual" exchange.

Companies that are listed on these exchanges typically sell for many more times their profits than do those just getting started. The principle is the same, however. Ownership of companies that have gone well past the risk threshold will cost multiples upwards of 10, 15, or more. In fact, as of this writing, there are some companies that sell for multiples of more than 100! If a multiple is a measure of how long it will take to recover the investment, you can already appreciate the fact that those who would pay that many times the company's profit either are expecting to live well beyond the normal life span or are very foolish indeed!

Diversification: Spreading the Risk

Putting all your eggs in one basket has never been smart. No matter how good the basket is, something can always happen to it. The last step in understanding why you should buy common stock is to understand the final reduction of risk.

If one business will give you a good return, why not invest in small pieces of a bunch of businesses? If you study companies—an easy job as you will shortly discover—you'll be able to eliminate from consideration all of the companies that are below average. You can then assemble a collection—a *portfolio*—of above-average companies that will perform better than the rest. And because you have your eggs in a variety of baskets, you will not have to worry about all of the risks that could blow a single company out of the water.

This is called *diversification,* and it's the final reason why ownership of common stocks is the place to be. When you own a few shares of a variety of above-average companies, you reduce your risk while retaining all of the benefits of owning businesses—those wonderful engines for adding value and making money.

Investing versus Playing the Market

The expression "playing the market" should be your first clue that this is something you don't want to do with your money. If you want to play, then you can certainly get the same kind of rush in the stock market that you get at the tables in Las Vegas or Atlantic City, and you can enjoy the same success that most people who play those tables enjoy—none! When you play the market, the odds are very much against you. So if you think that this book will help you play more successfully, you're reading the wrong book!

There is a basic difference between what I propose and what many unfortunate folks do. I suggest that you earn your money by participating in a business, not bet that you can make a killing by finding someone who will pay a lot more for the stock than you did. When you invest, you depend upon the successful businesses you have chosen to add value and create money.

Don't kid yourself! Playing the market is gambling in its truest sense. The risks that a player takes are enormous because the rewards aren't based upon the orderly supply of products or services for which people are willing to pay a fair price. A player relies upon a variety of totally unpredictable events or occurrences, as does a gambler at the roulette table. This is the playground of the traders.

Stock was first issued for the sole purpose of allowing more than one individual to participate in a venture. Later a market sprang up that allowed people to sell their shares to others, and it created a new kind of share owner, one who likes to speculate by buying and selling shares. The dynamics of that market well suits those who are eager to get rich in a hurry.

Psychology has always played a major role as shares were bought out of greed and sold out of fear. Until recent years it wasn't difficult for unscrupulous people to manipulate the price of shares by planting fears or by spreading excessively optimistic stories. They would then buy below or sell above the real value of the shares, before the enterprise itself was able to add to the shares' value.

Today the stock market does a roaring business while traders watch the minute-to-minute movement of the prices and frantically sell or buy shares when they move up or down by only a few cents.

The BFS/STS School of Speculation

Ask the average person what he thinks of the stock market and he will probably say it's scary. Everyone has either lost money on the stock market or can recite some horror story about someone they know who has. Like those who play the lottery, there are only a chosen few among traders who make the big bucks; the great majority have been burned.

Until recently the general public had a respectful fear of the stock market because it hadn't yet learned how to master it. As I write, however, many who should be intimidated are not, and that's even scarier. More and more people have come out of the woodwork and have thrown their life's savings into the market. And these folks have been rewarded on paper as the value of their investments has soared. They could have thrown a dart at the financial page and picked a winner in the bull market of the 1990s.

Except for the professionals, the market today is made up largely of folks who have no concept of the fact that they're really buying a company rather than merely buying its stock. These investors hold to what I call the *BFS/STS School of Speculation.* "BFS/STS" means "Buy from a sucker, sell to a sucker."

What is their methodology? It's simple. You have to first buy the stock from some poor sucker who doesn't know its true value as well as you do. And then you have to turn around and sell it to some other poor sucker who doesn't know its true value either or else he wouldn't buy it from you for the price you're asking.

What chance do you think the average investor—or you, for that matter—has of not being the sucker on at least one end of that transaction, if not both? Slim to none! If there is no rational means of determining the reasonable value of a stock, the only thing that provides the opportunity for people to sell their stocks at a profit is the presence of someone who is similarly unenlightened. The street has cynically called this phenomenon by another name: the "Greater Fool Theory." Each buyer admits to being a fool but relies on the next buyer to be yet a greater one.

On the other hand, if you buy stock in a growing company, having determined (in the fashion that you'll shortly learn) that the stock is worth a certain multiple of the previous year's profit, you'll have paid a fair price for it. Over the long term you'll see profits grow and with them the value of the company. As time passes, assuming the multiple you paid was reasonable, another buyer will be quite willing to pay as high a multiple as you did—perhaps higher. The same multiple times twice the profit means twice the price; your investment's value will have doubled. Long-term investing is not a gamble, nor does it depend on finding a "greater fool" to take your holdings off your hands.

WHY INVEST FOR THE LONG TERM?

The decision is yours to make. At this point, you may still prefer the rush that goes with betting on the long shots and you'd rather ride the hare to the finish line than the tortoise. Just so you know what you're missing if you do, here are some of the benefits of doing it our way:

Pick winners four out of five times.   Nearly a half century of experience with this methodology allows NAIC to boast that if you have done your homework diligently and conservatively, for every five stocks you pick, one will exceed your highest expectations, three will do about as you expected them to, and one will go down the tubes. This is called the *Rule of Five,* and you should keep it in mind when you worry about having some failures.

No one can predict when some calamity will befall a company. For example, not long ago a major food chain lost all of its high-level executives in an airplane crash. How could *anyone* have predicted that?

All kinds of risks can come without notice, but the odds are in your favor. If you do it right—and it's really not hard—you can enjoy an 80 percent success rate. That ain't too shabby!

Double your money every five years. If you're able to pick stocks that do you proud four out of five times, you can double your money every five years. With this "sure thing" philosophy, all you have to do is to watch the companies you've bought to make sure that, other than the occasional stumble that good management is allowed once in a while, your companies continue to perform as you expected. If their growth continues substantially as you anticipated, then the price of their shares will do the same over the long term, despite the fluctuations that occur every day.

Consider this: The S&P 500 is a dollar-weighted index of some 500 stocks that have been selected as representative of their industries and that meet certain quality criteria. Since its inception, the S&P 500 has produced an average annual return of around 10 percent. This means that if you had bought all five hundred of these companies, you would have increased the value of your investments by 10 percent after holding them for a year. Now this hasn't been the case every year, but the average has been around 10 percent.

Since this performance is for an *average* of 500 companies, doesn't it stand to reason that if you can eliminate the below-average companies and pick the best, your performance might easily be half again as good?

As a technamental investor, you will look for a return on your portfolio of 15 percent, which compounded annually will double your money every five years. (*Compounding* simply means that each year the earnings from the previous year are added to the value of the investment, and growth is then calculated on the new value.)

Doubling the value of your investment in five years is quite achievable. There are hundreds of thousands of folks just like you out there who are doing it all the time!

Maintain your portfolio painlessly. How would you like to be so confident in your investments that you check their performance only once a month, or every three months, or even once a year? Do you think that's smart—or even possible?

This is one of the great benefits of buying the company and not the stock. If you subscribe to the BFS/STS School of Speculation, you have to watch every movement of the price, the thing you're most concerned about. The price changes every minute that the exchange on which the stock trades is open. In fact, the price can even change during the night when the exchange is not open, which can drive traders nuts. Moreover, prices can fluctuate by as much as 50 percent above and below their averages during the course of a year. As a trader, you're afraid to miss a trick!

Long-term investors know that the price will fluctuate in the short term for a variety of reasons, most of them irrelevant. They don't have to worry about those fluctuations in price because they know one simple fact (and I'll repeat this later because it's important): *Changes in price that are not caused by changes in the fundamentals (sales, profits, etc.) are transient. What goes up will come down, and what goes down will come back up.* Because the price of a stock over the long term is directly related to the company's profits, there's really no point in watching the price zig-zag as it does every minute of every hour of every weekday. If you want to make money, you'll invest, not gamble. Watching the short-term fluctuations in the price is hardly different from sitting at the roulette table. It may be exciting, but it's not likely to beat your day job!

Everyone's a winner! This point may be redundant, but it's worth repeating. Technamental investing—this long-term, buy-and-hold, fundamental investment philosophy—produces no losers. If you perform the simple tasks related to studying a company before you buy it, and if you diversify enough so that the Rule of Five gives you at least 80 percent odds of being satisfied, you can't lose! Nor will you need to find a sucker to sell to, because when you're ready to sell something, you'll offer it at a fair value. Not only will you win, but the person who buys the stock from you at a fair price will make out just as well.

Defer taxes. As a bonus benefit, don't forget that there is no tax on your gain until you sell your stock.

There are only two main reasons for selling your shares: if a company's fundamentals (i.e., its operational performance) deteriorate so much that the company no longer meets your expectations, or if you need or want the money. (There's a third, unusual, occasion that I'll talk about in Chapter 12.)

Otherwise, let that company simply generate those profits, plow them back into the business, and make the value of your holdings increase year after year as its earnings grow. And defer paying taxes on those unrealized gains until you're ready to sell.

While you can *defer* the payment of taxes, there are only two circumstances that allow you to *avoid* paying taxes on gains: your death or the loss of your gains. Neither of these alternatives is palatable.

Traders, who are in and out of the market buying low and selling high, have to pay a tax on every cent of profit they earn—when they earn it. If they have to pay 20 percent of their gain, that's 20 percent less that they can reinvest and earn money on.

You may ask, "What about an IRA or a 401(k), where I don't have to pay taxes until I take out the money?" These investment vehicles can certainly be good when you want to move your money from one company to another that has a greater potential without incurring a tax liability. And the 401(k) is a great boon to many people who wouldn't otherwise discipline themselves to invest.

The biggest benefit of tax-deferred investments is that you can reinvest money that you would otherwise have had to pay out in taxes. And the money earned on that reinvestment can continue to grow without being taxed until later.

There's no free lunch, though. You will pay a substantial cost for this benefit later on. The taxes on your gains when you finally do take out your money are paid not at the capital gains rate, which can be as low as 10 percent, but at the full rate that applies to ordinary income (although by the time you reach retirement age, your tax rate will probably have come down some).

At this writing, the highest personal tax rate is nearly twice the capital gains rate! So unless Congress acts in a way that is quite out of character, you will have to do a great deal of optimizing to make up for paying almost double the taxes.

The least costly gains, therefore, are the gains in a non-tax-deferred portfolio. And it's a pleasure to watch the value of your holdings increase year after year without having to pay a tax on those increases in value.

If You're Retired and Don't Have a "Long Term"

Finally, I'd like to address the question of how this long-term philosophy can be of benefit to people in the "third third," people who are in their golden years, when it's time to make use of the funds they've accumulated for this time of their life.

My counsel to anyone at any age is to pretend that you're going to live forever. Not only will this give you a happier outlook from the time you wake up until the time you go back to sleep, but it will provide you with a better investment plan.

No matter how you slice it, a 15 percent return is better than a 6 percent return—more than twice as good—and you will be able to endure a lot of leaner years if you have more than twice the accumulation of wealth when times are good.

Since the early 1940s, when World War II brought the Depression to an end, there has never been a long-term catastrophe in the stock market. Even in the worst of times, good companies continue to earn; and many stocks buck the trend. To be sure, some of the weaker companies with poor management fold, but the well-managed, strong companies quickly scoop up their market share and life goes on.

Focus on investing in growth companies for the long term, and if the time arises when you need to take cash out of your account, sell off portions of your losers—the ones whose sales and profit growth is sluggish, not necessarily the ones whose prices are down.

This will assure you that when the market comes back up, which it surely will, you'll have a portfolio of winners. Have faith that the companies you own a piece of will perform well in the long term and so, therefore, will your investments. And gloat as you continue to rack up 15 percent years while your contemporaries are pulling down 6 percent and paying the taxes on it every month.

L E T ' S   T A K E   S T O C K   O F

The Reasons You Should Take Stock

- You can create wealth only by adding value to resources or by providing a service of value.

- Only investments in active businesses are capable of adding value.

- Owning a business, while very rewarding, is expensive and risky; but owning shares in a variety of successful businesses eliminates most of the risk while retaining most of the reward.

- Buying the stock of quality growth companies and holding it for the long term provides substantial, predictable returns.

- Short-term trading (BFS/STS) is unpredictable and stacks the odds against you because it relies upon winning at some loser's expense, and because there's no assurance that you won't be the loser.

- The benefits of long-term investing include care-free portfolio maintenance, the potential to double your money every five years, the deferment of taxes; and the fact that there are rarely any losers.

Finally, let's review the simple math that makes this method work:

1. Assume that 15 times earnings is a fair multiple for a good company, and

2. That the company earned a dollar per share last year.

3. You will therefore pay $15 for the stock.

4. In five years, the earnings will have grown to $2 per share.

5. At 15 times earnings, the price will then be $30.

The value of your investment will have doubled—in five years!

Hopefully you're satisfied with the logic behind this investing approach and can see its advantages.

Next, let's dispel any doubts you might have about whether you can be successful.

CHAPTER 3

Dispelling the Myths

There's a tremendous mystique out there about investing in stocks. So let's blow it away!

"Only people on the inside have access to the secret knowledge, which is surrounded by a huge, nearly impenetrable wall. The wall prevents anyone but the insiders from knowing enough to invest successfully on their own."

Baloney! It's a myth!

"Without a degree in finance or the letters MBA or CFA after your name, you just can't begin to know enough about business or the stock market to succeed."

So the professional community would have you believe. It's all nonsense!

Just think of all of the people in the investment business who have a stake in convincing you that you can't do it yourself!

For instance, where would the brokers be if you could make your own decisions without their help? Why, they'd be reduced to just taking your phone calls and executing your orders. Hardly more than you could do for yourself on the Internet—and you can do it after working hours to boot!

Money managers, mutual fund managers, analysts who make their recommendations in the avalanche of newsletters that you could be buried under if you let them just send the trial subscriptions, and all of the clerks, secretaries, computer technicians, chauffeurs (some of them make really big bucks), and the others who support them are all interested in keeping you in the dark because your ignorance is their bread, butter, and caviar.

Well, this is certainly an intimidating business. Just think of all of the things they know that you don't. And still they rarely do better than the market average!

Well, I've got news for you. Like the proverbial bumblebee, who floats through the air even though aeronautical engineers have proclaimed that she can't possibly fly, there are literally millions of folks out there, from grandparents to little school kids, who successfully invest in stocks. And you can too!

And it's not because the folks who do so are smart and the professionals are stupid. They're not at all stupid—at least not most of them. The problem is that they are working with money that's not their own. In order to avoid the liability that can go with handling other people's money, most mutual funds, banks, insurance companies, and money management firms have adopted a very conservative set of constraints. And the Securities and Exchange Commission (SEC) has also laid down some laws to protect the public. These prevent the pros from doing some of the things that you can do.

Some of the rules are so conservative as to be ludicrous; others have some merit to them but still stand in the way of excellent performance.

One of the biggest restraints on professional success is the way the professionals are rated. Their peers and the financial press judge the fund managers each quarter on the basis of what stocks are in their portfolios. So every three months there's a rush to "flush" stocks that are out of favor and replace them with "hot" ones. This vanity can be very costly to the fund's shareholders.

PETER LYNCH SAYS WE CAN DO IT

Without question, the most celebrated professional investor in history has been Peter Lynch. There have been others, like Warren Buffett and Sir John Templeton, who have made immense personal fortunes and who have shared their investment methods with the world. But the highest-profile investor, the consummate professional, is Peter Lynch.

Lynch has served as an inspiration to me and to millions of others who were initially bamboozled by the belief that we can't do a good job of investing in common stocks without help.

As the manager of history's arguably most successful mutual fund, Fidelity's Magellan, Lynch shepherded the fund's holdings from a relatively small $475 million or so to $9 billion in just over 11 years, from 1977 through 1989, when his book was published.

Lynch's wonderful *One Up on Wall Street* is a must-read. You should read it if only for the inspiration that he and his coauthor, John Rothchild, have given the world in this first light-hearted primer for bamboozled would-be investors. In the first paragraph of the first chapter, Lynch writes, *"Any normal person using the customary three percent of his brain can pick stocks as well, or better than, the average Wall Street expert."*

Take this to heart! How much simpler can it be said? And to whom can you look for greater credibility? There you have it: the quintessential professional telling you that you can do it. And you can!

NAIC HAS PROVEN WE CAN DO IT

More than five million investors have passed through the portals of NAIC since it was founded in 1951. Most learn and then leave once they have acquired the basics. But there's a solid core of several thousand volunteers who form the nucleus of NAIC's educational establishment. Beyond that, nearly three-quarters of a million individuals, including members of investment clubs, are active NAIC members.

If you would like to find out more about NAIC, point your browser to <www .better-investing.org>.

Thousands upon thousands of NAIC members do better than the average professional every day. And even the worst-performing NAIC members don't do nearly so badly as some professionals do.

Speaking of inspiration, track records, and publicity, how about the famed Beardstown Ladies? You probably remember when they burst upon the scene— an investment club composed of some 16 ladies from that small Illinois town.

Ranging in age from a youthful 41 to more than twice that age, the Beardstown Ladies learned how to select stocks and made money in the stock market.

You probably also remember the publicity when it appeared that their track record wasn't nearly so good as they had thought it was. Through an honest mistake they had miscalculated their returns. They had acquired a computer program to do their club's accounting, and after entering the data into the program, they thought the 23.4 percent return the program reported was for the previous nine years rather than for only the two years actually calculated.

How the financial press and the pros crowed! Here was proof positive that common people—and certainly an investment club made up of women averaging 70 years of age—could not do better than they. But they had missed the point: by using some very homespun, commonsense rules, the Beardstown Ladies had actually succeeded.

As it turned out, the ladies' annual return since the inception of their club was a very respectable 15.3 percent—this time verified by hawkeyed auditors. This is as much as we would hope for. And there are many folks out there just like you who are investing successfully because the Beardstown Ladies inspired them to do it!

Be like the bumblebee and pay no attention to the experts who tell you that you can't do it. Do it anyway!

I SAY YOU CAN DO IT—AND *EASILY*

So don't take Peter Lynch's word for it. Maybe you figure that he's in a different league and can't possibly be talking to you.

Be skeptical about NAIC's track record if you like. After all, if you haven't personally talked to all of those folks out there, you don't really know whom you can believe.

Perhaps you may even join the legion of cynics who can't look beyond the Beardstown Ladies' mistake and see the plain truth in their story and the moral to be learned from it.

But you certainly can't be enough of a skeptic to doubt your own common sense, can you?

I'm not only telling you that you can invest successfully; I'm telling you that you can do it easily, that it's well within your reach to understand the principles, no matter what level of education you have—or haven't—achieved.

Here I'm going to summarize what the rest of this book will tell you in much greater detail. If it makes good sense, if it seems logical enough to you and sounds reasonably easy, then you're well on your way!

HERE'S ALL THERE IS TO IT

To successfully pick good stocks, there are only two things that you need to determine about a company:

1. Whether the company is a good-quality business worthy of your interest as an investor
2. Whether the company's stock is selling for a reasonable price (no matter how good the company, it can still be a poor investment if the price is too high)

The Two Tests of Quality

There are only two things that you have to look at to determine whether the company is of good enough quality.

1. *Growth of revenue and earnings.* The first consideration is the company's track record. How successful has the company been in selling an increasing number of its products or services? And how successful has management been in converting those growing sales into profits for the shareholders?
2. *Efficiency.* The second consideration is management's ability to sustain that track record. How capable is management of controlling costs?

Don't worry at this point if you aren't sure exactly what these terms mean. They're defined quite simply in the next chapter.

Using the tools of technamental analysis described in Chapters 7, 8, and 9, you'll be able to actually see a company's growth and efficiency quite plainly.

The Two Tests of Value

When you're satisfied that the company would be a good one to own, *and only then,* you will assess two more factors to determine whether the price you must pay for its stock is reasonable. They are:

1. The *potential return* that you can expect on your investment. Is it sufficient at the price you're being asked to pay?
2. The *risk* that you must take. Is it reasonable for the reward?

You'll learn how to assess these criteria in Chapter 10.

If your company passes these two tests of value, there is an 80 percent chance that you have found a winner.

LET'S TAKE STOCK OF
Your Chances for Success

- In spite of the many obvious reasons that people want you to believe you can't be a successful investor without the help of investment professionals, there is abundant evidence to support the fact that you can! The consummate professional Peter Lynch says so. NAIC's five decades of success bear it out. And the simple logic of the approach makes plenty of sense.

- The two measurable criteria to determine the quality of a potential investment are the company's *growth* and management's *efficiency,* its ability to sustain that growth.

- The two measurable criteria to determine whether the stock is selling for a reasonable price are its potential *reward* and the accompanying *risk.*

- At least four out of five companies that pass the simple tests that measure these criteria should prove to be good investments for the long term.

And you can become wealthy with such a track record.

CHAPTER 4

Learning the Language

You're about to become a fundamental analyst, and that's the best kind! All of the acknowledged great investors are or have been fundamental analysts. So you'll join the ranks of the Peter Lynches, the Warren Buffets, the Sir John Templetons, and the Grahams and the Dodds.

But if you read any of the books that the successful professional fundamental analysts have written, although you may be inspired and excited, you're apt to be left with an inexplicable sense of intellectual discomfort. Why? Because there are few if any that will tell you in plain language how to make decisions.

It seems that what all of those books have in common—at least the ones I've read—is their interesting discussion of the various criteria that they look at, and sometimes a fine dissertation on what's bad or what's good. But I have yet to find a single book that will tell me what to do if I find something bad or good! It seems that no one wants to make a commitment and say, for instance, "If you come across a debt-to-equity ratio of such and such, you should not buy the stock."

And for good reason. Whether the debt-to-equity ratio—or inventory turnover ratio, or capital employed ratio, or liquidation lag value, or cyclical variation, or any of a number of other measurements of company performance—is excessive or not depends upon a bunch of other ratios and criteria. By the time you consider all of the factors that might affect a decision, the authors couldn't possibly tell you what to do.

Trust me. You don't have to worry about any of this stuff. I'm not pretending to be as experienced or as knowledgeable as any of these respected authors, but I am telling you emphatically that you can succeed even if you don't know any more than I do.

When you finish this book, you'll have some clear direction. And while this method isn't foolproof—you won't be right all of the time—it is predictable, and you will be right 80 percent of the time. And that's enough to make you very successful.

So let's get down to business.

FIRST, WHAT DO YOU NEED TO KNOW?

The first step in learning how to evaluate companies and their stock is to understand the terms that are used—the ones that you *do* have to know. You'll need to understand the language that's commonly used to refer to the things you'll examine and evaluate. What's good about learning this "foreign language" is that there are only ten terms that you need to know.

The rest of the fancy expressions that you may have been exposed to or may hear from the professional establishment are not required. This is because there's a sharp distinction between what you need to know to understand the company's results (on which you will base your judgment) and the tools that the company's management needs to know in order to produce those results.

When you drive a car, you don't need to know the micrometer settings for the spark plug gaps, the specifications for the fuel/air mixture in the carburetor, or anything else about the host of other things that go on under the hood. All you need to know is that it starts right up, it runs smoothly, and it stops when you put on the brake. If any of these things doesn't go right, you can simply tell the garage mechanic in commonsense terms what he needs to know to start diagnosing and solving the problem. That's his job. Fortunately, there's a whole lot more oversight to protect you from unscrupulous business managers than there is to protect you from unscrupulous garage mechanics.

When you look at a company, you need only to be able to tell how well it runs. You have neither the responsibility nor the authority to tell someone to fix it if it's not running right. You can't hire, train, or fire management. All you can do is find another company with which to replace it. Therefore, it's about as important for you to dig into those other terms and tools as it would be for you to know the amount and viscosity of the residual oil in your engine's crankcase.

Later, perhaps, after you've digested all of the basics and are comfortable with the use of the tools that you need to work with, your curiosity may lead you to explore some of those more cryptic things. That's the right time to dig deeper, not when you can be easily distracted into thinking that there's more to this exercise than there really is.

Even then, if you were to learn everything that a professional has learned about management's tools of the trade, their utility to you would be minimal. If you aren't in on all of the insider information that a company's management has at its disposal—and you won't be—you still won't be able to put those tools to much practical use. And even if you were to foresee a problem because you were using the more sophisticated tools, you simply wouldn't be able to predict what management would do when it discovered the problem itself or whether it had already put some fix in motion. Besides, management can—in fact must —focus only on its own company. You are the "owner" of many companies.

So let's concentrate only on the things that you need to know and forget about the rest.

The first term you already know about because we've discussed it at some length already. However, just to be sure, let's review what a *share of stock* is.

SHARE OF STOCK

It's absolutely imperative that you're clear on the fact that a share of stock is just what the name implies: a share, a piece of the action of an enterprise. It's not a kind of currency. It's not like a baseball card that has value in and of itself and can or should be traded. Its purpose is to give the person who owns it the right to share in the profit of the company that issues it and to provide evidence that he or she, (usually) along with many others, has an ownership claim to the company's value. We'll talk about how to assess that value in a few moments.

Shares of stock are issued by the company and are sometimes held by the stockholder, but more often than not they are held by a broker on behalf of the stockholder. Shares held by a broker are said to be held "in street name." But don't worry about that distinction for the moment. Suffice it to say that when you purchase a number of shares of stock, you're purchasing a fractional interest in a company, and that fraction, however small, represents your percentage of owner-ship of the company.

The next eight items are also quite elementary. So elementary, in fact, that they can be applied just as readily to Lucy's Lemonade Stand as to General Motors.

When you study any company, you will want to look at two things about it: how it has operated over a period of time and what its condition is at the end of that time. While as a rule Lucy wouldn't issue financial statements for her lemon-ade stand, she very well could.

To report on her lemonade stand's performance, Lucy would issue an *income statement*. ("I made $10 this week.") To report on its condition at the end of the week, she would issue a *balance sheet*. ("I now have $20.") Companies issue these reports every quarter (every three months) with a major report being issued each year showing the results for the entire year. I'll tell you later where you may find these reports. For now, let's just look at what's in them.

The company's performance is what "feeds" its condition. The more money a company earns, the better its condition. The income statement therefore feeds the balance sheet, and the items on each are quite similar.

I have somewhat oversimplified the notion that some things are "good" and others "bad." Expenses, for example, are good because the money is usually well spent and what it buys is necessary to make money. However, for our purposes, anything that benefits the company by having more of it is good; anything that will make a company better off by having less of it is bad.

THE INCOME STATEMENT

Because your biggest concern is the company's operation, you're going to want to look at the income statement first. Its purpose is to chronicle the company's performance.

While there may be as many as 50 items or more on the income statement, there are only 4 that are important to you. These 4 items represent categories that comprise all of the other items that can appear on an income statement.

Sales/revenue.   The first item is *sales.* For Lucy, this figure represents all of the money that she takes in over the counter for her lemonade. For a corporation, it's all of the compensation that it receives for the goods or services that it provides.

For some companies the word *revenue* is more appropriate because this more encompassing word goes beyond the marketing of goods or services and takes into account such odd things as rental income, interest income, and so on. For our purposes, however, we'll make *sales* and *revenue* interchangeable. Whatever the company brings in is sales. This is what a company would call its *top line,* meaning that this is the first thing that you'll find at the top of the income statement.

For Lucy's Lemonade Stand, sales would include one item only: lemonade. But a large manufacturing company may market many products or services. So the company will want to keep track of how many dollars come from each source so they can analyze what sells and what doesn't. These breakdowns are important for management's guidance but not for us. We're interested only in the total revenue. Keep this in mind when you look at a complicated annual report. You should just look for totals.

FIGURE 4.1 Income Statement

ABC Company
Income Statement
for Year Ending May 31, 1999

	1999
Sales	
Net sales	$ 757,414
Cost of sales	229,727
Gross profit	527,687
Expenses	
Selling, general, and administrative expense	265,565
Research and development expense	35,472
Depreciation	29,500
Special charge	55,000
Total operating expense	585,764
Operating income	171,650
Other income, net	15,787
Profit	
Profit before income taxes	186,337
Provision for income taxes	62,523
Net profit to shareholders	116,414
Earnings per share:	
Basic	$1.04
Diluted	1.03
Earnings per share (Normalized)	
Basic	$1.34
Diluted	1.32
Shares used in the computation of earnings per share:	
Basic	112,310
Diluted	113,380
Cash dividends paid per common share	$ .12

Not all sales are paid for at the time the sale is made or the product delivered. Most companies bill their customers for goods or services and are paid at a later date. These sales are still included in the sales figure because delivery has been made and the obligation has been incurred by the purchaser. The income statement will make no distinction between transactions with delayed payment and transactions for cash. The difference shows up later on the balance sheet.

Expenses. The second item you're interested in is *expenses.* For obvious reasons, you would consider these "bad." The higher your expenses are, the worse off you are.

For Lucy, the cost of lemons and sugar is about as complicated as it gets. For a manufacturer, expenses will range from costs related to the fabrication of each product to costs related to its delivery.

These *variable* expenses are known as the *cost of goods sold*, or COGS. Variable costs will vary with the number of units made. The more units produced, the higher the cost.

Fixed expenses, items like rent, salaries, interest on mortgages, and so on, are items that remain essentially the same regardless of how many units of a product are made.

Taxes are an expense as well. Taxes vary with the amount of profit (see below) so they are considered separately in the income statement.

Again, we don't need to keep track of these distinctions—at least for the moment. We need only be concerned with the total.

Profit. If we subtract the expenses from the sales, we come up with the *profit,* our third term. Profit is obviously "good."

Profit is what you have left after paying your expenses. It's what Lucy's been standing behind that table in the hot sun all week for. And it's what you as a shareholder of a company are entitled to a part of. It's the result of adding value and creating wealth. It's what the enterprise is all about.

Profit is not obscene, as some would have you believe. It's what the company uses to hire more people, buy more machines for them to work with, and create more jobs. It's what you want your company to make for you—and what it will ultimately use to reward you for allowing it to use your money.

This simple definition of profit leads us to the next term, to the figure that makes your company's performance more "personal." It converts the company's performance to a value that you can apply to your own share of the company.

Earnings per share. When you divide the profit by the number of shares of stock that you and all of your fellow shareholders own, you will have calculated *earnings per share* or *EPS*—a figure that represents just how much of that profit is attributable to each share of stock. This number is what's known as the *bottom line*, and it will, logically enough, be found at the very bottom of the income statement. From here on, I'll use earnings or EPS to refer to earnings per share.

If you were Lucy's dad or mom and agreed to fund her venture in return for half of the proceeds, your single share of Lucy's enterprise would be worth half of her profit. Your half of the profit would equal the EPS. In a large company, your share is only a small fraction of all of the ownership, so you'll receive a lot less than half of the profit. Your share of that company's earnings is the EPS multiplied by the number of shares that you own. If the company had issued a million shares and had earned a million dollars during the past three months, each of your shares would have earned $1 for you. If you had a hundred shares, your holdings would have earned you $100.

However, you wouldn't receive a check for that $100. If this company were to pay you and all of the other stockholders all of the earnings that your stock entitled you to in dividends, the company would go nowhere and you would have no reason to be interested in it as an investment. It's the portion of the profit that is retained by the company that fuels its growth, and it's that growth that's going to make you the money on your investment. In effect, your company is reinvesting your earnings back into itself, which is the best place for them to go, assuming the company's track record comes up to your standards. The most promising growth companies are usually those that retain all of their earnings and pay no dividends.

If the company is a very large, mature company, it will reward its stockholders by paying them a portion of the earnings while retaining the rest for growth. These larger companies have increased their revenues to the point where spectacular growth is no longer possible, so it's appropriate that they reward their shareholders with dividends.

Large, mature companies are not the ones that will make the most money for you, but some mature companies of especially high quality, like General Electric (GE), can provide stability to your portfolio and certainly have a place there.

You'll find most of the information you'll need in the company's income statement. As a long-term, growth/value investor, you are mostly interested in finding companies whose ability to produce earnings is sufficient to keep those earnings growing into the future. And as you now know, it's the growth of earnings that increases the value of your stock when you go to sell it to someone else down the road.

The company's track record, on which you base your judgment, is documented by not just one, but rather a series of income statements. You will extract just the basic information from each to analyze how rapidly and steadily sales and earnings have grown from year to year and quarter to quarter. Simple enough?

THE BALANCE SHEET

Most of us are blessed with two eyes, each of which has a slightly different perspective, giving us depth perception so that we can judge distance, size, and movement much more accurately than we could with a single eye.

The balance sheet affords you a second perspective of a company. It gives you a picture of the substance of the company and the value of your ownership of it.

Like the income statement, the balance sheet (see Figure 4.2) documents some very basic items that can be classified simply as "good" or "bad."

FIGURE 4.2   The Balance Sheet

ABC Company
Balance Sheet
Year Ending 5/31/99

Assets

Current assets:

Cash and cash equivalents	$ 129,359
Investments	60,078
Accounts and notes receivable, less allowance for doubtful receivables	
(1999 - $4,883 and 1998 - $5,957)	215,034
Refundable income taxes	31,308
Inventories	205,238
Prepaid expenses and other	40,691
Total current assets	681,708

Property, plant, and equipment:

Land and improvements	13,544
Buildings and improvements	92,396
Machinery and equipment	159,070
	265,010
Less, accumulated depreciation	96,137
Property, plant, and equipment, net	168,873
Investments	146,859
Intangible assets, net of accumulated amortization (1999 - $18,096 and 1998 - $14,427)	7,665
Excess acquisition costs over fair value of acquired net assets, net of	
accumulated amortization (1999 - $15,816 and 1998 - $11,102)	47,861
Other assets	14,990
Total assets	$ 1,067,956

Liabilities and Shareholders' Equity

Current liabilities:

Short-term borrowings	$ 45,137
Accounts payable	27,676
Accrued income taxes	17,088
Accrued wages and commissions	19,596
Accrued insurance	9,197
Accrued litigation	55,000
Other accrued expenses	27,736
Total current liabilities	201,430
Deferred federal income taxes	9,565
Other liabilities	324
Total liabilities	211,319
Minority interest	80,690

Commitments and contingencies (Note L)

Shareholders' equity:

Preferred shares, $100 par value: Authorized 5 shares; none issued	....
Common shares, without par value: Authorized 500,000 shares;	
issued and outstanding 1999 - 112,578 shares and 1998 - 112,043 shares	77,843
Additional paid-in capital	26,920
Retained earnings	687,828
Accumulated other comprehensive loss	(16,644)
Total shareholders' equity	775,947
Total liabilities and shareholders' equity	$ 1,067,956

Assets. Assets are everything that the company owns.

If Lucy came to you and asked you to invest in her lemonade stand, you might give her $20 to buy lemons and sugar, a pitcher, some cups, and a table to put them on. All of these, including any change she might have left after her purchases, would be assets. Assets are the things that the company owns and that it uses to add value, make money, and, closer to home, generate your earnings. Assets are generally classified as *liquid* or *fixed*. The $20 would have been a liquid asset, the nonexpendable items like the pitcher and table, fixed assets.

Such things as cash, factory buildings, machines, vehicles, postage stamps, and paper clips—all are assets. Some are more liquid than others; they are easier to spend because they are easier to convert to cash. Cash itself is the most liquid asset; money in a checking account is not far behind and is, in fact, easier to move around than currency.

The money that is owed to the company at the end of the period, its *accounts receivable,* is an asset that is nearly as liquid as cash because if the company is well managed and careful, the accounts receivable will soon be converted to cash. Other liquid assets are loans that the company has made, mortgages it owns, even stock in other companies in which management has invested spare cash so that it will earn something.

Machinery, vehicles, and other items that the company has purchased for its use are obviously less liquid because they are not nearly so easily converted to cash. Probably the least liquid of all of the fixed assets are land and the structures that sit on it.

You can lump all of the things the company owns into the single category called assets.

Liabilities. Liabilities are everything that the company owes. For obvious reasons, you would consider these "bad."

If you loan Lucy $20 instead of buying a piece of her action by becoming a shareholder, she incurs a liability. The good news for her enterprise is that after she pays you a fixed amount each week, she can keep all of the earnings above and beyond those payments for herself. The bad news is that no matter how many days it rains, she still has to make the payments every week.

Liabilities are recorded in the balance sheet in order of the length of the time the company has to repay them. Short-term liabilities such as *accounts payable*—the money the company owes for goods and services it has purchased and for short-term notes and loans—are called short-term liabilities, appropriately enough.

Long-term liabilities include such things as installment loans and mortgages on real estate. They also include bonds, debt instruments that must be repaid at the end of a fixed term and on which regular interest payments must be paid. Bonds constitute most of the long-term debt of companies that have funded some of their growth and asset acquisition by borrowing money instead of by issuing more stock to more shareholders.

When the company borrows money to acquire assets, it can benefit you as a shareholder because the increased profits that are generated by those additional assets are divided among fewer shares than they would been if more shares had been issued to cover the cost of the assets. This is called *leverage,* another of those nifty management tools that you don't have to be concerned with.

As you know from common sense, borrowing can also be a problem for the company and its shareholders. When times are hard, a demanding creditor can put a company out of business, forcing it to sell all of its assets to pay off the debt. Hopefully that won't happen to any of the companies that you own a piece of.

Equity.   Equity is what you have left when you subtract the liabilities from the assets. It is the "live" part of the company that grows. What's more important, the equity of the company is a statement of the value of that company—what you own a piece of. And it is "good."

At the end of each period for which the income statement shows more income than expense, earnings that are retained are added to the equity of the company.

Equity can include not only the tangible difference between assets and liabilities. A company can also own intangible things with real value such as brand recognition or customer goodwill. Any of these things can have a value attached and be a part of what you own as a stockholder. This kind of hard-to-wrap-your-arms-around value is part of a company's potential growth as well, and it is sometimes referred to as *franchise value.*

Book value per share. As with per share earnings, your portion of equity—the company's value—is determined by dividing the equity by the number of shares of stock issued. The result is called *book value* or *book value per share.* From here on, I'll simply use book value to refer to book value per share.

To "personalize" it again, you can see just how much your part of the company is worth by multiplying the book value by the number of shares you own. Thus, if the company is worth $100 million and it has 1 million shares outstanding, each share is worth $100. If you own 100 shares, they would be worth $10,000 (exclusive of the value of their potential earnings growth) if the company were to liquidate its assets and pay its liabilities.

For you as a growth/value investor, book value is not of much importance. Heaven forbid that you own stock in a company that has to liquidate its assets! However, we will have a use for both equity and book value later as we examine management's ability to obtain a return on the shareholders' ownership.

These eight terms: sales, expenses, profit, and earnings per share from the income statement; and assets, liabilities, equity, and book value from the balance sheet—all somewhat related—are all you need to know to understand how a company works. There is just one more term that's important, one that you will deal with frequently.

THE PRICE-EARNINGS RATIO

Last but not least, you will need to understand what the *price-earnings ratio (PE)* is and why it is significant. The PE is simple to calculate, but its significance may be somewhat more difficult to grasp. I've actually exposed you to the concept already in Chapter 2 when I used the term *multiple* to talk about the price of a business. You should know now why that price is expressed as the number of times a company's income one might be willing to pay for that business.

Whether you are evaluating a business as a potential proprietor or as a shareholder, the principle is the same and the notion of expressing the company's value as a multiple of earnings is the same. However, you're buying just a limited number of shares, not the entire business. Therefore, your multiple is expressed in terms of a single share.

The price-earnings ratio (PE, or multiple) is calculated by dividing the current price of a share of the stock by the earnings per share (EPS). The term is widely used because everyone acknowledges that over the long term the price of a stock is tied directly to the company's earnings—even if most short-term players disregard that reality.

For you as a long-term, technamental investor, the PE is the all-important relationship that you will need to explore in order to evaluate the price of a stock. To tie a will-o'-the-wisp figure like a stock's price to a solid number like a company's earnings is like trying to anchor a cloud to a rock! Let's look at the many faces of the PE to get the idea of it.

A measure of confidence. The price-earnings ratio is a measure of investor confidence in a company. What brings about that confidence is, of course, the company's ability to add value and make money, thus producing earnings. The more capable of producing earnings a company is—or appears to investors to be—the greater amount of confidence investors will have and the more they will pay for the stock. And this leads to another facet of the PE.

A measure of time. As I said earlier, earnings growth raises the price investors are willing to pay because they will be able to recover their investment in a shorter period of time. With no growth, the PE would actually represent the number of years it would take to recover one's investment. If the company earned $1 per share and the stock sold at a PE of 5, it would take five years at $1 each year to accumulate and recover the money paid for the stock. Who's going to wait that long to get their money back?

We might be willing to wait for three years if the company were good and solid. So for a company that's not growing, perhaps a PE of 3 might be reasonable.

Let's say, on the other hand, that a company earning $1 per share were to grow each year at 15 percent compounded. In those three years, we would be able to accumulate not $3 but $4 in earnings. We could therefore justify paying four times earnings (a PE of 4) because we wouldn't have to wait 4 years to make the $4. So in a sense, the PE is a way to look at time.

	Earned	*Accumulation*
First year	$1.15	$1.15
Second year	1.32	2.47
Third year	1.52	3.99

Time is money—or so they say. So it comes down to the fact that the PE is really another way we have to measure how much the stock is worth to us.

A measure of value. Veronica Lake, a movie star of my era, had a signature hairdo. One lock of her beautiful blond hair cascaded smoothly down over one eye and then joined the rest of her shoulder-length, neatly coifed tresses. Everyone knew her by her hair.

Golf pros have their signature clubs, and other athletes have their signature equipment, clothing, or even mannerisms. A signature is a particular trait or physical characteristic that is tied to an individual.

So it seems to be with a company and its price-earnings ratio. A company's ability to earn, or to grow its earnings, can be tied to its *fair market value*, the price at which you will find a willing buyer and a willing seller.

This *signature multiple* of earnings will be of interest to us when we evaluate a stock.

A forecasting tool. Most writers of traditional investment books won't let you read more than a few chapters before making some reference to the fact that the stock market is like the sea. This is a great metaphor, but most authors just don't carry it nearly far enough.

The stock market is indeed like the ocean because just like a cork floating upon its surface, the price of a stock is affected by many different influences at once. And each of those forces can either add to or subtract from the effects of the others.

The broadest influence is, of course, the tide that ebbs and flows regularly and in some places rises 50 feet or more above its low point.

Upon the tide are the broad, rolling waves caused by the various disturbances at the sea bottom. There are the large waves that are caused by storms and major changes in the atmosphere, and there are the various ripples and patterns caused by the whim of the local breeze that blows this way and that over a few square yards of the surface.

The cork is buoyed by a combination of all of these influences, some rising and some falling, all at the same time. If you were to try to predict where that cork would be in relation to sea level in the next moment, you'd have a tough time of it. You can't predict what a storm or even an underground earthquake will do to the cork at any given moment. And if you add to that the effects of the winds and the little breezes, it's hopeless!

However, you would be able to forecast, in general, where your cork would bob over the course of a day, instead of at a particular moment. This is because the tides are influenced by the position of the moon, by gravity, and by a variety of other factors that are all scientifically predictable—so predictable, in fact, that almanacs are published that forecast the tides for years ahead, right to the minute.

The stock market is also governed by a diverse set of influences. And just as the sea, it is predictable over the long term but not over the short term.

Probably the most widely watched reason for the long-term fluctuations of the price and PE is the rise and fall of the stock market itself. This can be a function of the economy's volatility. The economy is battered by the rise and fall of interest rates, by inflation, and by a variety of factors that drive consumer confidence or buying power up or down. Actual changes in the economy itself will cause longer-term changes in the market and the prices of its individual stocks. Speculation about such changes have a shorter-term effect.

In the shorter term, there are the ripples and wavelets. Every little utterance of a government official or company officer, insider buying or selling (which may or may not mean anything), rumor, gossip, and just about anything else can influence the whims of those on the Street. Many people will use these stories to try to make or break a market in the stock.

Over the life of a company, its *signature PE*—the "normal" relationship between a company's earnings and its stock's price—is virtually constant. It does tend to decline slowly as the company's earnings growth declines, which happens with all successful companies. For all practical purposes, however, that relationship is remarkably constant. And for that reason it's also remarkably predictable.

When a company's earnings continue to grow, so will its stock price. Conversely, when earnings flatten or go down, the price will follow.

The little fluctuations in the price-earnings ratio above and below that constant value are not so predictable because they are all caused by investor perception and opinion. They are like the winds that blow across the surface of the sea.

The broader moves above and below the norm are the undulations that are typically caused by the continuous rising and falling of analysts' expectations. When a company first emerges into its explosive growth period, the analysts expect earnings to continue to skyrocket. Earnings growth estimates in the 50 percent range or more are not uncommon.

As the company continues to meet these expectations, investor confidence booms along with it, and more investors pay a higher and higher price for the stock. The PE rises like a meteor right along with the price. The faster the growth, the higher the PE. This does nothing to alter the value of the "reasonable" PE multiple. It just means that investor confidence has risen well above that norm and that there will eventually be an adjustment.

Sure enough, one fine day when the analysts' consensus called for growth of 45 percent, the company turns in a "disappointing" earnings growth of only 38 percent. The analysts start wringing their hands because the company has not met their expectations, and some fund manager sells. Next, all of the lemmings on Wall Street follow suit. And not long thereafter you get a call from your broker telling you that you've had a nice ride, you've made a lot of money on the stock, and it's time to take your profit and get out. In the meantime, the broker has made a commission on your purchase and is hoping to make it on your sale as well.

After a while, after the price and the PE have plummeted and then sat there for a while, some analyst wakes up to the fact that a 34 percent earnings growth rate is still pretty darn good and jumps back in. Soon the cycle is reversed. The market starts showing the company some respect again. And you get a call from your broker.

Of course, as a smart technamental investor you didn't sell it in the first place! Because you were watching the fine earnings growth all along, you knew better than to sell, and you chose the opportunity to buy some more. In the meantime, your brokers' clients who were not so savvy had taken their profits (and had paid the taxes on them, by the way), and are now wishing that they had stayed in with you. By the time their broker called them again, the price had already climbed past the point where it made good sense to jump in again.

It's best to assume that any price—and therefore PE—movement that is not related to the company's earnings is transient. If the stories—not the numbers—cause the price to move, the change won't last. What goes up will come down, and what goes down will come up. You have to be concerned only when the sales, pretax profits, or earnings cause the change, and then only if you find that the performance decay is related to a major, long-term problem that is beyond management's ability to resolve.

Remember also that a sizable segment of Wall Street doesn't make its money on the ocean as you do; it makes its money on the ocean motion. Buy or sell, it makes little difference to them what you do. They make their money either way. But it sure makes a big difference to you!

LET'S TAKE STOCK OF

The Terms You Need to Know to Move Ahead

There are only ten terms you need to know.

1. **Share of stock**—Your evidence of ownership of a part of a company.

Eight terms to measure the company's performance and condition:

Performance (Income Statement)	*Condition (Balance Sheet)*
1. **Sales**— What it takes in ("good") Minus	2. **Assets**—What it owns ("good") Minus
3. **Expenses**—What it spends ("bad") Equals	4. **Liabilities**—What it owes ("bad") Equals
5. **Profit**—What's left ("good") Divided by shares outstanding	6. **Equity**—What's left ("good") Divided by shares outstanding
7. **Earnings per share**—Your portion	8. **Book value per share**—Your portion

And finally:

10. **Price-earnings ratio (PE, multiple)**—The relationship between the company's earnings and the price of its stock.

These terms describe the data that you will use to study your candidates. From these data you (or your computer) can easily calculate the additional values that you will use to decide whether a company is a good one to invest in and whether its stock is selling for a fair price. You'll learn later where and how you can obtain these data at minimum cost.

Next, we'll talk about the heartbeat of technamental investment: growth.

CHAPTER 5

Understanding Growth

Growth can be defined as an increase in whatever data you're looking at over a period of time. When you study a company, you're looking for the results of management at work—an increase in sales and earnings, quarter after quarter, year after year. This is the basis for your confidence in a company and its ability to grow and make money for you. Remember, your investment performance is directly related to the company's ability to generate a consistent increase in its earnings.

SALES GROWTH

While it's the growth of earnings that promises to double the value of your stock, earnings can't grow without sales growth. It's the growth of sales, after expenses have been deducted, that generates the profit. And it's the profit, divided among the outstanding shares, that produces the earnings. So without sales growth there can be no growth in earnings to increase the value of your stock—at least over the long term.

There are only a few ways sales can grow. And the quality of growth varies with those sources. Let's go back to Lucy's Lemonade Stand so this will be easy to understand.

In order for her sales to grow Lucy has to sell more lemonade each week. To do this she can sell more lemonade to her regular customers, increase the number of customers she sells lemonade to, add cookies or some other products, or pursue a combination of those options. She can also make more money from each customer by raising her prices.

To increase the number of customers she can put flyers in neighborhood mailboxes. She can pay her playmate Charlene to open another stand on the next block. If this puts her in competition with Peter, two blocks away, and she takes some of his customers, she might even be willing to take over Peter's stand for a share of the profits because he's decided he'd rather play baseball.

Adding new products makes sense because she already has the stand, the location, and the customer base. They like her lemonade and will probably try her cookies. And she can experiment with additional products—limeade, raspberry coolers, or whatever—to see whether it makes sense to offer them. Or she can raise prices—but only if she has no competition and if her customers will support it.

There's little or no difference between this and what a big company does to grow, but what management must do to accomplish these things is a bit more complicated.

Probably the healthiest growth in revenues is referred to as *organic growth*—growth that is generated by either marketing or research and development.

Successful marketing will add new users for the product from among those who have never used such a product before, or it will take customers (market share) away from competitors that sell a similar product. This activity might include creating new markets geographically—abroad, perhaps. Or the company might expand its customer base demographically—maybe marketing a product to older or younger users than were targeted before.

Research and development will add more products or services to put in the marketplace. Hopefully these will be related to the company's existing products or services and will not be outside of the company's customary business domain. Peter Lynch calls such unrelated expansion "deworsification." It wouldn't be smart for Lucy to offer pet food when her success is based upon her gustatory delights for the *human* palate.

Also effective, but perhaps less healthy, is the *acquisition* of other companies. A strong company gobbles up the weaker ones in the same or similar businesses. Where allowed by the government, it eliminates competition, adds the acquired companies' sales to the top line, and hopefully finds some economies of scale and some synergies that will benefit the bottom line as well.

What makes acquisition riskier than organic growth is that the acquiring company will likely inherit not only the acquired company's assets and additional business but also the problems that made the company weak enough to grab. Labor problems can be easy to turn around, given an enlightened corporate culture and the eagerness of the labor force to cooperate with new and benevolent management. But plant and equipment obsolescence, bad brand reputation, or other more deep-rooted, long-term problems can be harder to overcome.

Another means of growing the top line is to raise prices. This is a very risky step that works only in certain situations. Generally, competition limits those possibilities, and even if there's virtually no competition, the price doesn't usually go up without some decline in the units sold. There are some cases, though, where price increases add substantially to a company's revenues without a sacrifice at the bottom line. For example, consider a drug company that enjoys the protection of a patent for each new product as it emerges from its pipeline. It can take advantage of that unique protection from competition and push prices up with little fear of decline in units sold.

When you look at a company and consider it for investment, it's a good idea to ask yourself where the company's growth comes from. Is the growth organic? Or is it coming from acquisitions? Is the company adding products or invading new markets? How aggressive is the company's international business, or is there a potential to expand there? What, if any, are the company's barriers to competition?

If you can't answer these questions at first, don't worry! You'll learn as you go along. And as you will soon discover, you can do an excellent job of picking your stocks without going into detail about such things. You should know something about the product and its market though, if only on a basic consumer's level. Commonsense issues can and should influence you when it comes to feeling at home with your candidates.

EARNINGS GROWTH

Where can earnings growth come from? Let's look at Lucy's Lemonade Stand again.

Lucy has taken over Peter's stand. Charlene runs another stand next to the playground. Lucy financed this growth primarily from profits, but also by hitting up Uncle Harry for 30 bucks in return for a piece of the action. "By now," Lucy's Dad had told Harry, "she's up to about $50 a week and her business is growing pretty fast."

To be sure, earnings should be growing as fast as sales because it's her sales that produce the profit—after taking into account the cost of lemons and sugar and the 50 cents an hour she pays Charlene and little Douglas, who runs Peter's old stand.

Aside from the volume of sales—the source of earnings and the basic generator of growth—why might earnings grow any faster or slower? We're going to look at this issue in greater detail later. For now I'll just cover the high points.

There are only two other factors that will affect earnings: expenses and out-standing shares. We'll consider expenses first because they're easier to under-stand.

Lucy's lemon cost can rise or fall. It can rise because the cost of lemons at the store rises (a bad season in California), or because she has to pay someone to go to the market to get them. Her lemon cost can fall because the store's produce manager gives her a special volume price.

Lucy's labor cost can rise. Charlene had been working for a quarter an hour, but someone put a bug in her ear and told her she should be getting three times as much. She demanded 75 cents, but Lucy talked her friend back down to a half dollar.

Lucy has now started making enough money that her dad's going to have to show her income on his tax return. She's going to have to start saving up to reimburse Dad for the taxes. So she figures out the profits each week and puts aside a percentage of that to give her dad the following April.

Uncle Harry's share is just like common stock—he simply put money into the business, never expecting Lucy to pay it back. But he is entitled to a third of the profits.

If Uncle Harry had simply lent her the $30 with the expectation that she would pay him back in a year, it would have been a loan, and Lucy's expenses would have included paying him interest on that loan. Harry would then have held a bond rather than a share of stock. The downside to Lucy would have been the requirement that she pay Uncle Harry even when a spell of rainy weather kept the stand closed. The upside would be that she would owe Uncle Harry no more in good times than in bad. All of the extra money she might make from the money Uncle Harry lent to her would belong to her and her father—her original stockholder. Again, this is *leverage*—making money by using OPM (other people's money).

Lucy might have worked out yet another deal with Uncle Harry for the 30 bucks. He could have given her the money with no requirement that she pay him back. There would be two conditions, though. She would have to agree to pay him a fixed *dividend* every month so long as she stayed in business. And if the lemonade business folded, Uncle Harry would have first crack at whatever could be salvaged to recover his investment—even before her dad would. But as her profits rose, her payments to Uncle Harry wouldn't. This is the nature of *preferred stock*. Even though these *preferred dividends* represent a distribution to a shareholder, they are considered an expense, much like interest, and they would be paid before Lucy or her dad or any other common stockholders would be entitled to their shares.

But as it is, Lucy now has to split the take not only with her dad, but with Uncle Harry. So while every dollar's worth of profit meant 50 cents each to Lucy and her dad before Uncle Harry came along, it now represents a little more than 33 cents. But thanks to Uncle Harry, the business is now bringing in many more dollars of profit than it would have without his participation, so she's happy to split the profit with Uncle Harry too.

Any of these things can cause the earnings per share to grow at a faster or slower rate than sales. And all of them simply require common sense to understand. Let's apply them to a large company.

As we said, earnings growth is first a function of sales growth. Earnings, *over the long term*, can grow no faster than sales. Remember that when you look at a company, it's a good idea to understand where that sales growth comes from.

Earnings growth is a function of one of three things: sales growth, expenses, and shares outstanding. (Although tax is an expense like any other, it's dependent upon profits. When you evaluate growth, you'll find it of more significance to consider the profits before taxes have been paid. This will let you look more closely at how management handles the things over which it has some control.)

Expenses

As with Lucy's Lemonade Stand, for a large company variable and fixed expenses can fluctuate up or down for many reasons. Material costs can increase, the cost of labor can rise—all are expenses related to producing the product or service.

In addition, there are fixed expenses, things such as rent, interest on bonds, insurance, management's salaries, equipment leases, and the cost of replacing equipment that has become obsolete or worn *(depreciation)*. As would have been the case with Lucy if she had borrowed the money from Uncle Harry, fixed expenses have to be paid no matter how good or bad business is.

All of these expenses affect the bottom line. The *profit margin* is simply the percentage of sales that remains after all of these expenses have been paid.

Shares Outstanding

Earnings per share—your portion of the company's profits—are what drive the value of your investment. So, in addition to considering an increase or decline in the profit margin, you must look for earnings growth or decline based on the number of shares among which the profits are divided.

Before Uncle Harry got involved, Lucy had only her father to share the profits with. Now she and her dad have to share them with Uncle Harry, the new shareholder. This is called *dilution* because the amount of profit going to each shareholder is diluted when it must be split among additional shares.

If a company sells additional shares, the existing shareholders will see an increase in the equity of the company as the money paid for the stock goes in the bank. But the book value per share will not change very much if at all because the number of shares has increased, diluting the value of that equity for each share. And when the income statement comes out at the end of the period, they will find that the earnings per share (EPS) will have declined from what it might have been had the shares not been issued.

The issuing of *convertible debentures* is another consideration. These are instruments that are purchased as bonds—the money is lent to the company—but that may at a later date and at the discretion of the holder be turned in for common stock. There is a potential for greater dilution here. When someone decides to exercise the conversion option, the company's obligation to repay the loan will be over, so it will be the same as if the stockholder had purchased the stock earlier. The money is in the bank. Again, however, the number of shares among which the profit must be allocated will have grown to whatever extent those bonds have been converted.

Another source of dilution, especially with new economy companies, is the growing practice of issuing stock options as compensation. To be competitive in the labor market more and more companies are offering employees an opportunity to cash in at a later date on the company's growth.

Earnings must be reported both as *basic* and as *diluted* earnings. You're interested in the diluted earnings—as are most analysts—because they reflect the result of distributing earnings among all possible shares. This offers the worst-case view of earnings and represents the most conservative approach to assessing the company's performance.

Many times earnings will show growth despite the fact that neither sales nor profit margins have grown. In fact, either or both may have declined. When this happens, there is only one explanation: share repurchase. If a company has repurchased its shares, the opposite of dilution takes place as the company's profits are distributed among fewer shares. You'll find out later how to tell at a glance when share repurchase has caused earnings to grow without accompanying sales growth.

You will also learn later how to diagnose at a glance the reasons that earnings and sales are growing at different rates. For the time being, suffice it to say that any difference in the rates of growth can't last forever. The two must settle into a state of equilibrium eventually, or the company will go out of business. If earnings grow faster than sales, the cutting of costs or the buying back of shares cannot go on forever. If earnings grow at a slower rate than sales, the company will die if management isn't capable of stanching the outflow of money in expenses. And, of course, there's a limit to how much stock a company can issue when earnings per share is declining.

LET'S TAKE STOCK OF
What You Need to Know about Growth

- **T**he value of a stock is measured by the multiple of earnings (PE) that investors are willing to pay for it.

- The value of your investment grows when the company's earnings grow at a rate that increases the value of the stock at approximately the same rate.

- The rate of earnings growth depends upon the rate of sales growth but can, for a limited period, vary above or below it.

- Earnings per share is affected by expenses and by changes in the number of shares outstanding.

- You are interested in finding companies that are capable of producing earnings growth sufficient to double your investment about every five years.

With this understanding of growth under your belt, let's go on to learn about how to identify the companies that can deliver the growth you're looking for.

CHAPTER 6

Prospecting for Good Candidates

SOME SOUND PRINCIPLES

NAIC teaches its members four principles that have become something of a mantra. They represent excellent advice and are worthy of mention here:

1. *Invest a fixed amount regularly.* Successful investing requires discipline. This principle is especially important for young folks who have the opportunity to put aside a small amount on a regular basis, an amount that can add up over the years to become a substantial fortune. But it can also apply to clubs that collect dues that are to be invested on a regular basis.

    When you invest a fixed amount regularly, you enjoy the benefits of dollar cost averaging: you will buy more shares when they are cheap and fewer when they are expensive. This should provide for a lower cost per share over time.

2. *Reinvest all earnings.* Sound advice if you are going to maximize your investment benefits. The magic of compounding, of earning money on

your earned money, is very important. It makes the difference between being able to double your money every five years or putting that objective beyond reasonable reach. If you pull out your earnings every year instead of reinvesting them, it will take a return of 20 percent a year to double your investment. If you leave your earnings where they are, doubling your investment will take but 15 percent per year. The former is beyond reasonable reach, the latter an attainable goal.

3. *Invest only in good-quality growth companies.* As we've said over and over, growth is what drives the price of stocks. You will want to find those companies that, on the average, can double your money every five years.

4. *Diversify.* Without a doubt, it's foolish to put all your eggs in one basket. Having too high a percentage of your portfolio in only one company, a single industry, or a particular size of company can subject you to unnecessary risk. However, this principle is more often given too much emphasis than not enough. See Chapter 13 for a detailed discussion.

Of these four fine principles, the first two and the last are fairly mechanical and depend upon a simple sense of discipline. The third, however, is the most important and is the one that causes the most concern. That is why I have devoted most of this book to that topic.

One additional principle that is appropriate to mention here is: If it looks too good to be true, it probably is. This is one thing that many people find out from their own experience—unfortunately. When you learn how to analyze and evaluate a company, you'll occasionally find a stock that looks like a bargain. It rarely is. You'll be wise to be skeptical and suspicious—curious to find out why the price is so low rather than eager to make a killing.

Keep your expectations and ambitions modest and reasonable. You'll earn your success by seeking a win-win situation that results from adding value that someone is pleased to pay for. Once in a while you may be able to take advantage of a situation in which a stock is seriously undervalued by investors, but most of the time you'll find that you're prospecting among fairly valued stocks. That's where you will find your winners.

You can accomplish your goal of doubling your money in five years by investing in a business because earnings growth of 15 percent is a reasonable goal for a well-run business. When you look to do very much better than that, you're straying into territory in which someone else has to lose for you to gain. This is the BFS/STS scenario that grossly decreases your odds for success.

There are more than 10,000 publicly owned companies out there for you to select from. And those are just the ones in the United States. Some are, of course, much better candidates for your consideration than others. Of these 10,000 companies, fewer than 10 percent would probably make the cut as far as your quality standards are concerned. And perhaps only 10 percent of those might be available at the right price at any given time—and even this could be an overestimate.

HOW ABOUT A MUTUAL FUND?

"Aha!" you say. Based on those four principles that are important enough to commit to memory, it sounds like a mutual fund would be the perfect choice. Let's see:

The first principle says to invest a fixed amount regularly.

Check. That's what you do with a mutual fund. You commit to sending in a fixed amount every month. The discipline is taken care of and so is the dollar cost averaging. Perfect!

Reinvest all income.

Check. That's what they do. Your dividends remain in the account and are added to the value of the fund. Great!

Invest only in good-quality growth companies.

Check again. Not only can I select a fund that announces its intention to do just that but I can look at its track record to see how well it's done.

Diversify.

Perfect! A fund isn't limited to only as many stocks as I can keep track of in my spare time. It can own 1,000 stocks or 10,000 stocks and has a professional staff watching over them all day, every day.

What could be a more perfect way to apply the four principles?

Not so fast! True, investing in mutual funds offers the opportunity to do exactly what I've built a case for thus far—owning small pieces of growing concerns. And it's certainly much better than putting your money under your mattress or in a tin can buried in your backyard. If you pick the right fund, you should be able to do better than you would with a CD or a money market account, or with bonds.

I've made the point that your aim is to minimize your risks and responsibilities while still getting the best possible return from owning a business or businesses. I've led you down the road from starting your own business to owning shares of stock in a number of companies, and I've explained that you have to pay increasing multiples of earnings as you shed responsibilities and risks.

Mutual funds, however, are overkill. They carry you past the point where you can get the most return for the least cost.

Investing in a good mutual fund is a temporary alternative that you should pursue only long enough to develop confidence and skill in this simple and effective approach. It's a good way to build your beginning nest egg. However, I think you'll be paying more than you should for the privilege of relieving yourself of further responsibility and risk. Here's why.

First of all, the premise that you can satisfy the most important principle by simply selecting the fund that has the appropriate objective and the best track record is not the "no-brainer" that it sounds like. The government rigidly regulates funds—what they report and how they report—so you can find out about their track records if you know where to look and what to look for. Or you can seek the help of a professional who does. However, the government can't dictate what a fund chooses to advertise so long as it's accurate. Naturally, a fund will put its best foot forward, and if you rely on anything less rigorous than the prospectus, you will have a hard time comparing "apples to apples." There are, however, fine services like Morningstar at <www.morningstar.com> that have done a creditable job of standardizing the way performance is calculated and presented. But, it's often hard for the novice to tell how each fund's record is figured from what they usually have to go on.

But let's say that you could standardize performance figures and could look at several funds side by side, comparing them on that basis. What do you have to go on that assures you that their future performance will be anything like their history? Without being able to look at each stock in the fund's portfolio and to analyze it yourself (I suppose you could, but I think you'd rather have a life), you can't really assess the future.

More important, there's nothing that says that those same stocks will be there next week. When I talk about a "track record," it's truly apropos in this context, because trying to assess the future performance of a mutual fund is like trying to handicap a horse race by looking at the jockey's record. With a mutual fund you're looking at the record of the "jockey" that manages the fund. Not only that, jockeys change horses and fund managers move around too. There's nothing to assure you that the same manager will continue to manage your fund or that his success will necessarily continue if he stays on. You're betting your money on the jockey and not on the horse!

For that privilege you're likely to pay a commission either on the money you pay at the start *(front-end load)* or an even a bigger amount on the higher value that the fund should be worth at a later time *(back-end load).* There are also *no-load* funds for which no commissions are paid. But don't kid yourself! Someone has to pay everyone who manages the fund, sells it, promotes it, and does all of the paperwork. And after all of that the mutual fund company has to make a profit for its stockholders just like any other company. So you'll always find a management fee amounting to some percentage of your investment buried somewhere in the contract.

Having more than 15 or 20 good companies in your portfolio isn't going to be all that productive for you anyway. You don't need more companies to minimize your risk, and there are not all that many above-average companies out there. The more companies you own beyond a certain point, the more mediocre your portfolio's performance is likely to be. Warren Buffett, one of the most successful investors of all time, has fewer than 10 major positions and fewer than 25 companies in all—in his portfolio. Who are we to argue?

On top of that, because fund managers are handling other peoples' money and not just their own, there are many things you can do that they can't. You can take advantage of some opportunities that fund managers can't or won't. You can buy or sell all the shares of a stock without having to worry about whether your transaction will affect the price of the stock, while large-fund managers have to worry about whether selling their positions will affect the market for that stock because they control so much of it.

For me, however, the most compelling argument is this: While one fund may have a slower turnover rate for its holdings than others, its manager cannot sit still and wait out a bump in the road like you can. Those stocks are bought and sold all the time, and the fund managers have to churn those accounts to capture profits and to show off the portfolio every quarter. Every time they do it, they incur a tax liability that you have to pay, and at the end of the year you'll feel it.

So I suggest that you park your money in mutuals only long enough to earn some money while you find the stocks you want to buy individually. Once you've assembled your own portfolio, you can start paying *yourself* all of the money you'll save.

Your first job in assembling your portfolio will be to separate the wheat from the chaff and to select good prospects to study.

LOOKING FOR CANDIDATES

Candidate is certainly an appropriate word here. No candidate serves in office without being put in that office through an appropriate election process. And no candidate should become a part of your portfolio until it passes your stringent selection process. But without some candidates, we have nothing to elect or to select from.

We now know the terms. Let's apply them to our preliminary task of prospecting for good candidates for *study*—not yet for purchase.

What You're Not Looking For

Before I tell you about what you want in a company, let me take a moment or two to tell you about the qualities that you *don't* want. That way you'll be able to eliminate a whole lot of companies right off the bat.

Not old enough. Companies that have not been trading publicly long enough to have an audited track record are not good candidates. You don't want to bother with a company that hasn't had at least five years of public trading on one of the major exchanges.

This, of course, rules out initial public offerings (IPOs) and other such speculative situations. If someone suggests such an investment to you, check the financial pages in the newspaper for starters. If the stock doesn't appear in the NYSE, AMEX, or Nasdaq listings, tell your friend, "Thanks for the suggestion, but no thanks!"

Not big enough. Companies that, despite their age, have not grown to at least $50 million in sales are too small to be interesting. In fact, with rare exceptions, you're better off skipping companies that have not yet achieved $100 million in sales. Like landing fish below the limit, you should throw them back in and let them grow some more. Rest assured you won't miss out on anything.

Put the attractive "minnows" on your watch list when they're small. If they're capable of the kind of growth you think they are, they'll continue to grow until they have earned your confidence. And you'll still be able to get in before the rest of the world finds out enough about them to jump on the bandwagon.

Not earning yet. Companies with no earnings are not a good bet for reasons that you now know. Many companies have dot-com after their name but have nothing on their bottom line—no matter how big and popular they are. These companies may be the place to be in the future, but you are here and this is now. Wait for the start-ups to start making money—and then wait for them to make it for a while longer. I guarantee you it won't be too late for you to make money with them.

I guess this is as good a time as any to address the dot-com bubble. The stock market of the 1990s ought to be looked upon as a special case. It was a modern-day, real-live bubble, and many of us haven't lived through such a thing. The dot-com bubble has challenged all that we know and hold dear. And it's been an excellent example of what Charles McKay wrote about way back in 1841 in his wonderful book *Extraordinary Delusions and the Madness of Crowds.* If McKay had lived in the 20th century, he would have written with equal clarity and derision about the chain letters of 1935 and the dot-com bubble of the 1990s.

Webster's dictionary offers as a definition of the word *bubble:* "any idea, scheme, etc. that seems plausible at first but quickly shows itself to be worthless or misleading."

Generally speaking, an economic bubble develops when, on a large scale, buyers discard the rational assessment of the value of something and award to it a value that is based solely upon what they think someone else would be willing to pay for it.

Merchants and huge discount empires can't afford to mark up their merchandise to a level that exceeds the normal customer's willingness to pay for value received. Competition and availability of the merchandise keep the lid on. The exception, of course, is when the supply of something (like the Hula Hoop, Pokemon cards, or Beanie Babies) is limited and the prices become inflated for a while. But these are occasional events throughout history when the madness of crowds has prevailed.

One of the best-known bubbles of history was the tulip-bulb fiasco back in the mid-1630s. For much the same reason that companies without earnings have become sought after, tulips became so popular that the price was driven up until tulip bulbs were selling for as much as $100,000 apiece!

The story goes that on one occasion, a sailor, thinking it was an onion, ate a tulip bulb, the value of which was equal to a year's salary for him and all of his shipmates. Of course he landed in jail for many months for his culinary indiscretion—and I don't imagine the bulb tasted that good.

To give you a feel for just how full of hot air this modern-day bubble has been, Keith Mullins, emerging growth strategist at Salomon Smith Barney, pointed out in a report dated November 19, 1999, that if an investor had put his money into all of the stocks in the Russell 2000 (an index of small, publicly traded companies) at the beginning of 1999, he would have made 6.6 percent on his money for the year. However, if he had placed his money only in the Russell 2000 companies that *lost* money that year—that had no earnings—he would have made 49.7 percent on his investment! Mullins went on to say that the Russell Midcap Index was even more ridiculous. The gain for the entire index was a meager 8 percent, while investment in only the losers would have made you 107 percent!

If this bubble hasn't burst by the time this book is published, it will be a great surprise to me and to many others who are more knowledgeable than I am.

What caused the bubble? One could offer a potpourri of reasons. For starters: the presence of a lot of money that needed to go to work somewhere; economic euphoria; confidence in an economy driven largely by technological initiatives, many of which are paying off. In large measure, the bubble can be attributed to an uneducated public's expectations of the impact of the Internet on our lives.

Probably the biggest blast of hot air to pump up this bubble has come from the host of young people who have made millions in the technology sector, who have exercised their stock options and are looking for a way to make millions more.

The new venture capitalists say, "Never mind the earnings. Just get out there and cultivate the mind-share." (*Mind-share* is cyber-speak for the number of eye-balls that come to a Web site and hang out there.) Collectively, the new investors have billions of dollars, and they play only one level above the investors they hope will jump in when they take a dot-com public.

However, the venture capitalists' bubble can burst too—and will, just as soon as they discover that *someone* has to make the money to pay for things. It will burst as soon as the investing public decides that it's time to judge a stock they buy on the basis of how much the company earns, not according to how sexy its story seems to be.

Don't put your money into any company that doesn't have an established record of earning money for its shareholders, no matter how exciting its story.

Not familiar to you. You should reduce your risk further by eliminating from consideration companies that sell products or services that you either don't know about or have no interest in learning about. Peter Lynch often said that he steered clear of technology companies because he knew nothing about what they did. If you don't understand Internet technology, don't get involved with a company that sells routers, no matter how hot a company like Cisco (CSCO) may appear! There are plenty of other companies that you can nominate as good candidates.

Why avoid such a company? It's harder for you to understand such issues as the market for its products, the risks and potential pitfalls, the significance of new products, or the potential for competition—some of the commonsense factors that may lead you to make a decision at a later date about whether you should sell or hold onto the stock.

Keep in mind that your intentions are honorable. You're going to "marry" this company, not just have an affair with it. Just like in real life, the better you understand your mate, the better you'll get along with him or her—or in this case, it.

WHAT *ARE* YOU LOOKING FOR?

This book started with the premise that you should invest in common stocks because they are "live," not "dead" places to put your money. Let's talk for a bit about the "life" of a successful company.

Human beings start life with promise. They look cute and appealing (or red-faced and squalling), but no matter what they're like to begin with, if all goes well, they grow physically, mentally, and emotionally through infancy, childhood, adolescence, and finally adulthood and maturity.

Human beings start by being demanding and dependent. Along the way, they learn how to cope with life, how to be independent. And—again, if all goes well—they learn a set of skills; they learn how to contribute and how to get the most out of life by making that contribution. They also, hopefully, learn a set of values that makes life worthwhile.

FIGURE 6.1   Life Cycle of a Successful Company

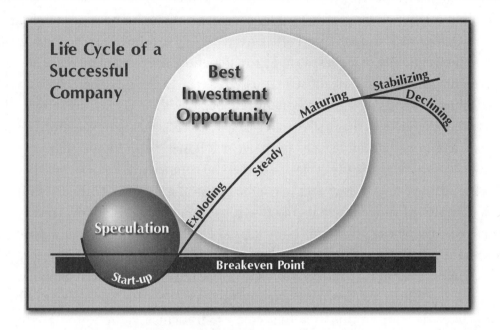

Some of life's phases are painful, some are awkward, and many are exciting, and eventually in the mature years things simmer down some. Then folks either capitalize on their experience and their resources to make life continually interesting, or at the other extreme they sink into maudlin reminiscence and dependency.

One could easily compare the stages in the life cycle of a successful business to all of these human phases of growth.

A company at start-up is certainly demanding and dependent. It requires an infusion of capital and sweat equity from risk takers. And as you can see in Figure 6.1, its earnings are predictably below the breakeven point.

It takes a while before the company can begin to stand on its own two feet and be productive. The process that most companies go through as individual ownership gives way to public ownership and professional management is often painful—akin to the worst kind of growing pains and adolescent turmoil.

Eventually the company breaks even, then learns to focus on what it does best. It begins to fine-tune its operations, to get focused, and to become solidly productive. It generates steady profits, develops a customer base or brand satisfaction and loyalty, and achieves sufficient credibility to sell its stock to the public.

At the beginning of this explosive growth period, the percent increase in sales and earnings can be spectacular. Obviously, it's easy to grow 100 percent in a year if sales and earnings were inconsequential to begin with. If a company sells $1,000 of goods or services in the first year, it's easy to sell $2,000 the next—much easier than it would be to double sales in the year following a million-dollar year. So growth rates early in the life cycle of a successful company tend to be sensational.

The adult years—those years when the physical growth in a human is superseded by mental and emotional growth—correspond to the company's most productive years. These years are characterized by the development of a positive corporate culture (in the best-run companies) and of a corporate ethic and set of values, whose results in productivity may not be traced directly to the top or bottom line, but without which success would be impossible. It's the degree to which companies develop in this area that creates "franchise value"—the premium above its peers in its industry at which its stock will consistently sell.

Eventually the successful company reaches a mature growth period when revenue becomes so large that it is difficult to maintain a consistent percentage increase in growth. Just like a human in the golden years, the company enters a period of stabilization—or it declines if it fails to rejuvenate its product mix or expand its markets.

You're interested in finding companies that are at least five years into their explosive growth period, businesses that have completed their adolescence, but have not gone past their prime into decline. Obviously, the longer the company has had a successful track record, the more stable and safe it's apt to be—provided its management copes successfully with maturity.

These are the standards you should stick with when you look for companies to invest in. Higher-risk situations involving companies early in their life cycle are speculative and not of investment quality.

WHERE DO YOU FIND
INVESTMENT-QUALITY COMPANIES?

You can find investment-quality companies everywhere. There are nearly as many good ways to prospect for candidates as there are candidates. Here are just a few:

The financial press. Read the financial newspapers. Subscribe to one of the many newsletters that are out there, or just accept the trial offers you will receive when you get on one of their mailing lists. Financial newspapers are full of exciting stories about "wonderful" companies that all try to outdo each other, bragging about their track records. However, none of the newsletters does any better selecting stocks than you can. It's fine to get ideas from them and see what the analysts are saying about some of the comers. But don't buy what the newsletters are selling until you do your own stock study.

Newspapers. Be sensitive to information about industries and specific companies in the regular newspapers. Look for exciting companies. Not only will you find good prospects in the financial pages, but frequently stories about exciting companies will appear in other parts of the paper when something newsworthy affects them. Buried in reports about discoveries or developments in the medical or scientific field will be the names of companies that are working with the new technologies.

The Wall Street Journal and *Investors Business Daily* are both great sources of information about likely prospects.

Television. Some commercials are not worth watching; they just provide you with a good opportunity to go to the refrigerator. But don't be too hasty. You'll find some commercials that are engaging and are marketing enticing products.

Whether you would use the products or not, you might see great value for the market they serve and have an interest in the companies that produce and sell them. Like newspapers, newscasts often have special features that reveal interesting discoveries or developments. With a little research you can dig up companies that are involved in those activities and that might prove to be great investments.

Your broker. Ask your broker for a suggestion or two. While we recommend that you *never* take a broker's suggestion and buy a stock without doing your own study, a good, conscientious broker who's interested in your success is an asset to you. Brokers have access to much more research material than you have at your disposal, so it's appropriate that you ask them for the information you want.

If your broker tries to "sell" you on buying an issue, be nice but firm and say that you want the research, not the advice. Ask the specific questions that you want answers to, but don't ask for the broker's opinion. You'd be surprised how soon your broker starts asking you for advice once you start to build a successful portfolio.

Common sense and a little observation are far better providers of stock tips than the average broker whose company may have its own interests at heart when it "suggests" he push a stock!

Many people prefer to use discount or online brokers. They offer some research resources, but they don't give advice and they don't pressure you to buy anything.

Your barber or beautician. You can get a good or bad tip from anyone. I once got a tip from a bellman in a hotel in Mexico City. He had overheard it from some visiting dignitaries and passed it along to me. Fortunately, I didn't go right home and buy the stock (I might have, since I didn't know then what I know now). I don't remember what the stock was any more, but I do remember that it turned out to be a bummer!

The point is, of course, that you can get a tip from anyone at any time, but you should do your homework on the company before you buy its stock.

The shopping mall or grocery store. Find out the names of the companies that produce the products and services that you use and think are excellent. This is a wonderful way to prospect because it takes into account the quality of the products, and you're familiar with the market and with the potential of the products or services.

Peter Lynch says that one of his greatest stock picks was L'Eggs, the hosiery sold in supermarkets. His wife came home one day enthusing about the notion that shoppers could so conveniently purchase hosiery while they were food shopping. He decided to take a look at the company and did buy it—but only after thoroughly researching it.

Products and services that you have specific knowledge of or experience with fit in here as well. If you're a doctor, you'll be familiar with pharmaceuticals. If you're a secretary, you may have had some good and bad experiences with certain brands of office equipment.

Your children's playroom. The fastest growing market today may be the children's market. Toys, clothes, books—anything and everything that kids might want—are selling like hotcakes. Kids have more influence in the home these days than ever, and parents are buying what their children want. This trend may continue until the next generation comes of age, so you might want to look at companies that provide things kids want.

The moral of this story is simply that you should be alert to the economics of what's around you. The booming children's market may be only a transient phenomenon—parents may have run out of money or patience by the time you read this. You will want to size up the trends of your time and look to your own common sense to decide whether they're just fads or are here to stay. If you identify some long-term trends, look for the companies that will let you profit from them.

The library. The library is a rich source for candidates to study. Not only are there plenty of magazines and other publications that are full of interesting articles and stories about intriguing companies, but there are also reference books that you can access. Some of these offer you names of companies to look at and the data that you need to study them.

The *Value Line Survey* is such a resource. To subscribe to this service, which is available either as a CD-ROM or in printed form, would cost you more than $500 annually. At the library you can find it for free, most likely in print. Probably the most highly respected source of data that you can access at the library, the *Value Line Survey* contains data for its basic list of around 1,700 companies and provides somewhat less information for an additional 1,800 businesses.

The *Value Line Survey* also provides you with lists of companies that meet certain screening requirements. For example, it lists all of the companies that have earnings growth rates above 13 percent per year and expectations of five more years of growth. It also offers a list of companies that are expected to do well over the next three to five years. We'll go into greater detail about *Value Line* later, when we discuss the various sources of information required for your studies. For now, suffice it to say that the *Value Line Survey* is a great source of possible candidates for your study, and you can kill two birds with one stone by accessing the data required for your analysis as well.

An investment club.   You can start an investment club or join an existing club. Investment clubs are an excellent source of high-quality candidates, and you have the added benefit of collaborating with others who want to learn as you do. If you belong to a club where everyone is as eager to learn as you are, your learning will accelerate as you go along.

NAIC's official guide, *Starting and Running a Successful Investment Club*, can help you start your own club. The guide is written by Thomas E. O'Hara and Kenneth S. Janke Sr., NAIC's chairman and founder and its president and CEO, respectively. Some of the guide is not easy to get through, but it contains a message that's been valid for 50 years and offers some especially good advice on the topics related to clubs.

NAIC events.   NAIC events are happening all the time, all across the country. Look for NAIC in your local phone directory or visit NAIC's Web site, <www.better-investing.org> to obtain the name and number of the regional representative. You'll soon be talking to a volunteer who can steer you to the next event, where you can form good associations with folks who have embarked on the same path that you're setting out on. NAIC not only can help you come up with good candidates for study, it can help you find a club to join, a workshop to go to that will help you learn more about what you're reading now, opportunities to network with others with the same interest.

NAIC online. Last, but certainly not least, is NAIC's online presence, the so-called I-Club, or online investment club. This is an army of more than 3,000 folks all over the country who have a common interest in NAIC's investment methodology and who are connected through the Internet or e-mail.

More than just a fantastic source of investment ideas, the I-Club is a great networking opportunity for those wishing to compare notes about the companies they're interested in, to debate the decisions that they make when evaluating stocks, to learn, and to share learning.

A lot of what you read in this book has come from the I-Club—from folks who have learned about this investment approach on their own—or has been published there first in answer to questions that arise from people just like you.

Active I-Club participants include people like Nancy Isaacs, an NAIC volunteer from New Jersey, who has taught more people than many a professor through her Socratic approach to learning—asking questions and demanding satisfactory answers until she is satisfied that she understands the topic completely.

It costs nothing to sign up and participate in the I-Club. Many people are simply *lurkers,* not writing a thing, just soaking up the information that's available there.

Don't overlook this resource! You can join simply by going to NAIC's Web site, <www.better-investing.org>. Unless the site has been radically changed, you will be able to just click on "I-Club List," which you'll find under "Community" on the left side of the screen.

I would be remiss if I didn't also mention NAIC's CompuServe Forum, which runs a close and closing second to the I-Club. Similar in content, but with a slightly different ambience, the forum is also a free area. You can join at <go.com puserve.com/NAIC>.

About Tips

Most tips, regardless of their source, fall in the category of either inside information or new product potential.

If someone offers you inside information, ask yourself, "If that information is so new, exciting, and secret, how did the person who told me about it know about it?" (If your stockbroker gives you the tip, you may rest assured that the market has already discounted the stock.)

In the case of new product information—"ABC Company is about to introduce a revolutionary new widget"—you have to ask yourself, "What percentage of current revenue can such a new product generate if that product or service is successful?" Usually the answer will be that sales of the new product will add only a tiny fraction to the current sales figures. If the company is so small that the new product would have a large effect on the company's bottom line, then the company is probably still too small or new to bother with, or the introduction of the new product is too risky to gamble on.

You can get a good idea from almost anywhere. There are as many suggestions out there as there are companies, and one might be just as good as another. So long as you clearly understand that you should *never, never, never* buy a stock on a tip without doing your homework, you're going to do just fine.

Electronic Screening

There's one other means of prospecting that should be mentioned here, and that is electronic screening using a personal computer. Screening is a method of filtering a large number of companies for only those meeting the criteria that you select. You can screen on a variety of different values: sales or earnings growth rates, PE multiples, company size, and so on. The list of criteria varies depending upon where you go to do your screening.

The cost ranges from zero for screening on the Internet to about $250 a year for subscribing to and maintaining a database on your own computer. (Some professional screening products, with the databases that go with them, cost upward of $20,000 a year.)

Internet sources. You'll find a number of Internet sites that offer screening opportunities usually free of charge. Since these change from time to time, you should consult a current listing of the most suitable sites. One of the best is Doug Gerlach's rich Investorama Web site <www.investorama.com>. Doug, the author of *Investor's Web Guide* and *The Complete Idiot's Guide to Online Investing*, is one of the most knowledgeable sources of Web-based investment information around today.

On Doug's Web site you'll find a consolidation of resources to suit your every need. As of this writing, Doug has listed some 25 sites with varying classes and kinds of data to screen on. There are descriptions of the sites to help you decide which ones might be most useful to you. To access this resource, point your Web browser to <www.investorama.com/directory/Quotes,_Charts,_Re search/ Screening/atoz.html>.

Screening databases and software. There are a number of desktop screening programs available as well. These provide data on a regular, subscription basis and give you the tools to filter that data for just what you want.

The most impressive of these products, in my opinion, is Stock Investor PRO, made available by the American Association of Individual Investors (AAII), another nonprofit organization whose mission, like NAIC's, is to educate individual investors and enhance their ability to make sound investment decisions on their own. While Internet sites that permit screening generally have only a few key criteria on which you may screen, Stock Investor PRO offers as many as 1,500 predetermined variables, plus the ability to create your own.

What to Look for and Where to Find It

You Don't Want

- Companies that are too small or young

- Companies that are too big or old

- Companies that aren't "in business" yet (i.e., that are earning no money)

- Companies in businesses you don't understand—or care to understand

You Do Want

- Companies whose sales are growing year to year at a rate consistent with company size

- Companies whose earnings are growing year to year at a rate that will allow doubling every five years

You can find information about good candidates almost anywhere, from the newspaper to your hair stylist. Your library and the Internet are two very fruitful places to find both good candidates and the data you will need for your studies.

Just don't buy anything on a tip! Consider no investment until you have studied the company using the methods that you will learn in detail in the next several chapters.

CHAPTER 7

Evaluating Company Quality

To buy a good stock, you only need to know if the company is a good-quality company and if the price you have to pay for its stock is reasonable. Frankly, if you can tell the difference between a straight and a crooked line and whether it slopes up or down, you can tell nearly everything you need to know about a company's quality. It's really that simple!

A good-quality company is one whose *growth,* upon which you rely to increase the value of your investment, is strong and stable, and one in which management's *efficiency* will enable it to continue that satisfactory growth. Both of these elements can be represented by lines on charts whose technamental interpretation requires no more than the simple skills I mentioned. In this chapter you'll learn how to quickly evaluate a company's growth. In Chapter 9, you'll learn to evaluate management's ability to sustain it.

THE CHARTS

Technamental analysis uses two kinds of charts to evaluate growth and efficiency. The first is a growth chart that is known technically as a semilog chart.

This is what you'll use to analyze the quality of sales and earnings growth. The other is a simple linear chart you can use to look at management's efficiency.

You can generate these charts painlessly on a computer using either electronic or printed data, or you can plot the charts by hand. If you have a computer, the disk accompanying this book will create them for you as will any of the software reviewed in Appendix B.

The illustrations in this book were generated quite easily using Microsoft's Excel spreadsheet program and printed data from the *Value Line Survey.*

If you're not a computer user, you can still do what's required using one of the printed forms available (described in detail in Appendix A). For this, you'll need only a ruler, business calculator, pencil, and eraser. A business calculator can be obtained for less than $25 at your local discount office supply store. One of the most popular is Texas Instruments' BA-35.

You need one that has four keys: "PV" (present value), "FV" (future value), "i%" (percent), and "N" (number of periods). It should also have a key that computes the result. It will be labeled "CPT" or something similar. These keys are used to solve problems that involve the time value of money. To solve for any of the four values, you simply enter the other three and press the "CPT" key to compute the result. With the calculator you can quickly determine compounded growth rates and rates of return and do all of the other calculations required for technamental analysis. Where such calculations are necessary, I'll indicate which keys to use.

CHARTING GROWTH

Chapter 5 was devoted to learning about the nature of growth, where it comes from, and how companies from Lucy's Lemonade Stand to General Electric generate growth in sales and earnings. That discussion gave you insight into the character and quality of growth.

You learned in Chapter 6 how to find a good candidate for consideration. And now you're ready to scrutinize that candidate's growth more closely to see if it has the character—the stability and strength—to be a good enough company to invest in.

FIGURE 7.1   Difference between Linear (Simple) Growth
and Compounded Growth

$1 growing at 15%	**Linear**	**Compounded**
Starting amount	$1.00	$1.00
End of year 1	1.15	1.15
End of year 2	1.30	1.32
End of year 3	1.45	1.52
End of year 4	1.60	1.75
End of year 5	1.75	2.01

You're interested in *compounded* growth as opposed to simple, *linear* growth. When the growth is compounded, you start with $1.00 and it grows 15 percent during the first year. You have $1.15 at the end of the year. The following year $1.15, not the original $1.00, grows 15 percent. See Figure 7.1 to understand the effect. As you can see, compounded growth at a little less than 15 percent will double your money in five years.

You can see from this chart just why it doesn't pay to pull money out of your account if you don't have to. The "Linear" column shows what will happen if you withdraw your gain each year. Leaving your earnings there will allow compounding to work its magic, doubling your money in five years.

Technamental analysis of sales and earnings growth means that you plot and literally look at that growth to appraise it, so you should know what a growth chart is and how you'll use it.

Some people have a knack for looking at a row or column of numbers, interpreting the numbers, and drawing conclusions from them. However, if you're like most people, when you look at a relationship between one set of numbers and another, it hardly sticks out like the proverbial damaged digit. So it doesn't do a whole lot of good to deal just with the raw numbers. You need a better way to visualize the numbers' significance. This is where a chart or graph is invaluable.

FIGURE 7.2   Sales Growing at 15%, Plotted on a Linear Chart

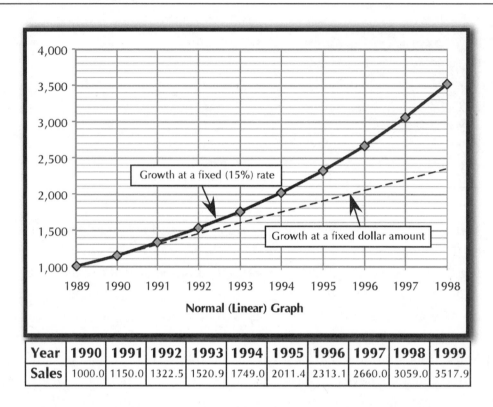

Year	1990	1991	1992	1993	1994	1995	1996	1997	1998	1999
Sales	1000.0	1150.0	1322.5	1520.9	1749.0	2011.4	2313.1	2660.0	3059.0	3517.9

At the bottom of Figure 7.2 there is a table with sales figures for ten years. Above the table the data are plotted on a regular (linear) graph. The sales figures (in millions of dollars) are listed along the left side (on the *Y*, or vertical, axis), and the years are shown along the bottom (on the *X*, or horizontal, axis).

This is one picture that's worth a thousand words. It should be obvious that you can best analyze growth when you can actually see it. But the chart tells you little about the rate of growth. Because the bold line curves higher each year, you might think the rate of growth is increasing, but, in fact, it's not. The rate of growth is the same each year.

If sales had increased at the same *dollar amount* (in this case, $150 million) each year rather than growing at the same *rate,* the line that depicts sales growth would be straight like the dotted line in the illustration. Although the dollar-amount line slopes up, the *rate* of growth is actually declining.

In the case of a linear chart like the one in Figure 7.2, it's easy to read the sales values because they are evenly spaced along the left side. But it's not easy to interpret the rate of growth except to say that the line climbs as it goes from left to right, indicating an increase—some growth.

But you're interested in seeing how a company's growth *rate* fares. You're looking for a business that maintains a fairly consistent record of growth; it must increase its *increase* each year. This is the *compounded* growth I spoke of above.

It's difficult for a company to maintain a steady growth rate forever. The bigger the company gets (i.e., the bigger the revenues become), the greater the revenues required to sustain that rate. (But then you only ask the company to sustain its rate for the duration of your lifetime.)

Look at the same data plotted on a semilog, or growth, chart in Figure 7.3. Again, sales in the example have grown steadily at 15 percent. The plotted data now show up as a straight line. The obvious advantage of using a growth chart is that a constant growth rate is easy to see, and changes in that rate can be spotted at a glance.

Any increase in the rate of growth will appear clearly as an increase in the slope of the line; and any decrease will reduce the line's slope. When you use a growth chart, the actual dollar amounts might be more difficult to determine, but because you're interested only in analyzing the rate of growth, this display is much more meaningful to you.

An additional advantage of using a growth chart is that sales figures in the millions of dollars can be plotted on the same chart as earnings figures in dollars and cents, so rates of growth can easily be compared. It makes little difference whether the number is 1 cent or $1 billion; it can be plotted on the same line on the same chart. (For more information about the growth chart, see "Plotting Tips" in Appendix A.)

FIGURE 7.3   The Same Data, Shown on a Growth (Semilog) Chart

---

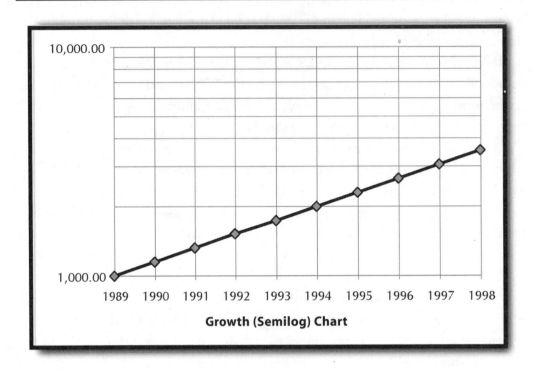

Growth (Semilog) Chart

In summary, we use a semilog graph, or growth chart, to analyze growth because

- a straight line depicts compounded growth at a consistent rate;
- a change in the rate of growth is easily recognized;
- a growth chart is useful for comparing growth rates, even the growth rate of sales revenue in the billions with that of earnings per share in dollars and cents; and
- you can fit more data on a smaller chart. Within three logarithmic scales or *decades*, for example, you can plot from $1 million to $1 billion, or from 10 cents to $10. Not too many companies are capable of growing more than that in 10 or 15 years.

ANALYZING GROWTH

When analyzing the trends in sales and earnings, look first at the general trend. Does the line slope upward? Look to see how steep or flat the sales and earnings lines are—the steeper the lines are, the stronger the growth. Of course, you can't tell the precise rate of growth just by looking. But you can get a general impression of a company's history of solid growth and its potential to continue being a strong-growth company.

Jim Jubak, senior markets editor for Microsoft Network's Money Central, then the senior financial editor of *Worth* magazine, referred to the growth chart in his book *The Worth Guide to Electronic Investing* (Harper Collins, 1996) as "perhaps the best single fundamental tool now available for grouping the character of a growth stock."

Probably the most important benefit that you can glean from your inspection of the growth chart of a company is that you will get a feel for the predictability of its growth.

The first key to successful investing, and the easiest task in your technamental analysis, is to recognize predictable growth. The only skill you require for this purpose is being able to tell a straight line from a crooked one.

The sun comes up each morning. That's certainly predictable. Your coworker brings a peanut butter sandwich to work today just as he has every day for the past year. Odds are that he'll bring one in tomorrow too. The more regular the behavior, the more predictable it is. And so it is with a company's growth. If your candidate's sales have been growing at a steady 15 percent every year for the past ten years as in Figure 7.3, you can probably be confident that it will do pretty much the same for at least the next year or two.

You can usually tell enough just by looking at a growth chart of a company's sales and earnings history to know whether it's going to be worth the trouble to continue studying that company. Because constant growth rates are shown as straight lines, you can tell at a glance whether growth is steady and positive.

Of course, you will rarely find growth to be perfectly steady. Rates vary from year to year, and in some cases the lines are punctuated by severe peaks or valleys. (Growth from a zero or negative beginning value is mathematically meaningless, so a growth chart cannot display a zero or negative value.)

When a company has had a really bad year, producing no earnings or experiencing a loss, that data will disappear off the bottom of the chart because there's no place to plot it. The dip will show as a break in the lines that connect the points on the chart. And that's okay because we're not interested so much in *how much* a company lost in a given year as we are in the simple fact that it *did* lose money.

Figure 7.4 shows the earnings of Hughes Electronics Corporation (GMH) during the period from 1990 through 1999. This company's growth is obviously inadequate and unpredictable.

You can easily see that Hughes made good money in 1990. It slipped some in 1991, lost money in 1992, and came back in 1993 and 1994. In 1995, Hughes declined seriously, but it began to come back in 1996 and 1997. Then it flopped again in 1998 and again lost money in 1999.

It's obvious that Hughes has declined over the ten years displayed. In view of what you already know about you're looking for, it's a no-brainer to decide with only a glance that you're not interested.

I suppose it could be said that the longer it takes to describe what you see on the chart, the less desirable the company is. For instance, compare the paragraph before the last with a description of the chart for Abbott Labs (Figure 7.5): earnings have grown at about 13.5 percent for the past ten years! You're looking for monotonous excellence.

The more erratic the growth (i.e., the more crooked the line representing that growth), the less confidence you will have in predicting whether growth will continue and at what rate, especially if in some years the company didn't grow at all.

Sales growth should be the most predictable of the statistics you analyze because very few short-term factors impact it—especially for a company that has annual sales of over $100 million.

The sudden onslaught of unexpected competition, a serious product failure, a major disaster, or a successful class action lawsuit against a company are among

---

FIGURE 7.4   Hughes's Earnings Growth

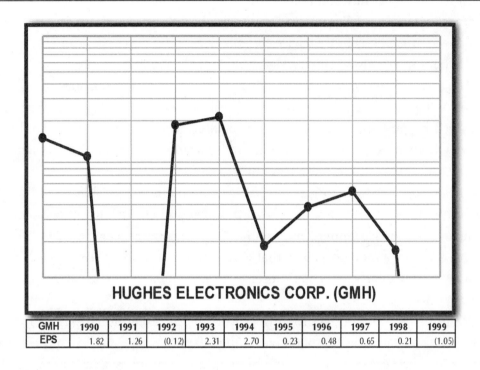

HUGHES ELECTRONICS CORP. (GMH)

GMH	1990	1991	1992	1993	1994	1995	1996	1997	1998	1999
EPS	1.82	1.26	(0.12)	2.31	2.70	0.23	0.48	0.65	0.21	(1.05)

---

the factors that can make a noticeable difference in sales growth. Aside from such major events, however, changes in the growth rate of sales are subtle and take place over a long period of time. They are brought about by less obvious factors like a less-than-successful marketing campaign for a single product, a decrease in standards or morale in the sales force, or long-term changes in management.

Earnings growth is apt to be a lot less predictable than sales growth because it's affected not only by the factors that influence sales growth but also by all of the things that chop away at the profit before it reaches the bottom line. Major changes in the cost of producing the product or service can take place from year to year, even from quarter to quarter, as can changes to the company's fixed costs, taxes, or the number of shares among which the profits are divided. All of these items impact earnings per share.

If you can see steady growth in earnings as well as sales, then you can be confident about predicting a company's future growth, but if the graph of year-to-year earnings looks like a roller coaster, you won't be able to muster up that degree of confidence. Management that's not capable of keeping expenses from fluctuating widely period to period likely lacks the skill you're looking for.

The *company's* success is based upon its ability to make earnings grow. *Your* success will be based upon how well you're able to forecast that growth. So you're interested in companies with steady, predictable growth. And you need only recognize whether the growth is stable enough for you to be comfortable—whether the line is crooked or relatively straight.

The bottom line? Looking at companies with patterns that swing wildly from high growth to none, it's easy to see that they just don't have it together, no matter what promises management may make in its annual report. Saw teeth in the growth chart are a raucous klaxon that warns you to stay away! You're looking for companies with charts that come closer to monotonous excellence than the others you can find.

What if the company is growing erratically but exceptionally fast? In most cases, the fastest growers do not have enough experience to stabilize or produce a track record you can rely on. You might highlight a company that bears watching for the future, but rapid growth, if erratic, is not necessarily the sign of a good prospect—at least for the moment. On the other hand, you won't turn your nose up at a company whose growth is both rapid and stable.

In Figure 7.5 are a couple of charts from real, live companies illustrating the extremes of what we're talking about. Which company would you want to buy?

Of course, the companies you look at will fall somewhere between the two extremes, but wouldn't it be nice if all of the companies you came across had growth charts resembling that of Abbott Labs? One way to make that happen is to use a screening program to filter out those that don't. You might also want to take a look at the Roster of Quality Companies that Inve$tWare posts on its Web site <www.investware.com>. The charts of all of the companies displayed there should be suitable for framing as far as the quality issues are concerned.

FIGURE 7.5 Abbott Labs (ABT) and ITT Industries (IIN)

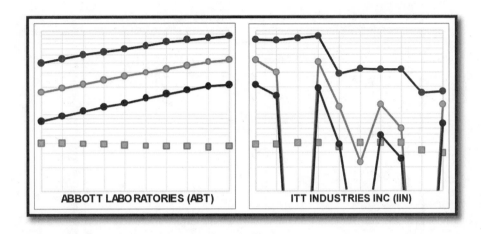

Deciding how straight the lines must be is a matter of developing your personal comfort zone. The best way to judge the degree of crookedness of a line is to visualize a straight line representing the general trend of the growth (see Figure 7.6). If you couldn't draw a line with a ruler that touches or comes fairly close to most of the points—at least for the most recent five years—you should probably find another company to study.

Until you gain experience and get a better feel for analyzing growth, you should stick with the admonition "If in doubt, throw it out." You may miss some good buys, but you won't be tempted to purchase stocks you shouldn't.

APPLYING WHAT YOU'VE LEARNED

Let's assess ABC Company's growth. Looking at the chart in Figure 7.7, what's your first impression?

1. Are the lines representing sales and earnings relatively straight, especially for the most recent five years, or do they zigzag from year to year?

FIGURE 7. 6   Using a Straight Line to Assess Degree of Crookedness

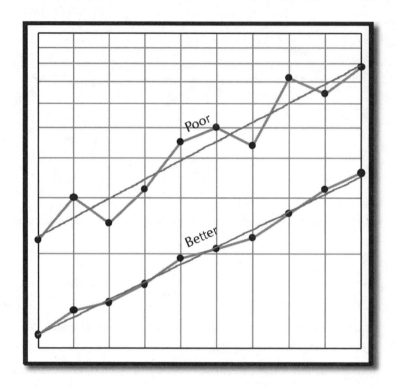

While there is a slight droop, there are no erratic swings from strong growth to flat growth and back. So you would have to say that ABC Company's growth is stable. (Compare this chart with the Hughes Electronics chart, Figure 7.4.

2. Is the slope from left to right positive or negative, strong or slight?

It's easy to see that the line slopes upward. As to how strongly it slopes, it would be difficult to tell the difference between 13 percent and 17 percent growth. You can get a feel for how strong the growth rate is by comparing the most recent year's approximate value with that of five years before. If value has doubled in the last five years, growth is at least 15 percent. In Fig-

FIGURE 7.7   Growth Chart for ABC Company

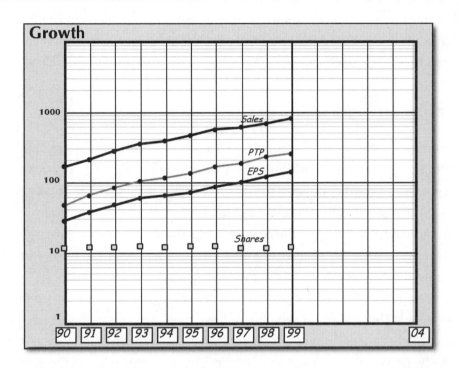

ure 7.7 the most recent earnings figure is about 130, and the figure for five years is about 60, so ABC Company is experiencing a growth rate of at least 15 percent.

3. Do the sales and earnings lines climb steadily as they go from left to right?

    Well, they did sag a little for a while. But then they settled into a comfortably stable straight upslope, which they have sustained for the last five years or more. So while growth slowed initially, it's been pretty steady for a significant period.

    You could feel comfortable forecasting that ABC Company will grow at or close to its recent rate. This business warrants further study.

Now that wasn't so hard, was it? This information is valuable and has already made a substantial contribution to your assessment of quality.

Not all companies have the same fine characteristics as this one, of course. The good news is that most of the ones that you should reject will scream caution to you from their growth charts.

Evaluating Strength of Growth

Presumably, when you first considered a company as a candidate, it met your requirements for sales and earnings growth—at least so far as a perfunctory look at the company's chart could peg it. You've confirmed this quantitatively because the line on the growth chart does slope up at an apparently good rate.

Now you need to know if the company has been growing fast enough. In the past, has it met your requirement to double your money every five years? If so, then it might be able to do so in the future.

To measure the strength of growth, you will need a line that sums up the trend of growth over the period for which you have data. The computer can do this for you, accurately calculating the position of a *trend line* that lies as close as possible to all of the points it's intended to describe. You can approximate the same thing visually with a ruler.

Eliminating Irrelevant History

Before a trend line can be useful to you, however, you will want to eliminate any *outliers*, irrelevant historical data reflecting events that have occurred in the past and are unlikely to occur again.

Including extraneous data in your measurements and calculations can easily skew the results enough to give you a false picture—most likely and most damaging, an excessively optimistic one. You should focus only on relevant history because you want to increase your odds of being right. If you take pains to be conservative, erring on the cautious side, you're far less likely to be disappointed.

After all, isn't successful investing a matter of keeping disappointment to a manageable minimum?

Briefly, outliers—irrelevant data—consist of two types:

- *Spikes:* one-time events, usually bad, that show up as a significant deviation from the rest of the data
- *Early rapid growth:* unsustainable growth that occurred in the past and is no longer likely

By avoiding companies whose growth is erratic and selecting only those whose lines have no major peaks and valleys, you will have disposed of businesses with spikes in their history. However, you'll want to be aware of the latter type of outlier because even though early rapid growth doesn't necessarily disqualify a company from your consideration, it can definitely throw off your forecasts (see Figure 7.8).

Getting rid of outliers is simple enough. If you're using a computer, your program will allow you to eliminate the earlier data from the calculation of the trend with a click of the mouse. If you're doing your study without a computer, when you draw your trend line with a ruler, simply don't include the early years in which the extraordinary growth occurred. Rotate your ruler clockwise, decreasing the slope of the line until the more recent, relevant growth fits closer to the line.

Once you've eliminated early years and you're satisfied with the remaining data, you can read the growth rate displayed on the computer screen. Or you can calculate growth using your business calculator. First enter the data for the most recent year as the "FV" (future value). (With a financial calculator you simply enter the data first, then push the appropriate key.) If your trend line passes through any of the data points, use the data represented by the left-most point through which your line passes as the "PV" (present value). If it doesn't, you may simply approximate the value where the line crosses the left margin of the chart. Then enter the number of years between the two points as "N" (time period). Punch the "CPT" (compute) button, then the "i%" key to solve for the growth rate.

FIGURE 7.8   Eliminating Early Rapid Growth

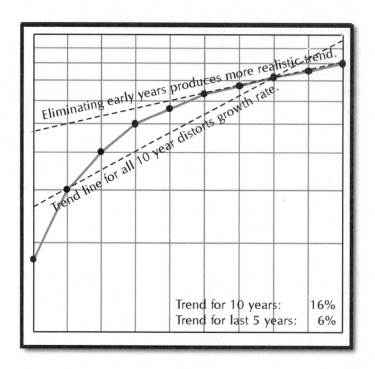

Eliminating early years produces more realistic trend.

Trend line for all 10 year distorts growth rate.

Trend for 10 years:	16%
Trend for last 5 years:	6%

Let's use ABC Company as an example again. In Figure 7.9 the trend line eliminates the first four years as outliers and fits nicely along the most recent six years. The 1999 earnings were 1.32. In 1994, five years earlier, they were 0.61. If you plug those numbers into your trusty calculator (FV = 1.32; PV = .61; N = 5), you'll arrive at a growth rate of 16.7 percent, more than enough to have doubled your money over that period. (The computer measures the precise slope of the line and comes up with 16.8. Close enough!)

FIGURE 7.9   Measuring Growth for ABC Company

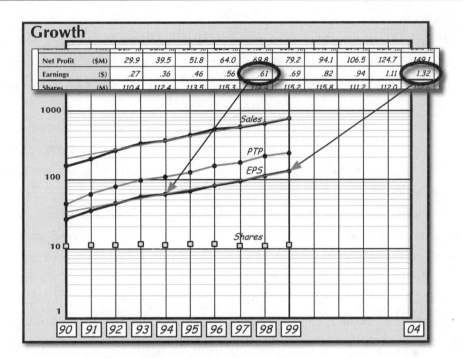

Note: ABC Company grew quickly in the early years. Eliminating irrelevant growth provides a more conservative view by which to judge history and a more reasonable starting point to estimate future growth.

REQUIREMENTS FOR GROWTH

Sales Growth

Because your goal is to double your investment's value every five years, it would seem reasonable that you should discard any company that isn't capable of generating sales growth at a minimum of 15 percent every year.

However, that isn't necessarily realistic; nor is it really necessary. Revenue growth can vary with the size of a company. The bigger the company, the smaller the growth rate you should require. Your goal is to have a *portfolio* whose average return is 15 percent or better. This doesn't require that all of the companies in it do that well.

Growth is bound to slow down as a good company grows larger. Small companies early in their life cycle grow at a very rapid clip because it's relatively easy to add new customers, find new markets, and grow sales from a small base. It's simple math.

In the interest of diversification, you're going to put some of your investment into larger companies to provide stability and strength when times are tough. And you're going to be willing to sacrifice a little return on your investment to buy that security.

Most mature companies, after reaching the point where they can no longer make as much money as they once could by reinvesting in their own growth, will begin to reward their stockholders with dividends, which make a contribution toward the total return. A 10 percent growth in earnings combined with a 3 percent dividend, for example, would produce a 13 percent total return, which is better than the S&P 500 has produced on average since its inception. And more and more large companies are capable of doing better than that. You may not double your money every five years through growth in the price of the stock, but you might make up some of the difference in dividend income. The stability and security of having an established business to serve as a sea anchor in stormy times could well be worth some sacrifice in the return on your investment.

Depending upon the size of the company, therefore, you should expect annual sales growth rates that vary from a low of about 7 percent to a high of about 20 percent. For a large, well-established company like a General Electric (GE), for example, which has sales well over the $4 billion mark, a growth rate of as little as 7 percent might be perfectly acceptable. (In reality, GE reports about $100 *billion* in sales and still manages to grow its earnings at around 13 percent!)

At the other end of the spectrum, a newer company well into its explosive growth period should show double-digit growth. While growth rates above 20 percent can't go on forever, you'll want to look for high growth rates as compensation for the increased risk. The more risky, fast-growing companies are needed

FIGURE 7.10   Trading Risk for Reward

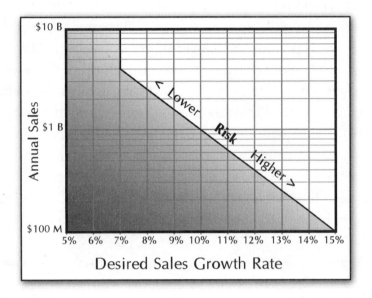

to balance the slower-growing large companies in your portfolio and contribute to an average growth of your investments of around 15 percent or better.

Some of the faster-growing companies will fall by the wayside, to be sure, but the successful smaller companies will eventually grow to become big ones. And you're going along for that long-term ride!

Figure 7.10 provides a rough guideline for the kinds of sales growth rates I suggest you look for. A growth rate in the light area of the chart is acceptable. For example, if a company's sales for the current year are in the neighborhood of $300 million, you would look for a growth rate of better than 12 percent. For a company with $1 billion in sales, you would want at least 10 percent.

Our guidelines tell us to look for a minimum of 7 percent growth in sales for a large company and at least 12 percent growth for a small company. Preferably a small company will have growth of 15 percent or more if we are to double our money every five years.

Earnings Growth

Because you depend upon earnings growth to double your investment every five years, as a rule you'd like to see 15 percent. There are several rationales for accepting something less, however. First of all, as I said above, it's not reasonable to expect every stock in your portfolio to produce returns at that rate. Your goal is for your portfolio to produce 15 percent. So, again, if you're looking at a larger company, you can settle for a lower rate as long as you keep the average high.

If sales growth is adequate and your first impression of this company is favorable, but earnings growth is just a bit short, continue your study. Your underlying interest is in the total return that the company can generate. It might just be that the current price of the stock is far enough below the fair price that you can realize a price appreciation of 15 percent or greater even with a smaller growth in earnings.

The current price (and therefore the PE) might offer some room for *PE expansion:* if you buy a stock at a price below its fair price, you can expect that the multiple of earnings will grow somewhat as the earnings grow. Of course, this is what the traders and short-term speculators all rely on, all the time. I'm just suggesting that if a company's earnings growth is a little short of your normal mark, a small component of PE expansion might make it possible to acquire a bargain.

Checking Quarterly Sales Growth

You're now at the point in your consideration of ABC Company where you can again exercise your prerogative to go on or to abandon the study. Your computer or calculator has told you that after you eliminate the data for the first four years, relevant sales growth for ABC Company is about 15 percent and earnings have stabilized at about 16.7 percent. So you're satisfied that both sales and earnings display satisfactory growth. At $757 million dollars, ABC Company's sales put the company in the lower part of the midsize companies. Twelve percent is the lower sales-growth limit for that category, so sales growth is just fine, and earnings growth is nicely above the desired 15 percent.

There's one more thing you might want to do before you go on to look at management's ability to sustain this desirable record. You might want to see if anything has happened recently to alter your opinion about the company's growth.

To do this, compare the sales figures for the sum of the most recent four quarters with the sales figures for the sum of the four quarters before that. Do the same for earnings. The percentage increases for both sales and earnings should be close to the growth you arrived at with your annual data.

The computer will do this nicely for you, but some computer programs don't display the entire four quarters. You may have to settle for just a comparison between the most recent quarter and the same quarter in the previous year. The advantage of using the entire trailing four quarters is that it will reduce the effect of a single hiccup and smooth out the numbers.

If you're doing your study manually, the Technamental Stock Study Worksheet provides spaces for all four quarters; NAIC's Stock Selection Guide offers space for only the most recent quarter. (See Appendix A.)

If you're a new investor, negative figures here, or figures that are significantly lower than annual growth rates, should tell you "no." Period.

If you're an experienced investor and have been doing technamental analysis for a while, you may decide to do some research, exploring the Internet, perhaps, to find out why the poor performance occurred and to assess whether the reasons are long term or short term in nature. If the problem is long term, you should not invest. If the problem's only a hiccup, you may decide to give management another quarter or two to correct it.

Remember, there are more candidates out there, so you shouldn't get hung up on any one stock just because you happen to like its story.

Let's look at the quarterly performance for ABC Company in Figure 7.11. (Note that the most recent reported quarter is the first quarter of the year 2000. Quarters are listed chronologically beginning with the second quarter of 1999.) Here you can see that sales growth, quarter to quarter, has been declining somewhat over the past few quarters.

Some companies are very much impacted by seasonal change, retailers especially because of the holiday activity. While that seasonal effect is easy to see from

FIGURE 7.11   Quarterly Performance

	Quarterly Sales					Quarterly Earnings per share				
	Qtr 2	Qtr 3	Qtr 4	Qtr 1	TTM	Qtr 2	Qtr 3	Qtr 4	Qtr 1	TTM
Last year	156.6	161.0	184.3	176.7	678.6	.27	.28	.30	.30	1.15
This year	183.3	192.3	205.1	192.2	772.9	.32	.33	.37	.35	1.37
% Change	17.1%	19.4%	11.3 %	8.8 %	13.9%	18.5%	17.9 %	23.3%	16.7%	19.1%

quarter to quarter in the actual sales figures, it does not affect year-to-year growth, the percent change from the previous year's quarter that you're analyzing. So a decline in sales over the course of the year may not be meaningful, but a decline in growth from year to year could be.

Quarterly performance doesn't carry quite the weight that annual (or trailing four-quarter) data do because anything can happen in a single quarter and never recur. However, it can be a good warning bell for you. You might find it prudent to give the company one more quarter to see if it can reverse the trend. However, I don't believe that these figures have declined enough to be alarming, and growth for the trailing four quarters is still well above our benchmark.

NOT MINUTES, MOMENTS!

It's taken a long time to read about analyzing growth, but what you've read about will take only moments to apply. If you're a computer user, you can see the quality of growth at a glance, eliminate the required outliers with a mouse click or two, and read the growth rates right off the screen.

If you're working by hand, once you've prepared the charts (the only tedious part), it will take you no longer to visually check the quality of growth than if you had a computer, hardly any longer to draw the trend line to exclude irrelevancies, and only moments more to plug the necessary numbers into the calculator to read the results. You should be able to complete the final step in less than a minute.

LET'S TAKE STOCK OF

What You Know about Evaluating Company Quality

- To be suitable as an investment, a company must be of good quality and have a reasonable stock price.

- The first technamental assessment of a company's quality is the analysis of its sales and earnings growth.

- Growth is best viewed using a growth (semilog) chart, which depicts a consistent rate of growth as a straight line and permits you to see at a glance whether growth is positive and predictable.

- The straighter the line showing growth, the more predictable it is, and the better the candidate.

- The steeper the slope, the stronger growth is, and the better the candidate.

- It's important to eliminate irrelevant data in order to properly measure historical growth and to provide a reasonable starting point for estimating future growth.

- Stronger growth is required of smaller companies than of larger ones to make up for the difference in stability and risk.

- You should check recently reported data to ensure that nothing has happened to undermine an otherwise good track record.

- Once you've become accustomed to the process, it should take less than a minute to analyze growth.

In the next chapter I'll take you on a tour of some of the growth scenarios you're likely to come across.

CHAPTER 8

Variations on the Growth Theme

The charts in this chapter illustrate some typical patterns of growth, both good and bad, that you'll come across in your studies. The purpose is for you to *see* the reasons why each pattern is good or bad so that when you encounter similar situations in your own research, you'll find them familiar and will know what they mean. Don't try to memorize anything. Instead, try to understand how the pictures translate into numbers and vice versa—what these patterns of growth mean and why they're acceptable or not. Bear in mind that these charts are caricatures— exaggerations of what you will typically find—to make the conditions a bit more identifiable. We'll look at each pattern and discuss its significance. After that I'll offer a few examples of actual companies so you can see what the patterns look like in real life.

Note that I have drawn the trend lines in gray on each chart. This should help you to view the historical growth realistically.

As I was writing this book, it was when I reached this point in the text that I dreamed up the term *technamental*. I looked at what I was doing and realized that I was charting, the favorite pastime of technical analysts, and even calling differ- ent types of patterns by different names just like they do.

But this process differs from technical analysis in a very noteworthy way. We are looking at what the company's *operations* did, not what the price of the stock and volume of shares traded did. Patterns of growth are significant because they can be used to predict what's coming, while stock price movement can't. These examples are intended to help you understand what actually happens in the life of a company, not the meaningless meanderings of the company's stock price in the short-term market. This is a crucial distinction, and it's the reason that I have chosen the term *technamental* to describe this approach. What we will be doing amounts to a technical analysis of the fundamentals.

THE CHARTS

Each chart displays, from top to bottom, sales, pretax profit, and earnings, respectively. If you do your charting manually, you may later find it interesting to plot some other data—shares outstanding, for example. But for now this is all you need.

Keep in mind that *sales growth drives pretax profit growth,* and pretax profit is a function of the expenses paid to produce the products or services and generate those sales.

Pretax profit growth, in turn, *drives net profit growth* (which is not displayed), and net profit is what remains after taxes are paid.

Finally, earnings per share results from dividing the net profit by the number of shares outstanding. Therefore, *the number of shares has a considerable effect on earnings.* A reduction in shares will increase earnings per share, and an increase in shares will reduce EPS.

You can distinguish trends in the profit margin by viewing changes in the space between the pretax profit and sales lines. An increase in the size of that space indicates an increase in the portion of sales that goes to expenses—hence a decrease in the profit margin. The narrower the space becomes, the smaller the percentage going to expenses and the greater the profit margin. Thus, you can tell by looking at the lines on the chart whether a change in earnings growth is caused by changes in the profit margin or by increases or decreases in the number of shares outstanding.

FIGURES 8.1 and 8.2   Monotonous Excellence and the Motorcycle

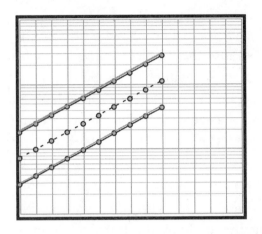 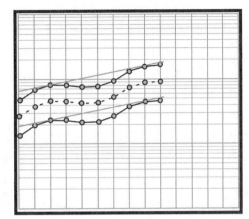

While you only need to go as far as I suggested in Chapter 7, rejecting all companies that don't exhibit strong, reasonably straight up-slopes, you may find it fun and interesting to interpret the dynamics between the lines. (You'll find a more detailed discussion of these variations in Chapter 13, "Finer Points and 'Fudge Factors.'")

As you study these charts, you should begin to see and understand the relationship between the sales, pretax profit, and earnings lines—and between these and the squares representing the outstanding shares.

Monotonous Excellence, Figure 8.1.   All of your companies should look like the *Monotonous Excellence* chart! Companies whose management can maintain "railroad tracks"—straight, parallel lines—are highly desirable. This is the kind of pattern that you will look for in all of your holdings.

Obviously, perfection is hard to find. So, your investment experience will likely include small compromises. The steeper the slope, the more forgiving you might be about stability—you'll swap a little zigzag in the line for faster growth. The smaller the company, the faster the growth and the less predictable the fundamentals might be. Of course, the larger and slower-growing the company, the more demanding you'll be in terms of predictability. But don't stray too far from the Monotonous Excellence model, especially when you first start out.

The Motorcycle, Figure 8.2.   The *Motorcycle* pattern is not strictly cyclical as its name seems to imply. I named it because the prime examples of cyclical companies are the motor makers—the automobile manufacturers. Strictly cyclical companies are those whose lines look like a roller coaster and whose high and low points seem always to be about the same. They usually depend upon a surge in economic good times to overcome the misery of the bad times. Stay away from strictly cyclical companies because you aren't interested in timing your investments by keeping track of when a cycle may or may not be at its high or low point.

There is a distinction, however, between a strictly cyclical company and one that has the kind of cyclical or undulating growth that is illustrated in Figure 8.2. You can test the slope visually by drawing your trend line between the peaks of the cycles. If the slope is steep enough to show substantial growth from one point in the cycle to the same point in the next cycle, the company may, over the long term, produce adequate returns. A cyclical-growth company is typically a well-run business in an industry that is affected by the rise and fall of the economy. Its growth usually ratchets up when its industry takes a beating and it is strong enough to acquire its weaker competitors' business. When the industry comes back into favor, the cyclical-growth company shoots ahead of where it was before.

As a new investor, you should treat a cyclical-growth company like any other. If the growth during the down phase becomes flat or negative as illustrated here, you should exercise caution. If, however, there is constant growth that varies in magnitude, if the cycle is predictable, and if growth doesn't fall too far below the desired growth rate in the down years, you might consider the company.

Companies with patterns like this are best purchased after comparing them with their peers in their industry (see Chapter 11).

The Bow and Arrow, Figure 8.3.   The "bow" part of the *Bow and Arrow* pattern is easy to see. Its path appears like a trajectory. If you were to draw a trend line that describes the growth for the entire period displayed, it would resemble the string on that bow (as illustrated by the dotted gray lines in Figure 8.3). This

FIGURES 8.3 and 8.4 The Bow and Arrow and the Arrowless Bow

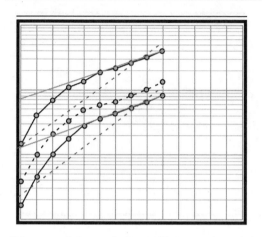 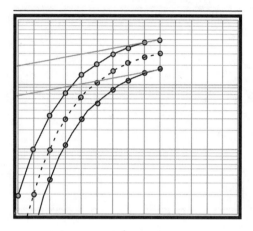

is typical of a company that is fairly early in its life cycle and has been enjoying superior but unsustainable growth. Some companies experience extraordinary growth longer than others, and what may be sustainable in one industry may not be in another.

Bow and Arrow companies show promise, but you must be careful not to measure historical growth by the "string." This is a good example of historical irrelevance. The early growth is irrelevant when you are considering a prospective growth rate for the future. As you can see by comparing the gray trend lines in the illustration, you should disregard those early years when measuring historical growth.

But how about the "arrow"? That's what I've called the part where the growth has settled down to a sustained rate. As you can see in Figure 8.3, the last five years' growth falls in a fairly straight line. The fact that growth has stabilized should enhance your confidence in forecasting: in the future this company should grow at a rate not too far below its growth rate for the past five years.

The Arrowless Bow, Figure 8.4. As the name implies, the *Arrowless Bow* is a bow without an arrow. Sure enough, in this chart you can see no settling down to a straight line. Like the Bow and Arrow pattern, this is typical of a company that

FIGURES 8.5 and 8.6   The Rocket and the Flatliner

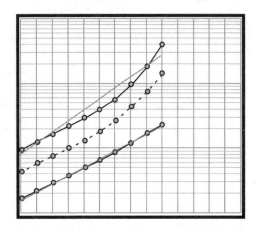 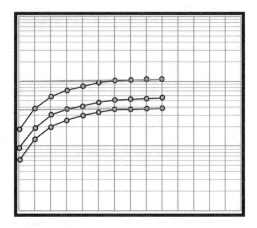

is early in its life cycle and continues to grow at a rapid but declining rate. But the Arrowless Bow company has not yet settled down to a rate that's sustainable.

For forecasting purposes, all of the data for an Arrowless Bow company are irrelevant. You wouldn't want to estimate future growth at a rate any faster than that of the most recent year, which I've suggested with the trend line. In fact, because growth has slowed every year, you can be nearly certain that the decline will continue. Nowhere in this picture can you find a clue about how low the sustainable rate of growth will be.

The Rocket, Figure 8.5. The *Rocket* is so called because it gathers momentum after liftoff. This company's growth, instead of suffering the customary decline, actually accelerates. This phenomenon is usually associated with acquisitions because it's very rare for a company of any size to introduce new products or create new markets that can generate sufficient organic growth to produce this kind of growth-rate increase. Goodness knows, it's difficult enough to perpetuate a rate, much less to increase it in the normal course of business!

When you see a Rocket pattern, you can often confirm that acquisitions are the source of growth. Look for a telltale decline in earnings growth while pretax profits are growing parallel with sales. This results from issuing shares to consummate the acquisitions, which tends to dilute and so reduce the earnings per share.

As the gray trend line implies, your assessment of historical growth should probably be based on the composite growth for the entire period. Surely the most recent growth is not sustainable for obvious reasons. It might even be more fitting to eliminate the most recent years as irrelevant and go back to the earlier years to measure what is sustainable. Be very careful that you don't overestimate future growth because of this kind of pattern. Growth from acquisitions is hardly sustainable.

The Flatliner, Figure 8.6. The "heartbeat" of the *Flatliner* company has slowed down and stopped. This business is dead! Sales and earnings are flat and have been so for a long time. While the Flatliner company is not losing money, it shows no potential for growth and should be avoided. The pattern is consistent, but that doesn't mean it's consistently good! The Flatliner is an income investment, if it's an investment at all. It's certainly not for a growth investor like you.

The Innocent Bystander, Figure 8.7. The *Innocent Bystander* is a company with an unblemished record, except that it had one bad year. Perhaps it had done too well before the apparent stumble. The company may have failed to write off everything it should have and then decided to take the hit that year and to do it right from then on. Usually a stumble like this results from an accounting matter, although a hiccup in revenues like the one that appears here could mean an internal problem in managing inventory or some other short-term, one-time issue that was resolved by a capable management team.

The performance during the bad year is data that you may eliminate as an outlier if you're satisfied that you fully understand what happened and feel it's safe to ignore it. A convenient rule of thumb is this: if eliminating the outlier decreases the slope of the trend line, then eliminate it. If eliminating the outlier increases the slope of the trend line, you should not eliminate the hiccup. You

FIGURES 8.7 and 8.8 The Innocent Bystander and Could Have Been a Contender

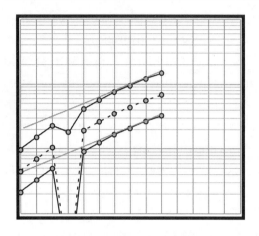 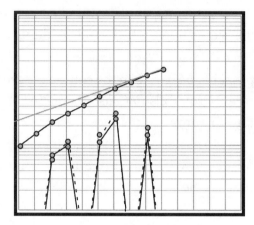

should wait until the bad year is far enough back in history to have little impact on the trend. If the bad year occurred within the last four or five years, you should pass the company up and go on to another study. You can look at this company again in a year or two.

Could Have Been a Contender, Figure 8.8. There's no question but that the *Could Have Been a Contender* company has had a fine record of sales growth, but its management has never been able to make money for its shareholders. This is better than your dot-com IPO that makes no money at all, but not by much.

Unless there's a good correlation between its top and bottom lines, a company like this is iffy at best.

The Disaster, Figure 8.9. A company with a chart like this is a *Disaster*. Need I say more? There's no point in continuing with a stock study when sales, earnings, or profits can't trudge uphill. A business doesn't have to look this bad to be an automatic discard, but when you see a bad one, you ought to be able to tell right away!

FIGURE 8.9 The Disaster

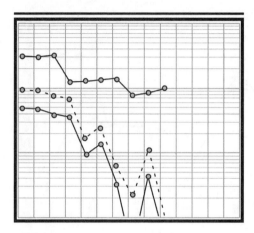

SOME REAL-WORLD EXAMPLES

Let's look at some companies in the real world to see if you can put into practice what you've just finished reading. Look at each chart, consider how each compares with the pictures hanging in this "Gallery of Growth," and see if you draw the same conclusions I do.

In each case, I've included the data as well as the chart so that you can begin to get a feel for how data look when they're plotted.

ITT Industries. Here's a company (see Figure 8.10) whose sales growth is obviously declining seriously. Profit margins have slipped badly as well, resulting in plummeting earnings. There's no point in bothering to continue with a study when sales and earnings are headed for the cellar as they are here. Companies in this condition are easy to spot. They are Disasters.

CompUSA. Here's a fine example (see Figure 8.11) of the Could Have Been a Contender syndrome. Revenues were growing beautifully; but what happened to

---

FIGURE 8.10   ITT Industries

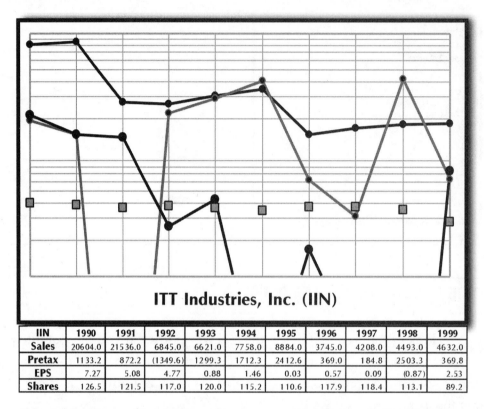

ITT Industries, Inc. (IIN)

IIN	1990	1991	1992	1993	1994	1995	1996	1997	1998	1999
Sales	20604.0	21536.0	6845.0	6621.0	7758.0	8884.0	3745.0	4208.0	4493.0	4632.0
Pretax	1133.2	872.2	(1349.6)	1299.3	1712.3	2412.6	369.0	184.8	2503.3	369.8
EPS	7.27	5.08	4.77	0.88	1.46	0.03	0.57	0.09	(0.87)	2.53
Shares	126.5	121.5	117.0	120.0	115.2	110.6	117.9	118.4	113.1	89.2

Note: Sales, pretax profit, earnings, and/or shares may have been scaled (multipled by a constant factor) in order to be conveniently placed on the chart. Such scaling affects only the positions of the lines and does not alter their movement relative to each other.

---

the profits, the earnings, and the shareholders' interest in the company? Unless this company learns how to steady its expenses and to manage itself properly, it won't be a predictable and healthy company in which a shareholder would want to own a piece of the action. (Note that CompUSA has been acquired by Grupo Sanborns, S.A. de C.V., a Mexican retail group, and is no longer publicly traded.)

FIGURE 8.11   CompUSA

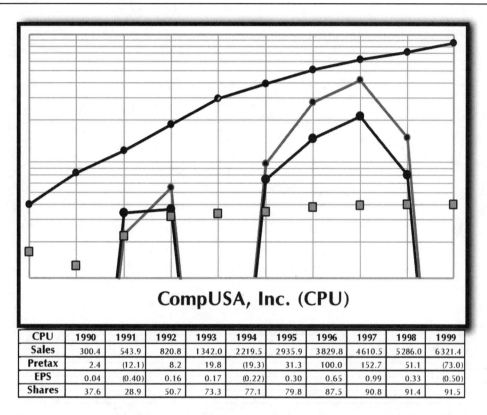

CompUSA, Inc. (CPU)

CPU	1990	1991	1992	1993	1994	1995	1996	1997	1998	1999
Sales	300.4	543.9	820.8	1342.0	2219.5	2935.9	3829.8	4610.5	5286.0	6321.4
Pretax	2.4	(12.1)	8.2	19.8	(19.3)	31.3	100.0	152.7	51.1	(73.0)
EPS	0.04	(0.40)	0.16	0.17	(0.22)	0.30	0.65	0.99	0.33	(0.50)
Shares	37.6	28.9	50.7	73.3	77.1	79.8	87.5	90.8	91.4	91.5

Note: Sales, pretax profit, earnings, and/or shares may have been scaled (multipled by a constant factor) in order to be conveniently placed on the chart. Such scaling affects only the positions of the lines and does not alter their movement relative to each other.

Apollo Group. Here's an Arrowless Bow (see Figure 8.12) that is in the beginning phase of becoming a Bow and Arrow. Note first that the trend line for the entire period—the "string" on the "bow"—would be much too steep a measure of the relevant growth for this company. When it comes time to forecast future growth, you will want to disregard all of the historical data and look just at the last couple of years. Because Apollo Group has not yet stabilized at a steady growth rate, your future growth rate estimate should be below the rate of the

FIGURE 8.12   Apollo Group

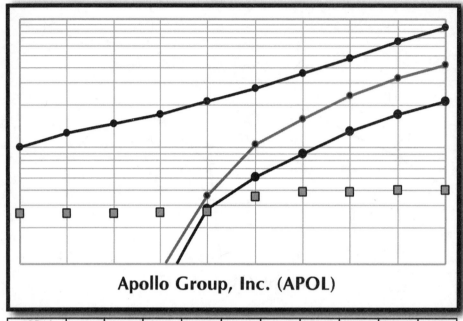

Apollo Group, Inc. (APOL)

APOL	1990	1991	1992	1993	1994	1995	1996	1997	1998	1999
Sales	52.9	68.8	81.9	97.5	124.4	161	211.2	279.2	384.9	498.8
Pretax	(0.4)	0.9	0.5	2.0	8.3	21.8	35.0	55.0	76.3	98.0
EPS	(0.01)	0.01	0.01	0.02	0.10	0.18	0.28	0.43	0.59	0.75
Shares	50.0	50.1	50.1	51.1	51.6	68.9	74.7	75.6	77.2	77.7

Note: Sales, pretax profit, earnings, and/or shares may have been scaled (multipled by a constant factor) in order to be conveniently placed on the chart. Such scaling affects only the positions of the lines and does not alter their movement relative to each other.

most recent year or two. Because the growth of the last two years or so is still excellent, you might continue to pursue this study. You could probably estimate future growth within your comfort zone (see Chapter 11) and see where the rest of the analysis takes you.

Tower Automotive. This is a company (see Figure 8.13) that seems to have reversed the normal trend because its revenue growth has accelerated instead of manifesting the normal deceleration. The plotted data curve up instead of down,

FIGURE 8.13   Tower Automotive

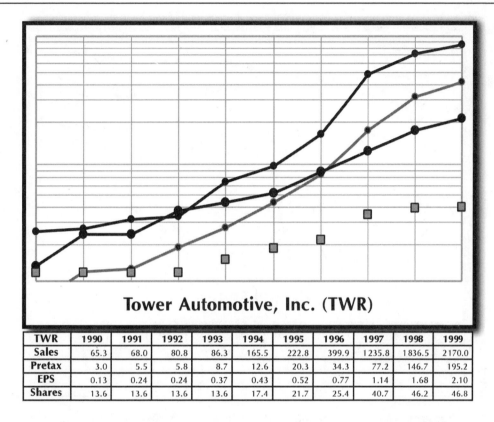

Tower Automotive, Inc. (TWR)

TWR	1990	1991	1992	1993	1994	1995	1996	1997	1998	1999
Sales	65.3	68.0	80.8	86.3	165.5	222.8	399.9	1235.8	1836.5	2170.0
Pretax	3.0	5.5	5.8	8.7	12.6	20.3	34.3	77.2	146.7	195.2
EPS	0.13	0.24	0.24	0.37	0.43	0.52	0.77	1.14	1.68	2.10
Shares	13.6	13.6	13.6	13.6	17.4	21.7	25.4	40.7	46.2	46.8

Note: Sales, pretax profit, earnings, and/or shares may have been scaled (multiplied by a constant factor) in order to be conveniently placed on the chart. Such scaling affects only the positions of the lines and does not alter their movement relative to each other.

and the "bowstring" would be displayed across the top of the picture instead of the bottom. Here's your classic Rocket.

Typically, this kind of growth results primarily from acquisitions. Adding the top line of the newly acquired companies to an already healthy top line can really paint a pretty picture. Note that earnings are growing at a substantially lower rate than sales. Usually, extensive acquisition activity is accomplished by issuing new shares. Such is the case at Tower Automotive, where the number of shares has

FIGURE 8.14   Alcoa

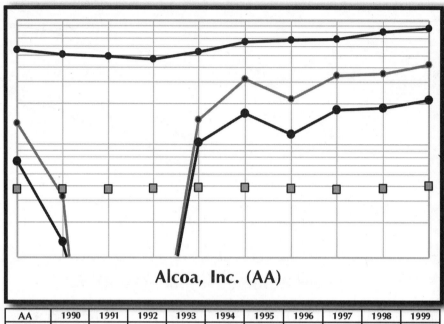

Alcoa, Inc. (AA)

AA	1990	1991	1992	1993	1994	1995	1996	1997	1998	1999
Sales	10865.1	9981.2	9588.4	9148.9	10391.5	12654.9	13128.4	13482.0	15489.0	16447.0
Pretax	474.1	114.1	(2049.0)	2.7	509.0	1131.1	768.8	1198.5	1251.5	1500.7
EPS	0.85	0.18	0.06	0.01	1.24	2.19	1.46	2.31	2.42	2.82
Shares	344.8	339.9	341.9	350.7	355.8	356.0	348.7	344.5	349.1	366.9

Note: Sales, pretax profit, earnings, and/or shares may have been scaled (multipled by a constant factor) in order to be conveniently placed on the chart. Such scaling affects only the positions of the lines and does not alter their movement relative to each other.

more than doubled in the past five years. A credit to the company is the fact that earnings growth has remained impressively high even with the huge increase in shares outstanding. With a company like this you should exercise caution because this kind of growth can't go on forever. Also, acquired companies often represent acquired problems.

Alcoa.   You're on your own here. Do you think Alcoa (see Figure 8.14) would be a good buy?

FIGURE 8.15 Clayton Homes

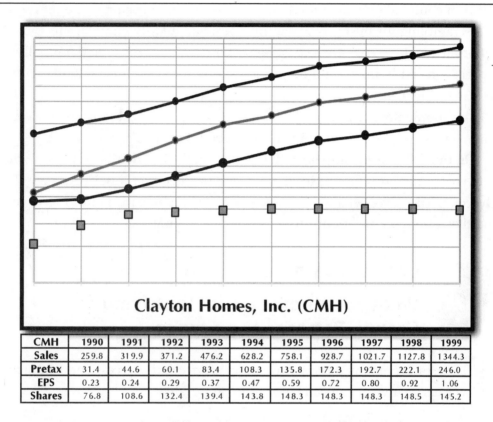

Clayton Homes, Inc. (CMH)

CMH	1990	1991	1992	1993	1994	1995	1996	1997	1998	1999
Sales	259.8	319.9	371.2	476.2	628.2	758.1	928.7	1021.7	1127.8	1344.3
Pretax	31.4	44.6	60.1	83.4	108.3	135.8	172.3	192.7	222.1	246.0
EPS	0.23	0.24	0.29	0.37	0.47	0.59	0.72	0.80	0.92	1.06
Shares	76.8	108.6	132.4	139.4	143.8	148.3	148.3	148.3	148.5	145.2

Note: Sales, pretax profit, earnings, and/or shares may have been scaled (multipled by a constant factor) in order to be conveniently placed on the chart. Such scaling affects only the positions of the lines and does not alter their movement relative to each other.

If you said no, you're in good shape. This Innocent Bystander is a marginal company for a new investor. On the other hand, an experienced investor might look closer at the recovery, questioning how long earnings growth can exceed that of sales, but be tempted to include this big stalwart in her portfolio.

Clayton Homes. It's hard to see in Figure 8.15 because the peaks and valleys are hardly discernable, but Clayton Homes is a Motorcycle company—an extremely well-run business in an industry that is very susceptible to hiccups in the economy. The prefabricated home industry's woes are exacerbated by the influx of competition when times are good—and the subsequent glut of product and scrambling for business when times are bad. Oddly enough, this industry suffers most when times are best, because many people who would normally buy a prefabricated home would be prone to seek more expensive housing when they're feeling flush.

You should now be in a good position to decide at first glance whether a company you're looking at is worthy of continued interest.

On the CD that accompanies this book, you'll find more companies whose data you can import into the technamental worksheet to try out your new skills. The companies have been selected because they illustrate the points I've covered, and they offer you the opportunity for some good practice.

LET'S TAKE STOCK OF

What You Know about Identifying Growth Patterns at a Glance

- As a company passes through its life cycle, its success and its potential as an investment can be sized up at a glance.

- Companies that are good candidates are easy to spot.

- More important, companies that are not good candidates are even easier to spot.

- As you become more experienced, you'll be able to gain more insight into what's in store for a company and why—just by glancing at its growth chart.

CHAPTER 9

Management's "Report Card"

If your candidate meets your growth requirements, the next step is to look at its *efficiency* and effectiveness. The fact that a company has exhibited the desired qualities in the past is no guarantee that it will continue to do so in the future. So you're interested in looking for signs that the future might be less rosy than the past.

Management has only two resources with which to generate earnings: *revenue* that comes in during the reporting period, and the *equity* of the company, which includes both the money that was paid by investors for stock issued and earnings retained from prior periods. As a beginning investor, you will be interested only in revenue. Equity can be an interesting and instructive measure under some circumstances, but it should be accorded no more weight on management's report card than social skills should be given on a kid's. I'll discuss equity later in Chapter 13, "Finer Points and 'Fudge Factors.'"

PROFIT MARGINS

To analyze the efficiency with which management uses the money it receives from the sale of goods or services, you will look at the return it earns on sales—the company's *profit margins.* Technamental investors like to look at the profit before taxes because management has no control over taxes.

The profit margin—the percent of revenue that remains as pretax profit after expenses have been paid—is calculated simply by dividing pretax profit by sales. So if a company sold $100 million worth of goods or services and spent $90 million on various expenses excluding taxes, the remaining $10 million in pretax profit would represent a profit margin of 10 percent.

$$\$100 \text{ (Sales)} - \$90 \text{ (Expenses)} = \$10 \text{ (Profit)}$$
$$\$10 \text{ (Profit)} \div 100 \text{ (Sales)} = 10\% \text{ (Profit margin)}$$

The higher that percentage figure, the more efficiently management has utilized the company's income. Trends in profit margins from year to year are an excellent indication of how capable and efficient management is—or isn't.

ABC Company, a nationally known producer of widgets and blivets, is fortunate. For every dollar it brings in, it makes an average of nearly 30 cents in profit before taxes. However, the percentages themselves are only important when you compare ABC Company with its peers in the same or similar industries. They are not nearly so important as the trend.

At one extreme, a food vendor is considered to be doing beautifully if it turns in a 4 percent profit margin. Because the grocery business relies on high volume and low markups of its products, the median profit margin in that industry is scarcely 2 percent.

On the other hand, a 25 percent profit margin in the computer software business would be very disappointing. The cost of hiring and retaining smart people is high, but much of the cost of developing new software products is incurred before a new product reaches the market. The actual expenses associated with the

FIGURE 9.1 ABC Company's Profit Margins

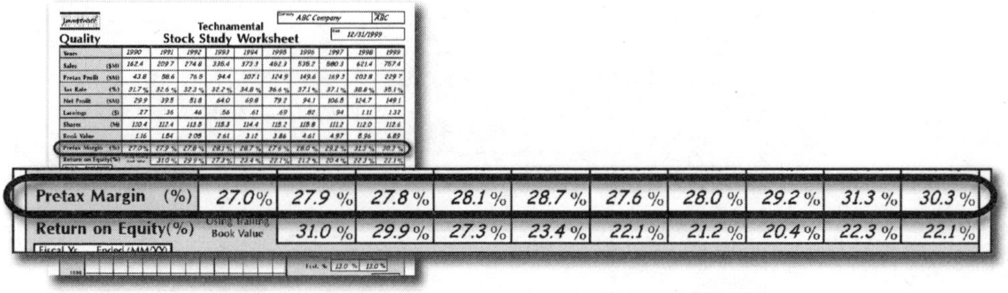

Technamental Stock Study Worksheet

Pretax Margin (%)	27.0%	27.9 %	27.8 %	28.1 %	28.7 %	27.6 %	28.0 %	29.2 %	31.3 %	30.3 %
Return on Equity(%) Using Trailing Book Value		31.0 %	29.9 %	27.3 %	23.4 %	22.1 %	21.2 %	20.4 %	22.3 %	22.1 %

distribution of software products are relatively low. Companies whose products are intellectual and those whose products are tangible are not comparable.

There are two issues concerning profit margins that should take priority above all else. The first and by far more important item is the trend. The second item is stability.

If profit margins decline over a period of time, it's usually evidence that management is not doing as good a job of minding the store as it should. Costs are climbing and management is not doing what needs to be done to keep them under control.

You can often analyze a trend quite easily just by looking at the figures (see Figure 9.1). You are particularly interested in margins for the most recent year or two, and you can compare them with the average for the last five years or so. If the most recent year's margin is higher than the five-year average, NAIC investors call it an uptrend. If the margin is no more than one-half a percent below the five-year average, then everything's probably okay.

As a technamental analyst, you may wish to plot the profit margins on a linear graph so you can see the trend clearly (see Figure 9.2).

As you can see, ABC Company's profit margins have been pretty steady and have been trending slightly up. Drawing—or simply visualizing—a line that rep-

FIGURE 9.2   Linear Graph of Profit Margins for ABC Company

resents the average pretax profit margin makes it easy to see where the margins have been going.

Buying a company jet or building a palace to house the corporate headquarters are examples of decisions that can erode profit margins over time. Some such decisions may actually improve efficiency or are otherwise beneficial in the long run, but the results of bad decisions will eventually show up in the profit margins, and when they do, it's not very pretty.

Figure 9.3 displays ten years of profit margins for Service Merchandise (SME). You don't need a chart to see the trend.

Service Merchandise is a discount retailer that competes with everyone from K-mart to Costco. Margins in the discount retail industry are normally low (averaging around 2.5 percent), but as you can see from the decline in the percentages,

FIGURE 9.3   Declining Profit Margins at Service Merchandise

Pretax Margin (%)	3.3 %	2.9 %	3.7 %	3.7 %	3.6 %	2.3 %	2.0 %	1.6 %	(4.0) %	(3.5) %
Return on Equity (%)			292.4 %	79.8 %	42.4 %	22.1 %	14.8 %	10.0 %	(20.6)%	(32.9)%

Pretax Profit Margins	Avg. 1.6 %
50%	
40%	
30%	
20%	
10%	
0%	

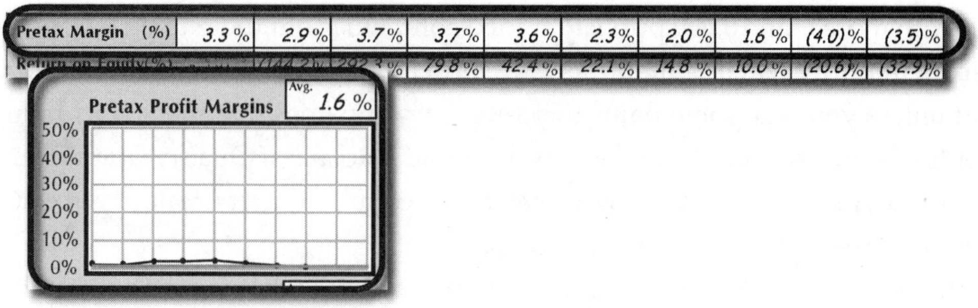

management at Service Merchandise appears to have taken a turn for the worse in 1994. The company lost nearly four cents on every dollar of sales for the last two years displayed. Needless to say, you would want to abandon your study of this company (if, in fact, you had even gone this far).

A flat trend is as good as an uptrend. If a company is operating as efficiently as it can, matching or bettering its peers in the profit margin department, then any attempts to cut costs could be counterproductive. On the other hand, a company that's improving its margins must have had something to improve. So while its efforts are certainly commendable and appropriate, the company with an uptrend is not necessarily better than another company that's already operating at close to maximum efficiency.

After you have become more experienced, there will be times when a little research will lead you to excuse a minor or temporary downtrend. But as a new investor you should never consider investing in a company whose profit margins are declining.

THE REAL WORLD

With more than 10,000 publicly traded companies out there to pick from, only a small minority will be suitable as long-term investments. This means, of course, that unless you take some pains to screen for companies that meet your requirements or find a source of suggestions such as the Roster of Quality Companies on the Inve$tWare Web site at <www.investware.com>, the great majority of companies you investigate will be unsuitable.

If you don't realize this up front and accept discouragement as a normal part of the process, you may tire of discarding company after company and give up. Worse yet, you may relax your requirements and accept companies that don't come up to snuff. Either way, you'll lose.

Remember, you need to own only about 10 to 20 good stocks; that's all! And there are plenty of companies to choose from to populate your portfolio. So be patient and disciplined.

To make you feel a little better about the prospects, I've listed below 48 companies that appear to have met our quality standards for at least the five years prior to this writing. A strong disclaimer: Don't buy any of these companies unless you are certain they meet your own standards for quality and price.

More than one of these companies is likely to have suffered a setback since reporting the data I used. And even if performance on our quality criteria has persisted—as I'm sure it has for most—you'll find the price for many of these stocks unattractive. When I assembled this list, I made no effort to assess the price, just the quality.

ACE Cash Express, Inc.	Charles Schwab Corp.
Affiliated Computer Services	Claire's Stores, Inc.
American Power Conversion	D.R. Horton, Inc.
Amgen, Inc.	DeVRY, Inc.
Blyth Industries, Inc.	Dollar Tree Stores, Inc.
Carnival Corporation	Estee Lauder Co.
CDW Computer Centers, Inc.	Expeditors International of Washington

Gap, Inc.

Gentex Corporation

Harley-Davidson, Inc.

Home Depot, Inc.

Kenneth Cole Productions

Kohl's Corporation

Kronos, Inc.

Lowe's Companies, Inc.

Microsoft Corporation

National Instruments Corp.

NCI Building Systems, Inc.

Omnicom Group, Inc.

On Assignment, Inc.

Oracle Corporation

Orthodontic Centers of America

Papa John's International, Inc.

Paychex, Inc.

Pomeroy Computer Resource

Quiksilver, Inc.

Reliance Steel and Aluminum

ResMed, Inc.

Schering-Plough Corp.

SEI Investments Co.

Staples, Inc.

Starbucks Corporation

Sun Microsystems, Inc.

Swift Transportation Co.

Sybron International Corp.

T. Rowe Price Associates

Technitrol, Inc.

Tellabs, Inc.

Tetra Tech, Inc.

Tower Automotive, Inc.

Walgreen Co.

Some of these companies have been around a long time and are familiar to you; others are not so well known. But all have been publicly traded for at least five years on the major exchanges and all have revenues of above $100 million.

Figure 9.4 shows a chart for each of the companies so you can see what they have in common.

The moral of the story here is that you should keep the faith. There are plenty of fish in the sea for you, even though the sea is enormous and there are more losers than winners.

FIGURE 9.4   Gallery of Quality Companies

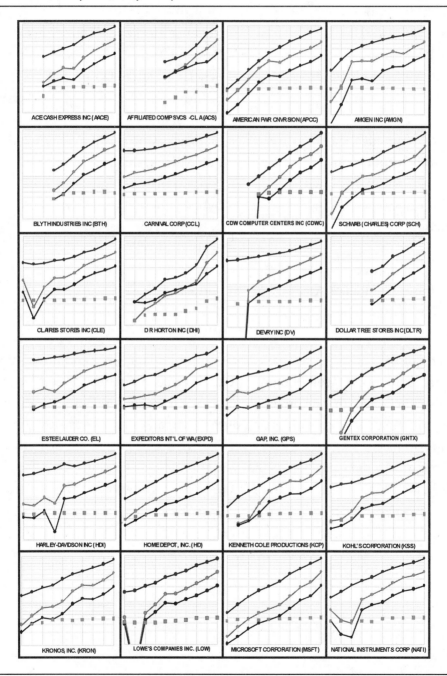

FIGURE 9.4   Gallery of Quality Companies (continued)

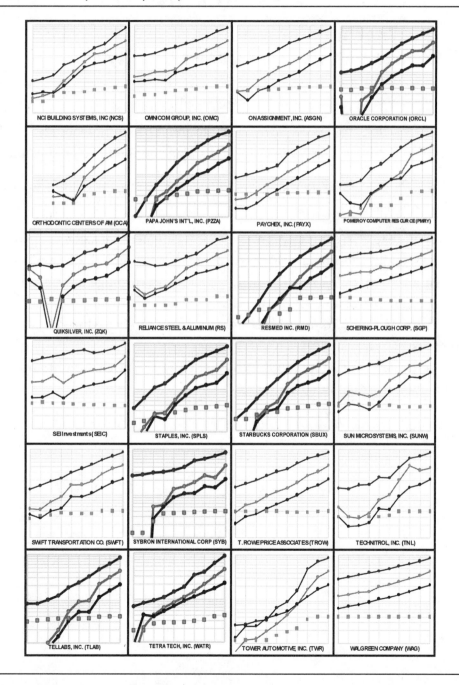

What You Know about Evaluating a Company's Quality

The two tests for quality that must be met are:

1. *Growth.* Sales and earnings growth must be strong enough to double your money every five years and stable enough to be predictable.

2. *Efficiency.* Profit margins must be stable, strong for their industry, and not declining.

You can tell if a company meets these requirements at a glance if you have the data and the technamental charts in hand. Nothing more is involved than making sure that the lines representing sales and earnings growth and profit margins are reasonably straight and are not sloping down.

Caution! If you compromise on quality, you can be seduced by the price. If in doubt, throw it out!

Your next step will be to find out whether the price is right and, if not, what the price ought to be.

CHAPTER 10

Evaluating the Price

You've completed the most important job, assessing a company's quality. Hopefully you won't have to find out the hard way that buying a good company for a high price is better than buying a poor company—even at what you perceive to be a bargain price.

Quality persists. Once you've determined that a company meets your quality standards, that status is not likely to change—at least for a while. As a result, you can collect a "watch list" of good companies and wait for them to hit an attractive price.

But how do you find out what that price should be? Like the other steps you've learned, this process is very simple.

As a long-term investor, your goal is to build a portfolio that will require little attention but will grow consistently in value over time, hopefully doubling every five years. To do this, you will need to think long term and push your horizon out at least five years into the future. When you think long term, you eliminate the noise and clutter of the short-term stock market and focus on the underlying driver of a stock's price—the potential growth of earnings. So let's look at the process of determining a fair price.

RETURN AND RISK

When it comes to evaluating the price of a stock, you're interested in just two things: the potential *return* and the *risk* you must take to get that return. If the potential return is worth the risk, the price is right. If it's not worth the risk, you should wait until it is.

In order to estimate the potential return, you'll have to come up with a reasonable estimate of how high the price might go. To do that you must draw upon history to forecast what earnings might be in five years and what multiple of those earnings you can expect investors to pay for the stock in the future. With those two estimates, you can readily calculate a hypothetical high price with which you can estimate the potential return.

You should also compare the current multiple of earnings with the historical average—the signature PE—to see how realistic the current price is compared with what appears to have been a fair price in the past. If the current price is depressed for some reason, the *historical value ratio (HVR)* will raise a red flag to tell you that you may have missed something in your quality assessment. On the other hand, the price may be high at the moment, in which case you should wait for it to come down.

To evaluate the risk, you'll repeat the process you went through to estimate the return, this time combining a low estimate for future earnings with the lowest multiple you would expect investors to pay. This will result in a conservative estimate of the stock's potential lowest price. If the *risk index* you calculate tells you that your potential gain is at least three times as much as you risk losing, your stock is probably selling at a fair price.

Again, there are some housekeeping chores that must be done to begin with. The computer does them nicely. If you're working manually, the chores are somewhat more tedious and time consuming, but they're not complicated—especially with your financial calculator.

ESTIMATING THE POTENTIAL RETURN ON YOUR INVESTMENT

Estimating the potential return on your investment requires three steps:

1. Estimating future PEs
2. Estimating future earnings
3. Calculating the return

Estimating Future PEs

Your first step is to look at the price—expressed as a multiple of earnings (PE) —that investors have paid for the stock at various times, both when they were confident and optimistic about the company (producing the highest PE each year), and when they were the least confident (producing the lowest PE). You'll then be able to draw some useful conclusions about those multiples.

Eliminating PE outliers. First you must eliminate PE outliers so that you'll be looking only at data that are historically relevant. Outlandish PEs, usually on the high side, are typically caused by one of two things: abnormally low earnings reported after the high price has been recorded for the year, or "irrational exuberance" on the part of investors who pay excessive prices not justified by the earnings.

If you're using a computer, the high and low multiples and the averages will have already been calculated for you. If you're doing this by hand, you will have completed those calculations when you prepared your worksheet.

The quickest way to find any offending PEs is to simply eyeball the average PEs you have calculated, looking for those that are obviously out of whack. Look at ABC Company's average PEs in Figure 10.1. It isn't difficult to pick out the ones that are out of line, is it? This case is pretty cut-and-dried. Average PEs of 56.3 and 48.2 in 1991 and 1992 are way out of line with the rest. However, you may not get off so easy the next time because PE outliers aren't always so obvious.

FIGURE 10.1   ABC Company's Price, EPS, and PE History

Look for PEs that are out of line with the rest.

Value								Company ABC Company		Ticker ABC
Earnings	.27	.36	.46	.56	.61	.69	.82	.94	1.11	1.32
High Price	9.7	32.4	30.5	16.5	14.3	19.9	20.6	27.0	41.2	45.8
Low Price	4.9	8.1	13.8	8.4	9.0	13.1	12.5	14.3	23.6	24.6
High P/E	35.9	90.0	66.3	29.5	23.4	28.8	25.1	28.7	37.1	34.7
Low P/E	18.1	22.5	30.0	15.0	14.8	19.0	15.2	15.2	21.3	18.6
Average P/E	27.0	56.3	48.2	22.3	19.1	23.9	20.2	22.0	29.2	26.7
Dividends									.10	.11	.12
Years	1990	1991	1992	1993	1994	1995	1996	1997	1998	1999

For less noticeable cases, plotting the PEs on a linear graph will help. In Figure 10.2, ABC Company's extraneous data hit you right between the eyes.

The dots in Figure 10.2 plot the high, low, and average PEs, and average PEs are connected to better show the trends. The upper and lower bands represent the average of the high and low PEs, respectively, and the band through the center represents the signature PE. The dotted lines have been included to show estimates of future high and low PEs, which we'll discuss shortly.

Eliminating the outliers takes only a mouse-click on the computer. If you're doing the study by hand, simply draw a line through the offending numbers and calculate your averages for the high, low, and average PEs without them as in Figure 10.3.

The barbed-wire fence. Imagine a barbed-wire fence that stands between the quality issues that we dealt with earlier and the value assessment we're currently embarking on. If you're not critical enough about quality, you can easily be seduced into believing that a stock is a bargain when you actually shouldn't touch it with a ten-foot pole. So I want to paint as graphic a picture as I can to help you

FIGURE 10.2   ABC Company: Linear Graph of PEs

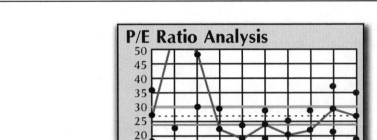

appreciate the consequence of trying to assess the value if you haven't paid enough attention to the quality.

Here's a statement that you may have to think about a little: *The worse a company performs, the better value it will appear to be.* Why do you suppose that is?

If a company is performing badly because management is not doing a good job of minding the store and sales and earnings have decayed, what will happen to the price? More people will want to sell than buy, and the price will go down, making the stock appear to be very cheap.

If you ignore the poor operational performance and just look at the price, you'll be in the market for someone else's mistake! Sure, you'll be able to pick up the stock at bargain-basement prices—but for a good reason. All of the benchmarks of a fair price that you're going to learn about in this chapter will look particularly good. You'll think you made out like a bandit when, in fact, whomever you bought the stock from will turn out to be the lucky one.

Fortunately, an alarm will go off if you bound over that barbed-wire fence recklessly or unawares. It's called the *historical value ratio.*

The historical value ratio (HVR).   Once you have averaged the relevant historical average multiples, you have what you need for a reality check on the current price. The historical value ratio (HVR) is a warning device that will tell you if you've missed something in your quality assessment.

In Chapter 4 I explained that the signature PE is the particular price-earnings ratio that is tied to a company. Over time a company consistently attracts investors at a certain multiple of earnings.

As time passes, prices rise and fall—with wide swings in the short term. Depending on which industry the company is in and the company's particular niche in that industry, investors will confer upon it a certain confidence level. This translates into a PE multiple that stays with it more or less throughout its life. Barring any serious problems, that PE will persist, although it will typically display a slight decline as the company's growth slows with the company's continuing success and increasing size.

Investors who buy stock in a company at a PE greater or less than its signature PE will find that the price tends to gravitate up or down toward that PE, and they will benefit or suffer accordingly.

To approximate the signature PE, remove the irrelevant historical data and average the remaining historical high and low PEs (see Figure 10.3). If you use a computer, there's no work to it; it's all done for you. If you're working by hand, don't be lazy! Calculate the average of the high, low, and average PEs from *all* of the years you have available (less the outliers, of course). The more data you use, the less effect variations will have on the average, and the more valid the signature PE will be. A large segment of the market has been overvalued during the past few years. Including the earlier PEs in the average can moderate the effect of the recent wilder times.

For ABC Company, with 1991 and 1992 removed, the ten-year average PE is about 23.8. (Had you not removed the outliers, the ten-year average would have been an exaggerated 29.6)

Now that you've come up with your signature PE, you can compare it with the current PE to see how today's price compares with the historically fair price of the stock (measured as a multiple of earnings). This comparison is the histori-

FIGURE 10.3   Calculating the Signature PE

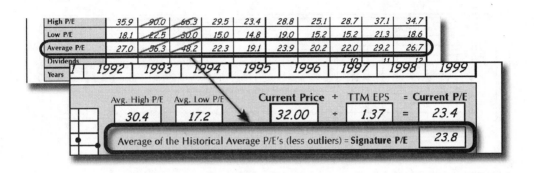

cal value ratio (HVR), which NAIC educators often call *relative value*. I use *HVR* because *relative value* is confused with terms used in other quarters for other things and because NAIC doesn't even mention relative value in its official guide. HVR and relative value are synonymous.

If you're using the computer, the HVR is calculated for you. If you're doing the study by hand, you'll first have to calculate the current PE (the current price divided by the sum of the earnings for the most recent four quarters) and then divide the result by the signature PE. (See Figure 10.4.)

The current PE for ABC Company is 23.4 (32 ÷ 1.37). When we divide this fig-ure by the signature PE (23.8), we come up with an HVR (or relative value) of 98.3 percent. This means that the stock is currently selling for a multiple that's just a trifle under the historical average; the price is reasonable in view of the past.

In general, you are looking for an HVR of right around 100 percent or a bit less. Obviously, if you can buy a quality stock today for a historically fair price, you should probably do so, provided the next steps show the reward and risk to be attractive.

However, what should you do if you find that the HVR is significantly above or below the 100 percent mark?

FIGURE 10.4 Calculating the Historical Value Ratio (HVR)

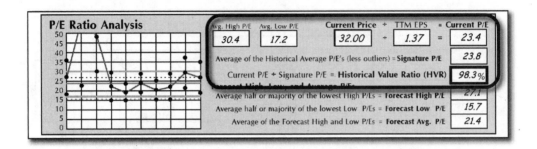

A low HVR is probably your biggest concern because it suggests that people who are buying the stock today might know something negative about the company that you don't know.

Think about it. Why would investors pay less for the stock than it has typically sold for? Is there something in the news that you haven't heard about? Has an analyst—or a number of analysts—announced a reduced expectation of future earnings based upon something they know that you don't know? Have you missed something in your quality analysis—or (shame on you!) recklessly jumped over that barbed-wire fence, failing to evaluate quality before moving on to look at the value considerations?

My strong recommendation to new investors is to start off by being mechanical. If the HVR is too low—below 85 percent—move on to another company and forget about looking at the risk and reward. You may miss a few good stocks, but you won't have to lose any sleep worrying about being wrong.

If the HVR is too high, above around 110 percent or so, put off buying it until the price becomes more reasonable. If you buy a stock whose PE is too far above the signature PE, when it later comes back down—which it usually will—the decrease in PE will reduce your gain considerably. There's simply no need to take unnecessary risks, especially when you're starting out. Your chances of having a superior portfolio are far better if you select stocks that you don't have to make any allowances for.

As you gain more experience, you'll find that you can make some intelligent exceptions in cases of high or low HVR; but for now, don't.

Completing your PE estimates. The next step will be to make a reasonable and conservative estimate of future multiples, both high and low. Again, I suggest that you do this task mechanically to begin with. Later you may think about moderating your estimates, but not until you have the experience to come up with good reasons for doing so.

Your mechanical process is simply to average the lowest half or majority of your data. If you have ten years of data, scratch out the highest five numbers and average the rest. If you have nine years of data, get rid of the highest four and average the remaining five, and so on. If you have only five years of data, you should average only the lowest three, and if you have fewer than five years, *you ought to be looking at an older company.* In no case would you forecast a high PE of greater than 30.

For ABC Company, the maximum high and low PEs occurred from 1990 through 1992 and in 1998 and 1999. Eliminating those and averaging the remaining high PEs, you would come up with a forecasting PE of 27.1. Had the result been greater than 30, you would have limited it to 30. (Note: The figures with Xs through them are the outliers. Those with a single diagonal line through them are eliminated to establish the forecast high and low PEs.)

Using the same process, you find that the average of the five lowest low PEs is 15.7. This is the forecast low PE. The average of the forecast high PE (27.1) and the forecast low PE (15.7) is the forecast average PE, 21.4.

In many cases, the high numbers you delete for both the forecast high PE and the forecast low PE will occur in the same years. As in the case of ABC Company, however, this won't necessarily be the case every time. So you should examine and eliminate the high numbers for the forecast high PE and the forecast low PE independently.

FIGURE 10.5   Averaging the Lowest Half or Majority

Value						Company	ABC Company		Ticker	ABC
Earnings	.27	.36	.46	.56	.61	.69	.82	.94	1.11	1.32
High Price	9.7	32.4	30.5	16.5	14.3	19.9	20.6	27.0	41.2	45.8
Low Price	4.9	8.1	13.8	8.4	9.0	13.1	12.5	14.3	23.6	24.6
High P/E	35.9	90.0	66.3	29.5	23.4	28.8	25.1	28.7	37.1	34.7
Low P/E	18.1	22.5	30.0	15.0	14.8	19.0	15.2	15.2	21.3	18.6
Average P/E	27.0	56.3	48.2	22.3	19.1	23.9	20.2	22.0	29.2	26.7

For both the high and low P/Es: If you have nine or ten years of data, average the lowest five. If you have only seven or eight, average the lowest four. If you have just five or six, average the lowest three. If you have fewer than five years of data, wait until you do have at least five years of data.

Forecast High, Low, and Average P/Es	
Average half or majority of the lowest High P/Es = **Forecast High P/E**	27.1
Average half or majority of the lowest Low P/Es = **Forecast Low P/E**	15.7
Average of the Forecast High and Low P/Es = **Forecast Avg. P/E**	21.4

A word of caution is in order here. In Chapter 6 I likened the life of a corporation to that of a human being. Many of the "hot" companies you'll be attracted to are still in a stage of "corporate adolescence." Be careful! They have not been seasoned as "adults" have. Many of them are the so-called new economy businesses whose managements have not had to deal much with economic downsides. Often the technology that such companies offer is unique. Their intellectual monopolies afford them the sort of protection that kids take for granted before they have to grapple with the cold, cruel world on their own. Like strapping high school football heroes, new economy companies think they're ready to conquer the world, but they haven't yet experienced an economy without euphoria or a market with healthy competition.

Citrix Systems (CTXS) comes to mind as an example. Not three months before I wrote this, Citrix could brag that of its 1,100 employees, more than 700 were millionaires! This was, of course, because their stock options looked fantastic on paper. From a high of around $122 at that time, the stock price recently plunged to around $20 on news of a disappointing quarter and has since continued to decline below $15. Citrix is an excellent company with great products and promise and a corps of smart employees and dedicated managers. But I'll wait to consider buying its stock until it has marshaled those resources and proved that it can survive its bump in the road.

The point? Don't even consider a fairly new company with a history of rising PEs and no sign of a downturn. Where investor confidence has never been challenged, a past without problems is definitely not a harbinger of an untroubled future. Companies that have been consistently meeting analysts' extraordinary estimates from the day they first attracted attention are an investor's disaster waiting to happen—and perhaps an opportunity when it does.

Estimating Future Earnings

In order to estimate earnings five years into the future, you will need to estimate the rate at which earnings will grow for those five years. Chances are that when you're looking at historical growth, you'll go on to forecast future growth. It makes a lot of sense to use the historical information that you've developed while it's fresh. That's the way all of the software is structured, as are the worksheets for those who do their calculations by hand. For purposes of this book, however, I held off on the discussion of forecasting until now rather than muddying the waters with value issues while we talked about quality.

Except in very rare cases, companies can't sustain extremely strong growth rates forever. A company's success alone is enough to work against the perpetuation of high rates. The bigger a company gets, the greater the level of sales and earnings it has to generate in order to keep up its rate of growth.

The first thing to recognize, therefore, is that growth rates of even the greatest companies will eventually decline. It's a fact of life. If you're estimating growth for the long term—not just for the next year—it's very likely that the historical growth rate of both sales and earnings will decline at least a little.

The next consideration when forecasting growth is predictability—the stability of past growth. If the lines that connect the annual dots are smooth, then it's relatively easy to forecast growth rationally. As I've noted, you're much more likely to see smooth historical growth lines on the chart for sales than for earnings because sales are influenced by far fewer things than are earnings. Therefore, you're going to have more confidence in your estimates of sales growth than in your estimates of earnings growth. You will estimate future sales growth at a rate closer to the historical sales growth rate than you will future earnings growth relative to the historical earnings growth rate.

Your aim is to produce estimates of future growth rates for sales and earnings that you feel comfortable with and that you believe are sustainable—not only for the next 5 years, but for the next 20 or more.

Some limiting rules of thumb.   Here are a couple of rules of thumb that will keep you inside the ballpark and out of trouble.

First, let sales be your guide. Because sales are more stable and are therefore more predictable, estimate sales growth first. Then, never estimate future earnings growth at a higher rate than that of sales. Earnings growth depends upon the rate of sales growth; differences between the two growth rates are only transient. Earnings growth at a rate faster than that of sales growth is simply not sustainable. Period.

Second, establish a sensible cap on growth estimates. Make it a hard and fast rule to *never predict future sales or earnings to grow at a rate greater than 20 percent*. Even 20 percent is rarely sustainable for very long, although in recent years a number of companies have demonstrated remarkable staying power at and above that rate and have held those high rates for more years than anyone could have imagined possible.

One case in point is the pharmaceutical industry. Many drug companies have discovered a formula for growing earnings that seems as elusive and incredible as perpetual motion. Using a combination of tax write-offs for research and development costs and the perpetual increase in the prices of patent-protected products, many drug companies have found a way to grow their earnings at a rate faster than sales growth—for decades. However, don't gamble that you may be the clever one to have found the next company or industry to perform the same feat. The odds are definitely against it.

Remember, your aim is to find companies that can provide you with a return of 15 percent or better. If you can't get that kind of return from investing in a company with 20 percent earnings growth, there's probably something wrong with the investment anyway! I would hate to have to rely upon any growth above 20 percent to produce my desired return. (Of course, any excess *beyond* my expectations would be gratefully accepted!)

With these constraints in mind, here are the commonsense considerations you'll take into account as you forecast the future.

Forecasting sales growth. If sales growth has described a perfectly straight line on the growth chart for all of the years that are plotted, it's easy to figure out what the future probably holds. You can feel comfortable estimating that future sales will grow at a rate close to, but a little below, their historical rate. In fact, you might consider rounding the historical rate down to the next lower percentage and letting it go at that. Walgreen's (WAG) is a good example of a company with a stable but slowing growth rate. (See Figure 10.6.)

However, the lines are rarely perfectly straight. If the line has a sawtooth pattern or zigzags as it climbs across the chart, sales growth is not predictable. Therefore, you can't depend upon steady growth in the future. This is more likely to be the case for earnings than for sales, but occasionally both lines exhibit the zigzag pattern.

A company with a zigzag pattern may have attracted your interest because of its comfortable uptrend. However, the more erratic the growth line appears to be, the greater the allowances you have to make for disappointment. Hopefully you will discard any company whose historical growth has meandered too much for you to be comfortable with a forecast.

FIGURE 10.6   Variations in Sales Growth

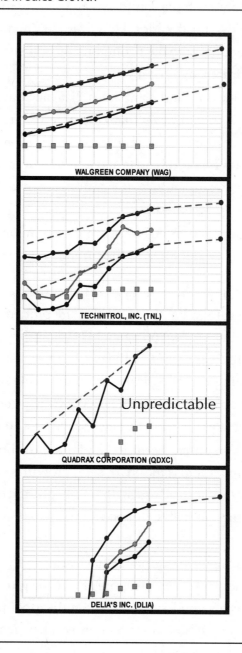

FIGURE 10.7   ABC Company's Growth Forecast

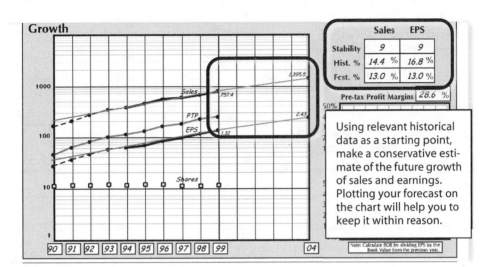

Be careful of younger companies. They will usually show rapid growth rates, then rapid decay. Be sure to take into account the decay as you project the growth into the future.

Forecasting earnings growth. The principle for estimating earnings growth is the same as that for sales, but earnings are apt to be less predictable. Because earnings are derived from sales, whatever volatility sales display, earnings will at least mirror. Compounding that volatility are all of the fluctuations in expenses, taxes, and the number of shares outstanding that come into play before you finally get to the bottom line.

To estimate the growth rate of earnings, use the relevant historical growth rate as a starting point and temper it with enough conservatism to make you comfortable, being certain that your estimate doesn't exceed your estimate of sales growth.

For ABC Company, after the outliers were eliminated, the historical sales growth rate came out at around 14 percent, earnings at nearly 17 percent (the computer came up with 14.4 and 16.8 percent, respectively). Just to be especially con-

FIGURE 10.8   Calculating the Total Return and the Average Return for ABC Company

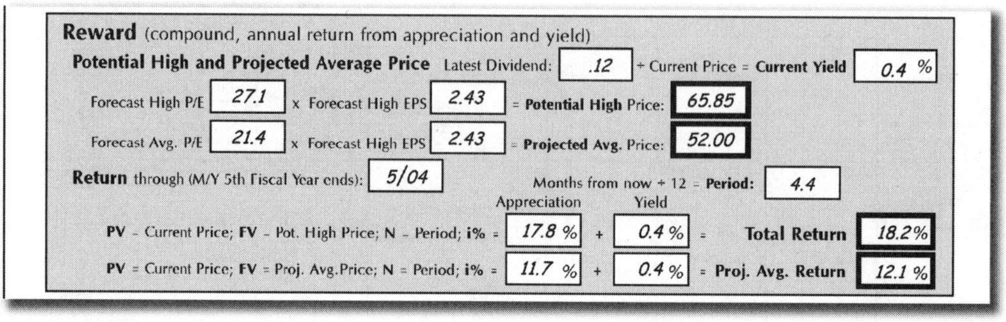

---

servative, I've chosen to estimate sales growth in the future at only 13 percent and, of course, earnings at a figure that is no higher despite past rapid earnings growth.

Now you can estimate what sales and earnings will be in five years. On the computer you will simply enter your estimated growth rates for sales and earnings into the appropriate fields and the computer will draw your trend lines out five years, calculating the sales and earnings at that point.

If you're working by hand, you'll use your business calculator to enter the data. Put in your sales information first, using last fiscal year's data as the present value: PV = 757.4; N = 5 (years); i% = 13. Now solve for FV, the future value of sales. You'll plot the result, 1,395.5, on the right margin. Next, you have only to replace the sales figure with the earnings figure (1.32) as the PV, and because the growth rate is the same, you're ready to solve for FV again. You will come up with 2.43, which you can also plot. You'll then draw your lines from the data for the most recent year to these newly plotted points.

Calculating the Return

Your *return* is the hypothetical profit you will make if you buy a stock at today's price and sell it in five years at its potential high price, receiving any dividends the company might pay over that time. Return is expressed as a *compounded, annualized* percentage.

As you can see, return has two components: *appreciation* (growth of the original investment), which is of primary interest to you as an investor in growth companies, and *yield* (the dividend income that you might receive along the way).

Appreciation. Your first chore is to figure out what the potential high price will be if earnings grow as you forecast and the PE meets your conservative expectation. It's simple. Multiply your forecast earnings by the multiple of those earnings you expect investors to pay (your forecast high PE), and you'll arrive at the highest potential high price you should expect.

We expect ABC Company to produce $2.43 per share in earnings in the year ending in May of 2004, and its stock could sell at a high multiple of 27.1. The product of the two figures is $65.85—the potential high price. That's simple enough, isn't it?

Now we need to figure out the compounded annual return. Again, the computer does the job handily so that all you have to do is read the return off the screen. If you're working manually, finding the return is just a matter of plugging the data into your calculator and reading the result. PV = the current price; FV = your forecast high price; N = the number of years in the future for which you're projecting—usually five. You'll solve for i%—the compounded annual appreciation.

As I implied above, the return calculation doesn't necessarily have a period (N) of five years. In the case of ABC Company, the last fiscal year ended in May of 1999, and the calculations for the high and low prices were for five years from then—May of 2004. However, the date of the study (and of the price) is December 31, 1999. So the price won't have the full five years to appreciate. In fact, it's expected to reach our projected high price by May 2004, which is only four years and five months from the date of the study for a period of 4.4 years.

So to come up with a more accurate hypothetical return (which, I'm afraid, is something of an oxymoron), you should plug in the exact number of years, and fractions of years, that are left before the end of the forecast period.

For ABC Company, therefore, we would use the following data: PV = 32; FV = 65.58; N = 4.4. Solving for i%, we get 17.8 percent as our compounded annual appreciation.

Yield. You're a growth company investor, so yield won't have much of an impact on your investment return. In fact, you're mostly interested in the companies whose policymakers feel that they can best increase shareholder value by plowing earnings back into their own operations to feed their growth.

Yield is nevertheless a part of your return, and if you're investing in a General Electric (GE) or some other large, established company to balance your risk and anchor your portfolio, you're definitely going to need to factor it in.

The simplest way to incorporate yield is to calculate current yield and use that as the yield component in your return calculation. To calculate yield, divide the dividend by the price of the stock. ABC Company last paid a dividend of 12 cents per share, so your dividend income is 0.4 percent of the $32 share price—not a significant amount. $(0.12 \div 32 = 0.4\%)$

When you add the 0.4 percent yield to the 17.8 percent appreciation, you arrive at a total return of 18.2 percent.

Average return. Another return calculation may be of interest to you: the *projected average return.* This is the same as the total return calculation above, except that the projected price (FV) in the equation is calculated by multiplying the high earnings by the forecast *average* PE rather than the forecast high PE. For ABC Company, the projected average return would be 12.1 percent. (See Figure 10.8.)

No matter how clever I may think I am, I can never seem to sell a stock at its high! It seems like someone else always gets a higher price for it right after I sell. However, I can usually plan on selling a stock at the average multiple. The projected average return—a total return based upon a lower selling price—is a more conservative view of the future. It's nice to know that I don't have to depend upon selling the stock at a higher-than-average multiple of earnings to make money.

I've set no deal-breaker goal for the average return, but I do feel good if it exceeds the percentage guidelines that I gave you in Chapter 7 (Figure 7.11) for minimum sales growth for a particular size of company.

DETERMINING THE POTENTIAL RISK

Evaluating risk, like estimating return, has several logical but simple steps:

- Estimating the future low PE
- Estimating future low earnings
- Calculating the risk

Estimating the Future Low PE

You've already estimated the future low PE! When you averaged the lowest half or majority of the low PEs (see Figure 10.5), you were forecasting the low PE. In our example, the forecast low PE is 15.7.

Estimating Future Low Earnings

To estimate the risk, you're going to use the same logic on the downside as you did on the upside to establish a price. Multiply the *lowest* reasonable estimate of future earnings by the *lowest* reasonable multiple of those earnings to come up with a reasonable estimate of the *lowest* price to which you might expect the stock to fall. First, you need to estimate the lowest earnings you could reasonably expect to be possible in the future. To be on the safe side, *let the earnings for the most recent four quarters* represent the lowest future earnings. How much more conservative can you be? This is a good growth company. You can't expect earnings to be lower in 5 years than they were during the past 12 months. If they should decline below that figure for very long, you will sell anyway.

Calculating the Risk

To calculate the risk, you'll have to figure out what the price would be if the company produced the lowest earnings that you forecast and the stock sold at the lowest PE that you predicted. Simply multiply the low earnings by the low PE, and you'll arrive at your potential low price.

In this example, ABC Company's earnings might remain at $1.37, and its stock could sell at a low multiple of 15.7. The product of the two figures is $21.51—the potential low price. Armed with that downside figure, you can now figure the risk: what you might lose if the stock price should go down to that potential low price instead of going up. The way you'll assess this risk is to calculate the risk index— a comparison of what you have to lose in the worst case versus what you have to gain if all goes well.

To calculate the risk index, divide the difference between the current price and the potential low price (your possible loss) by the difference between the potential high price and the potential low price (the "deal"—the range between the best and worst case). The result is the risk index, the percentage of the deal that is risky. We look for a risk index of less than 25 percent, meaning that less than a quarter of the proposition is risky. We would then have at least 75 percent to gain versus at most 25 percent to lose; so the reward is at least three times the risk.

FIGURE 10.9   The Risk Index

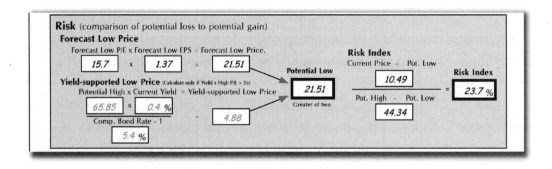

As with the historical value ratio (HVR), the benefits of considering the risk fall at both ends of the buy/don't-buy spectrum.

In general, the lower the risk index the better. If your risk is minimal or non-existent, there is no question that you're better off, *provided that there are no legitimate reasons for the price to be as low as it is or even lower.*

If the HVR didn't warn you that a company's price is depressed, the low risk index is a last-chance warning. If the HVR did not tell you that the price, expressed as a multiple of earnings, is lower than people have historically been willing to pay for the stock, the risk/reward relationship can tell you that the price simply appears too good to be true!

If you find that your risk is extraordinarily low compared with the reward—zero or negative risk—don't buy it unless you can satisfy yourself that the company is just fine, and it's only ignorant investors who are driving the price down (it happens). However, don't be too quick to dismiss the possibility that people who are selling the stock know something you don't!

The most important determination, of course, is that you don't buy the stock if there is too great a risk. In fact, I think it's safe to say that unless the reward is close to three times the risk, you should wait until the price is more favorable.

Let's put theory into practice with ABC Company. First, find the difference between the current price ($32) and the potential low price ($21.51). The result is $10.49. Next, calculate the difference between the potential high price ($65.85) and the potential low price ($21.51). The result is $44.34. Divide the first result by the second to arrive at a risk index of 23.7 percent, which is below our risk index limit of 25 percent.

TO BUY OR NOT TO BUY

No matter how you do your calculations—using a computer, a calculator, or an abacus—the bottom line is the potential reward and the amount of risk that you must accept to achieve it.

Always assuming you have done your due diligence concerning the quality issues, look to see if the hypothetical total return is sufficient to warrant adding the stock to your portfolio. If the stock appears to be capable of doubling its value in five years, it's probably a good buy.

If you have been cautious enough in your estimates of earnings growth and future PEs, and if the potential reward is at least three times the risk of loss, you'll have no qualms about buying the stock.

Would ABC Company be a good deal at $32? You bet! Suppose, however, that its risk index were a few tenths of a percent above the desired value of 25 percent? This brings up a final point of importance.

Use your good common sense. Investing is far from a precise science. What you lose in accuracy because you're building one estimate upon another, you gain by being conservative in your estimates. If you're careful to take the more cautious choice at every opportunity, you're rarely going to be disappointed at the outcome.

A small difference (a 1 percent difference in the risk index, in this case, would translate into less than 50 cents in the share price) is not enough to warrant waiting for the price to be just right.

If the price is more than just a little too high for the value parameters to satisfy you, however, you'll want to complete your study and wait for the price to come down to a reasonable figure.

FIGURE 10.10   Calculating the Buy Price

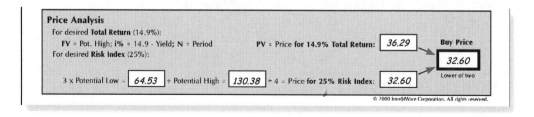

Price Analysis
For desired **Total Return** (14.9%):
  FV = Pot. High; **i%** = 14.9 - Yield; **N** = Period   **PV** = **Price for 14.9% Total Return:** | 36.29 | **Buy Price**
For desired **Risk Index** (25%): | 32.60 |

  3 x Potential Low = | 64.53 | + Potential High = | 130.38 | ÷ 4 = Price for 25% Risk Index: | 32.60 | Lower of two

© 2000 Inve$tWare Corporation. All rights reserved.

WHAT IS THE RIGHT PRICE?

Assuming that a company meets the quality standards, there are really only two criteria with which to determine if the price is right: the *reward* and the *risk*. From the information you've developed in your study, you can easily work backward and calculate the price at which each of those criteria is satisfied.

Some of the software will calculate a reasonable price for you, but it's easy enough to do with your calculator.

To satisfy the reward, or total return, requirement, plug the following information into your calculator: FV = the potential high price; i% = 14.9 *less the current yield;* and N = the period remaining until the forecast date. Solve for PV. For ABC Company: FV = 65.85; i% = 14.5; and N = 4.4. The present value of the stock, then, is $36.29.

Hypothetically, you could double your money every five years if you bought ABC Company at $36.29—fully $4.29 above its current price.

To satisfy the risk requirement, multiply the potential low price by three, add the potential high price, and divide the result by four (see Figure 10.10). The result is $32.60.

The lower of these two prices is the price at which you can feel quite comfortable buying the stock. This is a good price to look for on your watch list.

Remember that prices can fluctuate by as much as 50 percent on either side of their averages during the course of the year; so you might be pleasantly surprised when a price you thought beyond hope just happens to materialize one day.

What You Know about the Value Issues

The most important task in buying a stock is to determine that the company is a good company in which to own stock for the long term. However, no matter how good the company, if the price of its stock is too high, it's not going to be a good investment.

A stock price must pass two tests to be considered reasonable:

1. The hypothetical total return from the investment must be adequate—enough to contribute to a portfolio average of 15 percent, which is sufficient to double its value every five years.

2. The potential gain should be at least three times the potential loss.

To complete these tests, you have learned how to do the following:

- Estimate future sales and earnings growth

- Estimate future earnings

- Analyze past PEs (check the HVR)

- Estimate future PEs

- Forecast the potential high and low prices

- Calculate the potential return

- Calculate the potential risk

- Calculate a fair price

If you take each of these steps cautiously and shun excesses, the actual result is likely to be as good or better than the forecast at least four out of five times.

That's all there is; there ain't no more!

Well, that's not entirely true. But it's really all you need to build a great portfolio that will meet your expectations handily. However, to maintain that portfolio at peak performance, you will need to manage it well, optimizing its performance and preventing the companies that occasionally go south from damaging it. Portfolio management chores take a minimal amount of time, especially when you consider the value of the results. You can read about managing your portfolio in Chapter 12.

You will pick up a lot of useful information as your experience develops. However, I would be remiss if I didn't include in this book some additional tips gleaned from my own experience. You'll find them in Chapter 13. But be sure to heed the warning that accompanies that chapter.

In Chapter 11, we'll talk about comparing companies: What happens if you want to pick the best of two or more companies that might be good buys? How do you figure out which company in an industry is the best choice for your investment dollars?

CHAPTER 11

Comparing Companies

Sometimes you will be interested in more than just a single company—or even in a single industry. Occasionally, especially when you first start out, you'll want to consider a number of candidates for selection.

In the process of doing your stock studies, you have developed information about a number of companies that can now be of value in matching one investment opportunity against others that are competing for your investment dollars. The job of comparing is so easy that it would be foolish to pass up the chance to make sure the companies you select are the best of your candidates.

Under what circumstances might comparison be called for?

- **To consider a single stock.** You have studied a stock that you are particularly interested in—perhaps someone mentioned it as a tip or you read about it somewhere—and you are satisfied with its potential. You may want to look at other contenders in the same industry to see if there are any better choices.

- **To select one from a group of stocks.** You have studied a group of companies but have the money to buy only one or two for the moment. You will want to know which of them to select.

- **To study an industry.** You want to look at a particular industry that has attracted your attention to see which companies within it are the most attractive investments. You will, of course, need to perform the quality and value checks on each of the companies to develop the data necessary for meaningful comparison.

- **To select from among club choices.** You are in an investment club and want to settle on the best prospect from among several presented to the group.

- **To decide whether to switch to a different stock.** In the next chapter, you'll learn that there will be times when you should replace one stock with another that is of equal or better quality but that has a better potential for return. You may wish to compare the company you already own with one or more other companies to see if your portfolio could benefit from the swap.

For these or other reasons, you may find it desirable to compare investment opportunities with one another. This chapter will help you with that.

Probably the easiest way to compare companies is with a computerized spreadsheet program like Microsoft Excel or with one of the software packages that are described in Appendix B. If you have no computer, you can make your comparisons on a piece of lined paper.

CREATING A COMPARISON WORKSHEET

On a comparison worksheet (created with a computer spreadsheet program or on a piece of paper), you're going to list the criteria you will use for comparison along the left side of the page. You'll provide a column heading at the top of the page for each of the companies you wish to compare. Then you'll enter the information from your completed stock studies in the appropriate spaces and compare the stocks according to your criteria, circling or otherwise marking the winner or winners for each. The company with the most marks will probably—but not necessarily—be your best choice.

This simple procedure is a good starting place for a decision. With thoughtful deliberation about how much weight to give each criterion, and with some thought about the significance of other, subjective issues I'll talk about below, the worksheet can be of great help in making your decision.

Choosing and Prioritizing Your Comparison Criteria

The criteria that you will use for your comparisons will be pretty much the same as those you used for your stock studies, although you may decide to incorporate additional criteria of your own. You should give first priority to the quality issues, then consider the value issues.

It's entirely possible that you will find a company whose quality criteria are more favorable than those of another—its growth and stability are more impressive—but whose stock is selling for a little higher price than you feel you should pay, while the other is a bargain at the moment.

Naturally, you'll want to weigh those considerations carefully, and you could be confronted with a dilemma: Should you buy a company of suitable quality at a great price? Or should you buy a company of better quality at a less attractive price? It could be a tough call. Perhaps the answer will lie in the urgency. Can you afford to wait for the price to come down on the better-quality stock?

Some of the additional criteria that will be factored into your comparison are informational, not quantitative. For example, even if you're not comparing companies within a specific industry but are simply looking for the best investment, the industry may still have a place in your decision. If the numbers are similar, you may want to give the edge to a company in a more vital or secure industry, depending upon your personal experience, perceptions, or interests. Quantitative measures aren't the only useful comparative criteria.

Setting Up Your Worksheet

Here's a list of basic criteria that you should list on your comparison worksheet. I have briefly described each item and have indicated whether the winner will have the higher or lower value on that criterion compared with its competitors. I have also referred to the chapter in this book where you can review each criterion.

Quality

Historical sales growth. Growth rate of sales *for relevant years*   (Higher)
(Chapter 7)

Historical earnings growth. Growth rate of earnings *for relevant*   (Higher)
years (Chapter 7)

Future sales growth. Your estimate of future sales growth   (Higher)
(Chapter 10)

Future earnings growth. Your estimate of future earnings growth   (Higher)
(Chapter 10)

Sales predictability. (Chapter 7)   (Higher)
Using the computer you will find the value of R^2. In the jargon of statisticians, R^2 is the *coefficient of determination*, which measures on a scale from one to zero the extent to which the plotted points on which a trend line is based fall on, close to, or well away from that line. If all of the points lie on the trend line, R^2 is 1 (or 100%). If none are close, R^2 approaches zero. Most financial software products (including the compact disk that comes with this book) will provide you with the R^2 value for trend lines you are evaluating.

If you are working manually, you will make a subjective judgment about sales predictability based on your visual assessment of the degree to which the growth line approaches your goal of monotonous excellence. A 10 would indicate a perfectly straight growth line, and a 1 would be assigned to a line that describes wildly fluctuating growth.

Earnings predictability. (Chapter 7)   (Higher)
Evaluated in the same way as sales predictability
Note: *Value Line* has a measurement called "Earnings
Predictability" that doesn't relate directly to the stability criteria
we've discussed; still, *Value Line* users may apply that
measurement here because it addresses the same issue.

Average profit margin. The average of all available data—a   (Higher)
  minimum of five years (Chapter 9)

Profit margin stability. Evaluated subjectively in the same way as   (Higher)
  sales predictability (Chapter 9)

Trend in profit margins. Comparison of the most recent year's   (The more
  profit margin with the average profit margin. If the most recent   positive the
  year is higher than the average, the trend is up. Record it as   better)
  ("++," "+," "=," "−," or "− −") (Chapter 9)

Value

Current PE. Calculated using the most recent four quarters of   (Lower)
  earnings (Chapter 10)

Historical value ratio (HVR). Current PE compared to signature   (Lower, if
  PE (Chapter 10)   above 85)

Risk index. Risk of loss from decline in price, expressed as a   (Lower)
  percentage (Chapter 10)

Total return. Compounded appreciation and income if stock were   (Higher)
  to sell at high PE (Chapter 10)

Average return. Compounded appreciation and income if stock   (Higher)
  were to sell at average PE (Chapter 10)

Miscellaneous Information

Current price   (N/A)

Number of shares you can buy with the fixed amount of money   (N/A)
  you would like to spend

Industry   (N/A)

Exchange where stock is traded   (N/A)

As you go along, you may come up with other items that are of importance to you and can have a bearing on your decision. Don't hesitate to list and prioritize additional criteria.

Be sure to put the name and/or ticker symbol of the company at the top of the list so you can easily identify it as you add the data. If you are listing the criteria by hand, you might want to numerically prioritize them and then list them in order of importance. If you create the list on your computer using a spreadsheet program, you can simply type in your criteria, assign each a number indicating its level of priority, then sort the list when you are finished.

When you've completed your prioritized list, make a master copy of it from which you can run copies from time to time so you won't have to construct the list again. If you're using a computer, it's simple enough to save the spreadsheet as a template and bring up a fresh document each time you perform your comparisons.

SELECTING STOCKS TO COMPARE

Before you select stocks to compare, eliminate any companies that fall below your baseline quality standards. Then determine what your objective is in making your comparison.

Is it important to you that the companies you compare be in the same industry? Or are you simply looking for the best overall investment? You may just want to be sure that the company you've tentatively chosen is the best in its industry. Or it may be that your portfolio's diversification goals suggest that you add a company in a particular economic sector or industry.

One advantage of comparing companies in similar industries is that comparisons on some of the criteria may be valid only within an industry. For example, a company's profit margins will be on an "apples to apples" basis when you are comparing companies within the same industry, but profit margin comparisons will be irrelevant if you are considering companies in different industries. You simply can't compare Microsoft's profit margins with Home Depot's. However, you can compare the *trend* in profit margins to determine whether each company is controlling its costs properly.

There are some very good reasons to compare companies within a single industry, but this isn't essential if your objective is to come up with the most profitable option regardless of industry.

How many stocks should you compare? No more than five. If you work with more than five, the comparison becomes both unwieldy and less meaningful; you'll be conducting a screening exercise rather than a comparison, and you'll have a tough time selecting the winner.

ANALYZING THE RESULTS

Once you've selected stocks to compare, it's time to enter the result from the completed stock study for each criterion in a column under the appropriate company's name and ticker symbol. When you have finished, you will have a column of significant numbers and other data for each of the companies side by side.

The next step is to compare each of the variables, circling or otherwise marking the favorable values. It's best to circle more than one company's result on a criterion when the values are not too far apart. It's less important to pick a single winner in each of the categories than it is to pick the values that seem better than most of the others.

The trouble with computer programs that do all of this for you is that they mark only the highest value, no matter how close the winner is to the runner-up. Sometimes a company that is perfectly good will lose the contest by a tiny fraction of a number.

The lesson here is to be judicious about selecting the winners. For the comparison to be most effective and do you the most good, you should ponder each item and make a conscious decision about its meaning and importance. Many investors foolishly look at each item, decide whether higher or lower is better, and circle the highest or lowest value on that line. The wisest approach is to consciously consider each criterion. Remind yourself about what makes it important to you.

And think about the significance of half a percent or a couple of pennies—or a couple of million dollars—when you decide whether or not to circle a value.

If you've marked your values properly, you will have a number of rows in which there are several marks—in fact, some rows may have a mark for every company.

Don't play favorites! It's easy to yield to temptation and favor the company you started with. (Suppose you're a member of an investment club and are comparing your own candidate with the companies that others have proposed. It's not hard to imagine succumbing to the temptation to play favorites, but the rest of the members probably won't let you get away with it!)

Here's a trick: Don't use any rhyme or reason for the order in which you assign the companies to the columns. Or assign them alphabetically. Just don't follow the normal instinct and put the stock you first decided to study in the first column. One fellow I know just calls the companies "A," "B," "C," and so on. You'd be surprised at how much better a job you'll do of comparing the variables if you judge the values on their merits alone rather than associating them with particular companies.

When you've finished marking the data, you may then add up the marks and see which companies come out with the greatest number. If your criteria are relatively few, you'll have a pretty good start for deciding which company you will want to go with.

It's also a good idea to make room on your comparison worksheet for notes so that you can look back and remember the things you considered when you made your decision.

It's important not to select a company simply because it's numerically superior to the others. The numbers serve only as a guide. The most important judgment is your overall subjective assessment. You might prefer industries you're familiar with and companies whose stores you shop in and are impressed with. These and other subjective criteria should be used for tiebreakers if you come up with two or more companies that are close on the quantitative measures.

Comparison can be fun as well as valuable (see Figure 11.1). Many times I've started the exercise with a successful stock study and scant interest in going

FIGURE 11.1   A Simple Comparison of Five Retailers

Comparison Worksheet

	Company 1		Company 2		Company 3		Company 4		Company 5	
Company	Home Depot		Lowes Com.		Kohl's Corp.		Dollar Tree		Walgreen	
Ticker	HD		LOW		KSS		DLTR		WAG	
Quality										
Historical sales growth	28.8%	x	22.3%		20.8%		28.7%		12.6%	
Historical earnings growth	27.5%		40.1%	x	30.9%		38.7%		14.7%	
Future sales growth	20.0%	x	20.0%	x	20.0%	x	20.0%	x	12.5%	
Future earnings growth	20.0%	x	20.0%	x	20.0%	x	20.0%	x	12.5%	
Sales predictability	10	x	10	x	10	x	10	x	10	x
Earnings predictability	10	x	6		10	x	10	x	10	x
Average pretax profit margin	8.4		5.6		7.8		11.7	x	5.3	
Profit margin stability	9	x	9	x	9	x	9	x	9	x
Profit margin trend	+	x	++	x	+	x	+	x	=	x
Value										
Current PE	48.6		23.7	x	70.4		28.0		40.8	
Historical value ratio (HVR)	134.3		93.3	x	206.5		110.7		143.7	
Total return	10.2%		27.6%	x	1.0%		10.2%		6.4%	
Average return	8.1%		21.8%	x	0.8%		7.4%		5.0%	
Risk index	52.2%		8.2%	x	93.7%		24.3%		66.7%	
Miscellaneous										
Current price	48.56		41.69		54.94		40.63		27.75	
Number of shares $1,000 will buy	20.6		24.0		18.2		24.6		36.0	
Industry	Retail		Retail		Retail		Retail		Retail	
Where traded	NYSE		NYSE		NYSE		NASDAQ		NYSE	
Scores	7		11		6		7		4	

Notes: *LOW scored the most points. Earnings growth is lots higher than sales growth (profit margins are improving)--can't keep this up too long! (However, return is based upon both sales and earnings growth at 20%.) Except for the price, HD could have been a wise choice. LOW is increasing profit margins; but HD already has great margins for industry. LOW is opening new stores in our neighborhood and seem eager to get our business. LOW's reduced stability was from early years.*

Picked LOW because I don't know when HD's price will come back down to within reason. LOW's return looks excellent.

through the motions of checking to see if I might have overlooked something better, only to find that there was an alternative that was clearly superior. Often, you'll find that the "good deal" you contemplated buying has given way to a "great deal"—just because you were objective enough to keep an open mind and take a look.

LET'S TAKE STOCK OF
What You Know about Comparing Companies

- There are times when it's a good idea to compare one investment opportunity with another in order to select the best alternative.

- The easiest way to compare companies is to select and prioritize the essential criteria and place the companies' performance on the criteria side by side for analysis.

- Some criteria are merely informational, not quantitative.

- Minor numerical differences are not important in weighing one company's performance against another.

- Marking the winning numbers and counting those marks is a good starting point for making a decision, but subjective judgment that includes other considerations such as the company's industry or the quality of your own experience with the company should also influence your final judgment.

CHAPTER 12

Managing Your Portfolio

Before I tackle the issue of portfolio management, I need to clarify just what *portfolio management* really means because there are a few misconceptions.

WHAT IS PORTFOLIO MANAGEMENT—REALLY?

Many folks think that *portfolio management* means tracking their portfolio—watching the prices and checking how much they've gained or lost on their holdings. It's not. Tracking merely tells you how well or poorly you may have managed your portfolio—after the fact. Portfolio management is a proactive process; it involves taking some action.

Other investors believe that they're managing their portfolios when they watch the market and then sell stocks when prices reach predefined targets or when returns exceed predefined goals. Wrong again! Let me say emphatically that contrary to popular opinion, portfolio management does *not* require you to sell the stocks whose prices move into disappointing territory or languish there. All of your stocks can fit that description from time to time—and probably will—without any long-term consequence to fret about. As I've said elsewhere, excursions of 50 percent on either side of the average price are not at all unusual in the best of times, and for the best of stocks.

If all things were textbook-perfect, the price of each of your stocks would grow in lockstep with earnings, the PE would hover closely around the signature PE, and at any time you would be able to sell the stock at the same multiple of earnings that you paid for it—perhaps more—and make a tidy profit.

But that would be against the law, Murphy's Law: If something can go wrong, it will. Remember that in the short term, prices are driven by investors' whims and by a whole variety of hot issues that can either warm investors' hearts or ignite the flames of discontent.

Actual fundamentals like sales, pretax profit, and earnings are reported only quarterly, so changes in the fundamentals aren't responsible for short-term price fluctuations. Rumors, stories, insider tips, analysts' upgrades or downgrades, and other "soft" stuff, as opposed to hard facts, drive short-term price changes. And some of that soft stuff can influence your stocks' prices long enough to challenge your patience.

The soft stuff can be related to a particular company (a rumor about a change in management), a single industry (rumors of new competitive technology that threatens the existing participants), a market sector (a small increase in interest rates that can affect consumer cyclicals), or the market as a whole (consensus by analysts that the sky is falling after the chairman of the Federal Reserve Board makes a speech).

In Chapter 4, when I was discussing the character of the PE, I stated that "any price (PE) movement that is not related to the company's earnings is transient. If the stories—not the numbers—cause the price to move, the change won't last. What goes up will come down, and what goes down will come up."

I hope that this statement will fortify you with abundant patience when prices remain depressed for long periods—sometimes very long periods—as they inevitably will. At such times, you might want to repeat it to yourself as a mantra to help bolster your confidence that prices will eventually return to the fair and reasonable state as a rational multiple of earnings. (You should also repeat the mantra daily when prices balloon to way *above* where they should be for a very long time.)

You will find, in fact, that a time of price decline offers a good opportunity to add to your position, provided the company continues to operate as you had hoped. Stock prices retreat because of declines in investor confidence, and investor loss of confidence in good-quality companies is groundless far more often than it's justified.

You might argue that the landscape is littered with the remains of companies in which investors lost confidence for good reason. But such companies don't usually qualify as quality companies. Or if they were quality companies at some point, they would be among the 20 percent of companies that fall by the wayside for reasons that were simply unpredictable.

To be sure, portfolio management is the practice of monitoring your portfolio and taking whatever actions are necessary to enhance its performance. But watching the daily stock prices is not where it's at. In a very real sense, when you buy stocks you buy companies—or at least shares in them. So portfolio management involves monitoring the companies, not their stock prices. This is a major distinction and one that you must embrace.

THE SIZE OF YOUR PORTFOLIO

You now know how to intelligently select the stocks that can help you accumulate substantial wealth over the years. Hopefully you're going to put these methods into practice and build a strong portfolio of somewhere between 10 and 25 stocks—although there's no hard-and-fast rule about how many you should own. If you own 10 or 11 stocks, you have enough baskets for your eggs to ward off a calamity. Beyond that, it's all a matter of your comfort level—and your equipment.

The best rule of thumb is to hold no more companies than you can easily keep track of. This number can vary depending upon whether you do all of your chores by hand, as many people have over the past half century, or on a computer. Needless to say, it's a whole lot easier to keep track of stocks when the work is automated. Computerized portfolio management is so much easier, faster, and more accurate than the manual alternative.

However you keep track of your holdings, one of the best things about the technamental approach is that your portfolio management tasks will be far less demanding than they would be if you were a trader or even just a longer-term short-term investor.

DECIDING WHEN TO SELL

When should you sell your stocks? At what point should you take your profit and get out?

The answers to these questions are "never" and "never," respectively.

Well, that's not entirely true. There are, in fact, three occasions when you might want or need to sell your stock. First of all, if you want the money—or need it—you'll obviously have to sell your stock to get it.

Second, you may discover that you have one of the one-out-of-five companies that the Rule of Five warns you about. You'll want to get rid of it before it does serious damage to your portfolio.

Third, you should always have an open mind about replacing one of your stocks with another one of equal or better quality and a better potential for return. Replacement may be a good strategy if the price of one of your stocks has been bid up so high as to offer little or no return based on earnings growth.

Scenarios two and three involve, respectively, the *defensive* and *offensive* portfolio management strategies that I'm going to tell you about. Beyond these three situations, for all practical purposes there are no reasons to sell your stock.

You're investing for the long haul. And the beautiful part of this discipline is that over the years most of the stocks you buy will do just fine—even if you put them in a drawer and forget that you own them! You've selected companies that can and will continue to grow their earnings. If that earnings growth deserves nearly as much investor confidence as it did when you bought into the companies, your stocks' value will grow right along with the growth of those earnings forever—or for a lot of years, anyway.

But if you *don't* just throw your stocks in a drawer and forget about them, you can do even better.

DEFENSIVE STRATEGY

To *defend* is to protect from harm. In a ball game, it also means to prevent a loss. Each of these meanings is apropos and denotes a certain degree of urgency.

A defensive strategy is necessary to protect your portfolio from harm and to prevent loss. Your goal is for your portfolio to average at least a 15 percent return, and you can't afford to retain for too long any bad apples that risk your achievement of that result.

Pursuing a defensive strategy is not very time consuming. However, it's mandatory that you do spend the little time required to do this job—if you're intent on accumulating wealth.

Some people consider a glass half full, and some consider it half empty. It's the same way with the Rule of Five. To the pessimist it means, "For every five stocks you own, one will go bad." When I cite the very same statistic, my preference is to say, "For every five stocks you own, four will do just fine—one of them much better than you expect." I suppose I tend to be the optimist.

Defensive portfolio management strategy deals with the stocks about which the pessimists wring their hands. The objective of defensive strategy is to protect your portfolio from being damaged by companies that for no predictable reason fail to perform as you had expected—or that fall from grace after having performed well for a while.

Defensive strategy deals strictly with quality; it has nothing to do with value issues, which are price related. I'll talk about value issues when I discuss offensive strategy.

So long as your companies continue to grow their sales and earnings nearly every quarter at about the rate you have forecast, you have nothing to be concerned about. Unlike the trader who sweats out every moment-to-moment fluctuation of the price, you're concerned only with the long term and with continuing growth in the earnings of the company. Remember, when earnings grow and are multiplied by a reasonable PE, you'll see a continuing increase in the stock's value.

What to Look For

So what do you look for when you pursue a defensive strategy? Look at each company's sales, earnings, and pretax profit each quarter, comparing them with the figures from the same period of the previous year. Calculate the percentage change for each item and check to be sure that it is close to the growth rate you expected when you bought the stock.

Check each company's sales figure first. This should be the most stable figure, so if sales growth has slipped below your expectations, you know that something of major importance is the cause.

Next, examine pretax profit to see if it's growing at the rate that you expected earnings to grow. This is the most important item after sales: Declines in profit growth will ultimately affect earnings, but companies can sometimes stave off the impact on earnings for a quarter or two by making adjustments in their provision for income taxes and in the number of shares outstanding. If you're lucky, when you check pretax profit you can spot a problem before it reaches the bottom line.

If you catch a problem in pretax profit before it reaches the earnings line, you may be able to respond before other investors see and react to the coming unfavorable earnings report; you may be able to get out without the loss that you might have taken if you were to wait until the earnings took the hit and the rest of the pack responded.

After checking for a decline in sales and pretax profit, do the same for earnings growth.

What to Do If You Detect a Decline

What should you do if you find a disappointment in any of these statistics? Should you call your broker and put in a sell order right away?

Not at all. You didn't subject the company to all those tests for nothing! And you don't want to sell it without a very good reason. After all, the company's management has proven itself able to solve problems in the past. This may be only a single event. One bad quarter does not a loser make.

Remember that companies whose growth has been extraordinary and that are still early in their life cycle will experience a slowing growth rate. This shouldn't be alarming. Compare the growth with your expectations, not with the stock's historical rate of growth. This is precisely why you selected a *sustainable* growth rate for your expected future growth when you decided to buy the stock.

If a company has been growing its sales, pretax profit, or earnings at more than 20 percent, even for an extended period of time, you shouldn't worry if its growth slows to a more reasonable rate. It's only when the growth rate continues to fall below your expectations that you need have any concern. On the other hand, as with any other falling object, if growth is falling fast, you should take its momentum into account when you decide on a course of action. You might benefit from reevaluating the stock and making a more modest growth rate prediction. Certainly it would behoove you to look closely at the reasons for the declines in sales, pretax profit, or earnings.

If the decline in growth is not huge but is still enough to claim your attention, you should give the stock another quarter. You shouldn't be alarmed unless two consecutive quarters are disappointing.

Anything can happen at any time, and management may need a quarter or two to deal with an unexpected turn of events. It's too much to expect a company to enjoy total serenity and perpetual good times. Important to you is the way management handles adversities when they do arise. You've taken pains to "hire" competent management. Unless the problem is serious and long term in nature, likely to be beyond management's ability to fix it, it's best to let management have a shot at making the repairs before you do anything rash.

A decline in growth to a level below your expectations is certainly a red flag, however. If the problem repeats itself two quarters in a row, or if the decline is substantial—for example, the company *lost* 5 percent instead of growing at 15 percent—it's time to do something about it.

What action should you take? Should you sell the stock? Not necessarily. The first thing you should do is to investigate. Find out what the company says about the reasons for the decline. In its quarterly report the company has likely offered some explanation for the change. Read it and consider how plausible the explanation sounds. Submit it to the test of your own common sense.

If you don't understand the company's explanation—if it sounds like so much gobbledygook to you—don't be afraid to challenge it. Call the company's investor-relations person and require a clear explanation. It doesn't matter how few shares you hold. You are one of the owners, and you have a right to an explanation—in a fashion that's understandable to you.

I've found that most investor-relations people are patient and eager to please shareholders. The enlightened ones recognize that while individual and club investors don't buy as many shares as institutional investors do, they are collectively the most valuable stockholders. Individual and club investors are neither as fickle nor as disloyal as the institutional investors who play the pro game on Wall Street.

A company that has a strong base of individual investors who are in it for the long term benefits in a great many ways. The best investor-relations professionals treasure such stockholders because the stability they bring makes the company's shares more sought after and its new issues easier to sell.

Sources of Information

Where should you obtain the periodic information that you need for your defensive strategy? You can request that your companies send you their quarterly reports. (Most companies used to send them to their shareholders automatically, but many have decided to avoid the expense.) In the quarterly report you will find information not only for the current quarter but also for the same period of the year before. And you are likely to see the percent changes already calculated for you.

There are a number of locations on the Internet where earnings are reported just as soon as companies announce them. These sites can also give you a schedule of when to expect those earnings reports.

You should draw up a schedule so that you will know when to look for the necessary reports. Such a schedule will set you free because the rest of the time you'll know that you have no pressing portfolio management chores. Defensive strategy is crucial to protect your portfolio from harm, but it's not onerous to implement because you need only worry about each company four times a year.

Approximately 60 percent of publicly traded companies match their fiscal years with the calendar year. This means that their books are closed at the end of March, June, September, and December, with the fiscal year ending on December 31. Other companies close their fiscal years at other times for various reasons. Many retailers, for example, close their books at the end of January rather than the end of December. This is so they can focus all of their resources on the intense activity that accompanies the holiday season and can include the most recent holiday business in the year-end results.

A company can't complete its financial statements without completing a number of accounting chores after the period ends, so there is a certain amount of lead time required. You can't expect on April 1 to read a company's earnings report for the quarter ending March 31—even on the Internet.

The Securities and Exchange Commission (SEC) requires all publicly traded companies with more than 500 shareholders and $10 million in assets (you're not likely to be interested in any smaller companies) to report their quarterly results (called 10-Qs) within 45 days following the end of each quarter, and their audited annual results (called 10-Ks) within 90 days following the end of the fiscal year. And many companies take all of the time allowed.

The most reliable source for the final figures for each period is the SEC, which reports the figures on its EDGAR Web site at <www.sec.gov/>. You might also try one of the kindred sites like Free Edgar, <www.freeedgar.com/>, or Edgarscan, <edgarscan.tc.pw.com/>. You can often get more timely figures from other Internet sources that report them as soon as companies release their earnings reports publicly. These sources include <www.yahoo.com>, <www.prnewswire.com>, <www.moneycentral.msn.com>, and <www.infobeat.com>. Some of these sites—Infobeat, for example—will automatically e-mail news about all of the companies in your portfolio to you at no charge.

The final defensive consideration is to recognize that the money you take out of a poor stock is not going to do you any good if it's not invested in a company of better quality than the one that you just got rid of. So if you're going to take your money out, go back to your stock studies to find another place to put it. That's important! Money not invested is likely to be *losing* ground. You can't win if you don't play!

OFFENSIVE STRATEGY

Now that you know how to keep from losing the game on defense, let's take a few minutes to talk about winning it on offense.

Offensive strategy doesn't share the urgency of defense. Here, you're concerned not so much with preventing loss or protecting your portfolio from harm as you are with enhancing the value of your holdings. You can implement your offensive strategy whenever the spirit moves you.

Offensive strategy involves analyzing the companies whose stock you hold to determine whether their potential is as good as it should be. Obviously you bought your stocks with the idea in mind that their prices would go up over time.

And, sure enough, they did! Isn't that the idea? For your stocks to grow and continue growing in value? Of course it is!

In discussing defensive strategies, I made the point that nothing ever goes textbook perfect and that prices can fall, and even stay down for a long time, for a variety of reasons other than the fundamentals. The same lesson applies on the upside. Stock prices can go up for reasons other than the fundamentals. Investor confidence can be buoyed up by a variety of factors that affect the stock, the industry, the market sector, or the market as a whole.

More often than on the downside, the "hot" issues that warm investors' hearts are not related to the fundamentals at all. It's rare, of course, to see spectacularly pleasant surprises rather than unpleasant ones surfacing in earnings reports, but it's not at all unusual to see prices driven sky-high by stories and rumors. And then there are times when stock prices are inflated well beyond the bounds of common sense. Stimulated by a mix of economic euphoria, a surplus of money in the hands of those who don't know what to do with it, and a belief that the law against free lunches has been repealed, along will come times like the dot-com bubble of the 1990s.

Under such circumstances, it's entirely possible for the price of one of your stocks to rise too much. If the price is so high that you would be hard put to justify adding the stock to your portfolio if you didn't already own it, you might now find it difficult to justify keeping it.

All of the price-dependent value measurements you made when you first considered buying a stock are still valid for judging the stock's current potential to increase in value. The lower the price, the greater the potential gain. This means that a stock that has performed better than you had hoped may suffer because its *potential* is not as good as it would be if the price were lower.

Confused? Let's back up a bit, then. First of all, once you buy a stock, the next likely question is when you should sell it. Portfolio management certainly deals with that question.

Defensive strategy, you learned, is both urgent and necessary. You *must* sell your potential losers—companies whose quality standards have slipped—or they can wreak havoc with your portfolio. Defensive strategy is easy enough to implement. It takes little time and the process is pretty cut-and-dried.

But making money is quite different from not losing it. And you're now concerned with when to sell your stocks to make the most money.

The Role of Price

As a long-term investor, you should set no price goals. Yes, you've anticipated what the price of a stock might be in 5 years, but that number is a moving target! You should push your time horizon out 5 years from whatever point in time you look at your investments or prospective investments. No matter when you look at a stock or at your portfolio as a whole, you're concerned with 5 years *from that moment.* (You should actually be concerned with 10, 20, or more years out, but your 5-year benchmark does put your estimates beyond the point where price is affected by short-term volatility.)

Let's say that you own a great company and it's performing better than you hoped it would. Now the price has gone up to where you're tempted to take your profit and hit the road. Whoa! Stop! Time out!

What are you going to do with the money? Spend it? Or are you going to try to find another investment that will do as well for you as that one did? Chances are, you're going to look for another winner—or you should, unless you need or want the money for some immediate purpose.

But wait! What's wrong with the company that you're thinking about selling? Is it still a good company? Is it still churning out those earnings the same way you would want its replacement to? Is the company still top-notch? Does it meet all of the criteria that you would hope a new investment would—except for the current price? Then why sell it?

If you sell the stock, you're going to have to pay taxes on the gain plus the commissions on both that sale and the new purchase. These expenses erode the amount of money you can invest in the new stock. Put those things all together, and you'll have to find some other compelling reason for selling, because capturing the profit isn't a good reason.

Think about it. When you sell your winners, what do you have left? You've got a portfolio full of losers! And that's not too smart, is it?

So read my lips. Never, never, never, never sell a stock because of the price! Is that clear enough?

Replacing, Not Selling

"Okay," you might say, "if I'm supposed to sell only if I need or want the money or if the company goes bad, perhaps I'll never need to think about selling at all."

As I've said, price shouldn't be a consideration for selling. However, there's a whale of a distinction between *selling* and *replacing*—a critical difference that I hope to make clear now.

The most important rule of offensive portfolio management is simply this: Unless you have found an investment of equal or better quality than the one you now own—one with a greater potential for return and with less risk—you should stick with what you have.

You did your homework to find the stock. It's performed as well as or better than you expected. You've made money on it so far—at least on paper. You will have to pay taxes and commissions if you sell it. So when do you put your offensive strategy to work?

Your offensive portfolio management strategy is implemented only when a stock is *overvalued*. How do you know when a stock has become overvalued? A stock commences to become overvalued when (1) the risk grows to be greater than the reward; and/or (2) when the potential return over the next five years is less than you want it to be.

These criteria are familiar, aren't they? You encountered the risk-to-reward comparison when you looked at the value issues. A risk index of 25 percent tells you that the reward is three times the risk. It stands to reason, then, that at a risk index of 50 percent, risk and reward are equal. A risk index above 50 percent indicates that risk exceeds reward.

Return is the other criterion. If you're looking for a 15 percent return from a company and the potential return falls below 15 percent, the stock has then commenced to become overvalued. Its price has been rising, but the earnings on which the future price will be based have probably stood still; therefore, the potential future price based upon those earnings has not increased.

Overvaluation is a matter of degree. A stock can be slightly overvalued or greatly overvalued. Your eagerness to replace the stock should grow the more overvalued it becomes. But how can you say that at a certain price the stock will become *too* overvalued? That can change tomorrow if new earnings are announced. At that price, does the stock become sufficiently overvalued to warrant its replacement, especially when taxes and commissions are involved? It's pretty difficult to put in a sell order based on anything so slippery.

Implementing the Strategy

How, then, do you actually implement an offensive strategy? This chore will take a little bit longer than your defensive strategy will, so I suggest that you set aside some extra time to complete it thoughtfully. You'll be convinced that it's worth the time you spend on it if you figure out how much per hour you stand to gain—paying yourself the dollar value of the improvements you can make in your portfolio's performance, compounded over the long term.

If you're computerized, you can accomplish these tasks in a heartbeat, but if you're not, it's still well worth the time.

Redo your stock studies optimistically.   Check all of your stock studies to make sure that the data are up-to-date. Redo each study with new data and using the latest price. And this time, you're going to do your studies optimistically.

Throughout your stock studies I've cautioned you to be conservative. Our byword has been, "When you come to a fork in the road, turn right!" I've told you that every time you have an estimate to make, a judgment to apply, you should err on the side of underestimating rather than overestimating. It's certainly better to be safe than sorry, and you will always be happy if things turn out better than you expected.

The purpose of underestimating future performance is to avoid the temptation to buy stocks that are less than the best, or to pay more than you should for the ones that you do buy. You shouldn't have to rely on perfect performance to realize your objectives.

The conservative approach to portfolio management is just the opposite. It entails being *optimistic* rather than *pessimistic*. Why? Because you should not be in too much of a hurry to sell. The more optimistic you are, the less likely you are to sell before you should.

There are two opportunities to act on your optimism when you're redoing your stock studies. The first opportunity arises when you're estimating future sales and earnings growth. When you are looking to see if one of your stocks is overvalued, redo your study estimating what future earnings will be if growth continues at the existing historical rate—rather than reducing the rate as you did before. Do this within reason, of course, but place the cap at 25 or 30 percent rather than at 20 percent. You don't actually expect earnings to continue to grow that fast for the next couple of decades; rather, you are making allowances for the best possible world rather than the worst.

The other opportunity to act optimistically is when you estimate the future PEs. After eliminating any irrelevant outliers, average *all* of the high PEs, and use that average, along with your optimistic earnings estimate, to calculate your high price. (You will recall that earlier you averaged only the lowest high PEs from the years in question.)

You may do the same with your low-price components. Your estimate of future low earnings should stay as it was, probably based upon the most recent four quarters; however, your low PE can reflect all of the historical low PEs rather than only the lowest of the low PEs from past years.

Complete the study on each of your holdings and record each company's risk index and total return.

Select the stocks that are overvalued. Sort your studies in order, starting with the one that has the highest risk index. You may put aside—and plan to keep—the companies with a risk index below 50 percent, after ensuring that the total return is within reason for that size company. The total return doesn't have to be 15 percent when you are implementing your offensive strategy. The price may be growing just a little ahead of the company's earnings, or the company's lower risk may warrant a little less of a return. Remember, your goal is a *portfolio average* of 15 percent or better.

Replace the overvalued stocks if you can. Start with the company that has the highest risk index. You may find that even though you've used an optimistic forecast, the risk index is still 100 percent or higher—all risk and no reward. This happens when your current price is as high as your projected high price or higher. If the risk index is over 100 percent, plan on seeking a replacement for that company.

Any time that a stock has appreciated to the point at which you have the reverse of your desirable condition so that you are risking three times as much as you stand to gain (the stock has a 75 percent risk index), you should consider replacing it. Seek a stock of equal or better quality that has the potential for return that you sought in the first place.

So that you will be ready when you need replacements, your best bet is to maintain a watch list of high-quality stocks, any of which you would own if the price were right. If you need a new stock, you can simply put in your order for one on your watch list that is in an appropriate price range.

If you can't find an appropriate replacement, hang on to what you have and keep looking. You could do much worse. Keep an eye on the risk and return. If the return reaches the point where it's less than what you could get from the money market with virtually no risk (now about 5 percent), then sell your stock and leave the money in your money market account until a persistent search turns up another stock that fits your need.

When you leave the money in the money market account, you have "replaced" the stock with an investment of high quality (but no risk) and a better potential for return. You have not "sold" it. In no case, though, do you want to stay in that situation longer than you have to. The sooner you put your money to work again, the better.

Deciding on a Good Replacement

Make use of the comparison worksheet that we discussed in Chapter 11, adding four more rows to the bottom of the page. Label the rows: Cost of Trade, Number of Shares, Value, and Projected Value.

Put all of the information from your completed stock studies in the columns as you would for a normal comparison. It's a perfect way to lay the challenged company next to the challenger and check the quality issues. Remember, it's important that your replacement be of at least as good quality as the company you're replacing.

Next, fill in the information required on the added lines, completing the information for the challenged company first.

	Challenged	*Challenger*
Cost of Trade:	None	Commissions on sale and purchase, plus tax on sale (capital gains or normal income tax if appropriate, none if in tax-deferred portfolio)
Number of Shares:	Shares owned	Value of challenged company ÷ Current price of challenger
Value:	Shares × Price	Value of owned shares of challenged company less cost of trade
Projected Value:	PV = Value	Same
	i% = Total return	Same
	N = 5	Same
	Solve for FV	Same

FIGURE 12.1 Challenging an Overvalued Stock

Comparison Worksheet

		Challenged		Challenger									
		Company 1		Company 2		Company 3		Company 4		Company 5			
	Company	Cisco		Tetra Tech									
	Ticker	CSCO		WATR									
Quality													
	Historical sales growth	37.3%		40.5%									
	Historical earnings growth	35.0%	x	27.7%									
	Future sales growth	25.0%	x	20.0%									
	Future earnings growth	25.0%	x	20.0%									
	Sales predictability	10	x	10	x								
	Earnings predictability	6		9	x								
	Average pretax profit margin	30.5	x	12.4									
	Profit margin stability	7		9	x								
	Profit margin trend	-		=	x								
Value													
	Current PE	178.8		27.9	x								
	Historical value ratio (HVR)	536.9		109.4	x								
	Total return	-8.1%		22.4%	x								
	Average return	-15.0%		16.4%	x								
	Risk index	148.5%		19.5%	x								
Miscellaneous													
	Current price	64.38		22.88									
	Number of shares $1,000 will buy	15.5		43/7									
	Industry	Cptr. Hdwr		Waste Mgt									
	Where traded	NASDAQ		NASDAQ									
Challenge													
	Cost of trade	N/A		612									
	Number of shares to sell/buy	100		255									
	Value	6,438		5,826									
	Projected Value	4,220		16,007									

Note that earnings growth is at maximum of 25% for challenged stock; but challenger is held to maximum of 20% .

Additional Challenge Data

CSCO	WATR
No. of shares to replace	Comm to sell $12
	Comm to buy 12
No. of shares x Current price	Tax on gain _588_
	Total: $612
Current Value projected for 5 years at Total Return rate (-8.1%) for a decline.	CSCO's value divided by the share price for WATR
	CSCO's value less costs.
	Current Value projected for 5 years at Total Return rate (22.4%) for an increase.

Projected Value
PV = Value   N = 5
i% = Total Ret.   Solve for **FV**

Notes: *CSCO, with forecast earnings growth at 25%, using a high P/E of 46.1 to forecast a high price of 45.1 shows a potential decline over the next five years. WATR, while not in the same industry, would be a suitable replacement. WATR has been issuing more stock which causes earnings to grow slower than sales. I'll make nearly $12,000 more with WATR over five years!*

Compare the projected values of the two companies to see whether there's enough difference after paying the cost to warrant making the replacement.

If the quality issues favor the challenger and the difference in return is sufficient, consider making the swap.

Tax Implications of Replacing Stocks

The tax implications of replacing stocks are not as straightforward as they might seem. If, for example, you have all of your stocks in a tax-deferred portfolio—an IRA, 401(k), or the like—there would seem to be no tax consequences to consider. You won't pay taxes on your gains until you take out the money; and those taxes will be at the standard income tax rate at the time you do.

If you're not in a tax-deferred situation and have owned your stock long enough for proceeds from a sale to be considered as capital gains, you will pay a tax on the money you make on the sale. In some cases the capital gains tax amounts to only about half as much as you would pay in standard income tax—or even less.

When pondering a decision to replace your stock, you may want to take into account the effects of taxes. Of course, if you're really a long-term thinker, you're going to realize that the only way that you can avoid paying taxes on investment gain is either to die or to lose the gain. Neither of these alternatives is palatable. So you might as well face it: you're going to pay taxes on the gain at some point, no matter what. The only difference is that in a tax-deferred portfolio, you can sell a stock and then reinvest all the money you took in from the sale. The entire amount of those proceeds will grow, but you'll pay higher taxes later at regular rather than capital gains rates.

If you have a non-tax-deferred portfolio, you will have to pay the taxes in the near term. This means that although the cash flow situation in your account may allow you to reinvest the full proceeds from the sale right away, soon you're going to have to use some of those proceeds—or money from somewhere else—for

---

FIGURE 12.2   Summary of Offensive Strategy

Risk index	Return	Tax-Deferred	Non-Tax-Deferred
Less than 50%	15% or more	Keep	Keep
50% to 67%	15% or more	Replace	Keep
Greater than 67%	Less than 15%	Replace if possible	Replace if possible
Greater than 67%	Less than 5%	Money market	Money market

---

taxes. And whatever the amount of those taxes, the money used to pay them won't be earning money for you.

However, if your sale meets the requirements for capital gains, then you're still ahead if you replace a stock now because (a) you're paying less tax now than you would later at the regular income tax rate, and (b) the benefit you gain by owning a stock with a greater potential for return will hopefully make up for some of the loss.

Figure 12.2 sums up your offensive strategy as I suggest you implement it.

LET'S TAKE STOCK OF

WHAT YOU KNOW ABOUT PORTFOLIO MANAGEMENT STRATEGIES

Two strategies will help you make the most of your investments: a defensive strategy and an offensive strategy.

Defensive strategy implies preventing damage and deals with the quality issues that you have learned. You detect and replace companies whose growth in the fundamentals—sales, pretax profit, and earnings—fall significantly below the expectations you had when you bought the stock. This way you can avoid serious damage to your portfolio's performance.

Offensive strategy deals with the value issues and is less urgent. This strategy involves finding the stocks whose prices have appreciated so much that their potential return and risk are no longer desirable. You'll challenge the overvalued stocks to find others of equal or higher quality that have a better potential for return. If you fail to find acceptable replacements, you will keep the overvalued stocks until suitable replacements can be found.

You should *never* sell your stock in a good company just because it reaches some arbitrary target price or just to capture profits. Remember: selling your winners will leave you with only losers.

CHAPTER 13

Finer Points and "Fudge Factors"

So far I've given you strategies that are effective and easy to implement and that will keep you out of trouble. Now I'm about to share with you some things that may be confusing, sometimes counterproductive, and will possibly get you *into* trouble!

As you gain technamental investment experience, you'll find that there are times when one or another of the strict guidelines or rules of thumb that I've given you can be relaxed in favor of a wise alternative. And that's truly the best way for you to discover those things—to grow into them.

These "Finer Points and 'Fudge Factors'" will not do a thing to improve your portfolio's performance. Some of them will only make it easier for you to justify buying companies that you might otherwise not consider. And there's a risk that, by using these additional points as a rationale for making such decisions, you might make some bad ones.

Don't be too hasty to add any of these less conservative practices to your repertoire. Above all, don't think that you need to know about them or that your investment prowess will suffer if you don't digest and embrace them. These finer points are the stuff of my experience. I would feel that I had shortchanged you if I didn't at least put them out there for you to reject or accept as your common sense, experience, or confidence guides you to.

GATHERING DATA FOR NONSTANDARD INDUSTRIES

Some industries are special and report their revenues or sales differently than do other businesses. A prime example of this is the banking and financial services industry. Especially in this day and age, banks are more than just institutions that borrow your money and lend it. The main product of a bank is money. Because a bank borrows the money it lends, usually from the Federal Reserve, it must pay interest on that money. So, for a bank the conventional way to report revenues is to deduct the interest paid for the money from the interest received from the borrower for that money and report that income as *net interest income.*

Banks are also involved in other profitable enterprises, such as mortgage and credit card servicing and investment brokerage. So banks have other profit centers that contribute to their bottom lines and revenues that must be counted as *noninterest income.*

Another departure from the typical business is the way that banks provide for bad debt. Because banks are highly regulated, they must take special precautions to fulfill their fiduciary responsibility to those whose money they work with. A portion of revenue is set aside as a *loan loss provision* and must be deducted from revenues reported because it is not available to the bank for any other purpose than to cover bad debt.

Because of all these differences the most informative way to report bank revenues is to combine net interest income and noninterest income and subtract the loan loss provision from the result.

Most of the data sources provide these items, but not all do. The closer you come to including these three items, the more accurate your revenue analysis will be.

There is another item that is not always available but should be included so that your analysis will be accurate. That is the *tax equivalent adjustment*, an accounting adjustment that factors in the portion of a bank's income that comes from tax-exempt securities and then reports that income as its taxable equivalent. The tax equivalent adjustment is smaller and less important to your analysis than the other elements of revenue, but it is still good to know its value, which should be added to the calculation of revenues if it's available.

Sometimes you will find that usable information is reported annually but not on a quarterly basis. The *Value Line Survey* reports only "Loans" instead of the "Net Interest Income" on a quarterly basis. In this case, because quarterly revenues are not used for any calculations, you can use the loan information as just a measure of activity.

ASSESSING QUALITY

Evaluating Growth

Forgiving spikes. Some perfectly good companies have slipped now and then, have had a spike in their corporate lives, or have otherwise faltered and then learned from their mistakes. Companies like these can be perfectly good investments. Compromising on the straightness of the charted lines just a little can open wide new vistas to you, exploding the number of companies you might consider as candidates.

If you find that a company has had a single event that caused a spike in an otherwise acceptable growth picture, you can probably get away with eliminating it as an outlier and pretending it didn't happen. You might even forgive two or even three such events, but only if they happened quite early in the company's history. They say that time heals many wounds, and a company that's been able to get back on track and demonstrate that it's there to stay can be treated with respect. On the other hand, if a company's strength or stability has been marginal during the period since those events occurred, you will probably want to avoid investing in it.

In a nutshell, a long-ago hiccup that is followed by an exceptionally good run of stable and predictable growth can usually be safely overlooked.

Preview of coming detractions. Comparing the slope of the sales and earnings lines can tell you some interesting things about the direction a company is headed.

Look carefully at the direction of the sales and earnings lines. Are they behaving in concert? Or are they diverging or converging? If the sales and earnings lines run pretty much parallel, you'll know that management is probably controlling its costs efficiently and capably. Barring the repurchase or issuance of shares or the unlikely benefits of a tax break, the profit margins remain fairly stable. Expenses, and therefore profits, are increasing right along with revenues.

But what if earnings are growing either more quickly or more slowly than sales? What can you learn from this? First of all, I believe that plotting pretax profit and the number of shares on your growth chart is well worth the extra time and trouble. Then the questions that are raised when the growth of earnings and sales is dissimilar can be answered at a glance. You will want to notice whether the pretax profit line parallels the sales line or the earnings line. See Figures 13.1 through 13.4.

If sales are growing at a faster rate than earnings and pretax profit is growing at a rate closer to earnings than to sales, the profit margin is likely decreasing—a bad sign (or there's been an increase in the tax rate).

If sales are growing at a faster rate than earnings and pretax profit is growing at a rate closer to sales than to earnings, then the number of shares has been increasing (or there's been an increase in the tax rate).

If earnings are growing at a faster rate than sales and pretax profit is growing at a rate closer to sales than earnings, then the number of shares has likely been decreasing as the company repurchases them (or there's been a decrease in the tax rate).

If earnings are growing at a faster rate than sales and pretax profit is growing at a rate closer to earnings than to sales, the profit margin is likely increasing—usually a good sign (or there's been a decrease in the tax rate—still a good sign but not likely, at least for the long term).

FIGURES 13.1 through 13.4   Dissimilar Growth Rates for Sales, PTP, and EPS

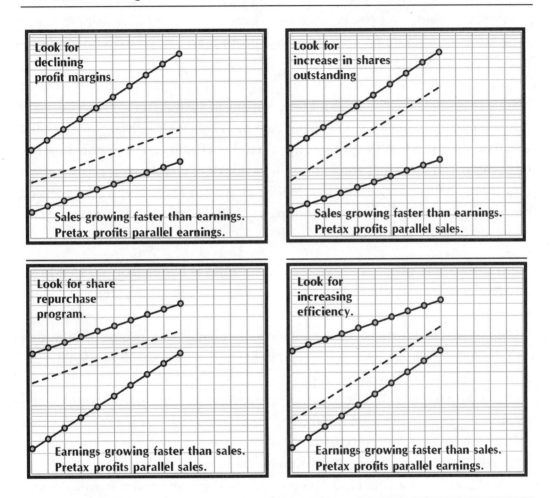

Changes in the tax rate are the least likely reasons for these dissimilarities in growth rate—especially when the dissimilarities persist for more than a single year. Uncle Sam and his cohorts in the statehouses are not prone to bestowing gifts on industry. But factors such as carryover losses, in which the full tax benefit of a loss could not be claimed in the year of the loss, can distort the otherwise normal role of taxes in the progression from the top to the bottom line.

Evaluating Efficiency

Profit margins. As you become more experienced, you may want to look a little more deeply into companies whose profit margins have declined—especially if you already own them.

There are some scenarios, such as an acquisition, that can produce a reduced margin temporarily but be good for the company in the long run. When you study the facts that surround an acquisition, you may find to your satisfaction that what you thought was a trend really was not a trend at all and can be overlooked. But until you're confident that you know what to look for, you shouldn't spend much time trying to make such exceptions to the rule work for you. If you see a reduced profit margin, you're far better off putting your study for that company aside and going on to another company.

Trend. Some people believe that an uptrend is better than no trend. An uptrend certainly would indicate that management is taking steps to reduce expenses.

However, you might ask yourself if the uptrend might not also be an indication that the company's efficiency left something to be desired—that it needed the improvement which is now under way.

Or if the company has already been operating efficiently—its margins are better than average—might not an uptrend result from cost-cutting measures that could prove to be counterproductive?

Understanding the causes of an uptrend, like most of the things your curiosity will lead you to, is a matter of common sense and does not require an MBA. Reading the company's news reports, press releases, and annual reports is a good way to find out about such things as what steps are being taken to cut costs when margins are increasing—or decreasing.

Return on equity. The second item on management's report card is return on equity—the return management is able to produce with the equity of the company—the investors' ownership. This is a widely used measure; but I believe that its value to analysts and investors is overrated as it's usually calculated.

Remember that the company's assets—everything it owns (its cash, machines, buildings, computers and other office equipment, airplanes, and so on)—have as their purpose the production of income or the curbing of costs. You would like to assess how effectively the management of your company puts those assets to use. You must also take into account the obligations that the company has against those assets and reduce the value of the company accordingly.

Return on equity (ROE) is calculated by dividing the company's net profit by its equity. Comparing the profit with the unencumbered assets offers another view of management's effectiveness.

Often ROE is calculated using the company's EPS and its book value. In most cases, either method is fine unless changes have occurred in the number of shares outstanding during the year.

What does ROE tell us? At its simplest, the ROE is supposed to answer the question, "Given the amount of money this company is worth after paying off its debt, how much profit does management bring in for every dollar of that value?" It's an important measure of management's effectiveness and efficiency. And it's an interesting number because it doesn't matter whether management is using a lot of OPM (other people's money)—or none at all—to bring in the return. ROE just addresses how efficiently management is making use of *your* share of the company. Debt, or leverage, is simply another tool that management has at its disposal to increase growth and shareholder value.

There is a caveat, however. I believe that return on equity is of practically no value to you unless it's calculated using the equity from the beginning of the period in which the earnings are produced rather than from the end. Unfortunately, however, most of the time you'll find that ROE has been calculated using the equity at the end of the period instead of the beginning—or an average of both. Let me explain.

Return on something usually means the profit you make on whatever that "something" is. If you have $10 and make $1 with it, you figure your return on that $10. Logically, you divide the dollar by the ten-spot and arrive at a 10 percent return. Simple enough.

Return on equity is typically calculated, though, using the book value at the *end* of the period for which the earnings were reported instead of the book value the company started the period with. All of the earnings not distributed in dividends are therefore retained as a part of that equity or book value. This means that those earnings are a part of both the top and bottom of the ROE equation. Excluding any consideration of dividend disbursements, calculating ROE this way is the equivalent of dividing that dollar you made by 11 bucks instead of 10—the 11 including the dollar you just made! It's recursive, and therefore, in my opinion, it isn't nearly as meaningful as it could be. Trends tend to be mathematically distorted and of little value.

The problem is compounded if dividends are involved. Company A and Company B both report $1 in earnings for the year, and both start with a book value of $5. Company A retains the entire dollar to equity. Company B, however, pays 20 percent out in dividends, retaining only the remaining 80 cents. Did one company perform better than the other?

Calculated using ending equity, the ROE for Company A would be 1 ÷ 6, or 16.7 percent. Company B's ROE would be 17.2 percent, which would seem to indicate that the management of the company paying dividends was able to get a better return on its resources than its competitor!

Had we calculated the return on beginning equity, both companies would have earned the dollar on $5 for an ROE of 20 percent.

I would likely find the company that did not pay dividends to be more interesting and at least as desirable as the one that did. Certainly the notion that a higher ROE is better (as typically calculated) is not valid in this case.

Many accounting and business schools teach their students to use the *average* of the equity from the beginning and the end. This might be a little better, but in my opinion it still doesn't serve a very useful purpose for you.

If you calculated ROE using the previous year's equity, as shown in Figure 13.5, then the relationship between the earnings and the equity that contributed to producing them is quite clear—a straightforward indication of the growth in the company's value and your share of it.

FIGURE 13.5 Return on Equity (ROE) Using Previous Year's Equity.

Earnings	($)	.27	.36	.46	.56	.61	.69	.82	.94	1.11	1.32
Shares	(M)	110.4	112.4	113.5	115.3	114.4	115.2	115.8	111.2	112.0	112.6
Book Value		1.16	1.54	2.05	2.61	3.12	3.86	4.61	4.97	5.96	.89
Pre-tax Margin (%)		27.0 %	27.9 %	27.8 %	28.1 %	28.7 %	27.6 %	28.0 %	29.2 %	31.3 %	30.3 %
Return on Equity(%)	Using Trailing Book Value	31.0 %	29.9 %	27.3 %	23.4 %	22.1 %	21.2 %	20.4 %	22.3 %	22.1 %

1999 5/99	Quarterly Sales
Date last quarter ended 8/99	Qtr.2 Qtr.3 Qtr.4 Qtr.1 TTM

Return on Equity Avg 24.4 %

50%
40%
30%
20%
10%
0%

04 Note: Calculate ROE by dividing EPS by the Book Value from the previous year.

In general, profit margins are the most important item on the management report card. ROE (when calculated as I recommend) will generally not trend down unless profit margins, sales, or earnings growth does—in which case you're going to be looking for another company anyway.

ASSESSING VALUE

Estimating Future Growth

I've given you some suggestions for conservatively forecasting growth; however, there are as many different thoughts about how conservative such estimates should be as there are people who estimate. Still, no matter how experienced I get, I'm perfectly content to stick with the rules of thumb I've given you already.

What about the analysts' estimates that you can find in the *Value Line Survey*, on the Internet, in financial newsletters, or in the newspaper? Can they give you some idea of what the future holds?

Professional analysts are playing a serious game among themselves. Their reputations—and their incomes—are based on their accuracy. The more often they precisely predict earnings growth, the higher *their* stock rises within their peer group and the professional financial community. They're judged about as critically for underestimating as they are for overestimating. So either way, if they're off the mark, they can suffer.

Believe it or not, your goal is not to be accurate. Your goal is to be right. You're rewarded when your prediction is accurate, but your rewards are even greater when you prove to have underestimated. Because you have *your* money riding on your prediction, you will need to be right at least 80 percent of the time, and the best way to ensure that you'll be right is to be conservative—not unreasonably conservative, but conservative nonetheless.

As a rule, I estimate growth based upon relevant history, tempered by a reasonable decrease to elevate my confidence that I will be right. If after I have made my best estimate I find that the analysts' mean estimates are the same as mine or lower, I knock off a percentage point or two just to make sure that I'm being cautious enough to have a better chance of being right.

Companies aren't allowed to publish their own forecasts, so analysts are the ones who create earnings expectations. The surprises come when the analysts are wrong.

David Dreman, author of *Contrarian Investment Strategies: The Next Generation* (Simon and Schuster, 1998), offers some statistics taken from a study of all companies followed by a minimum of four analysts—about 1,000 companies—over a 23-year period. Dreman suggests that analysts' estimates of earnings four quarters out were off by at least 5 percent 124 out of 125 times. And when the analysts were estimating five years out, the odds against their being right were 30 billion to one!

Obviously some professionals are right more often than others. My point is that you have as good a chance of being right as the professionals do. The more you nestle your estimate down into your comfort zone, the more likely you are to be inaccurate on the low side—which is a fine place to be.

Estimating Future PEs

Without doubt, the most frustrating aspect of your stock studies will be trying to keep your PE forecasts within reason. This will likely be the constraint that condemns more stock candidates than any other.

I've given you a method for forecasting future PEs conservatively enough so that you will be right most of the time. By "averaging the lowest half or majority" of low values for your high and low PEs and sticking with a cap of 30 (see Chapter 10), you should rarely if ever overestimate what the future holds. But you're probably going to feel all too often that you may have underestimated.

Many investors simply use the average of the historical high and low PEs for the future value. I think that's a good idea only if you make a conscious decision to use that average after thinking carefully about it and believing that the historical high and low PEs are reasonable. This method is not conservative enough for me—especially in these times.

The PEG ratio. Many people deliberately estimate below the average just to be on the safe side. And some people use the *PEG ratio.*

The PEG ratio is calculated by dividing the PE by the estimated growth rate. For example, a company that is selling at a PE of 15 times earnings and whose earnings are expected to grow at 15 percent will have a PEG ratio of 1 to 1.

What is the value of the PEG ratio? Probably its most common use is in screening. Some experienced investors will not even look at a company that's valued at a PEG ratio of more than 1.5 or, at the most, 2 to 1.

Some investors use the PEG ratio to test the historical PE to see if it's reasonable to use as an estimate of future PE. Others use a PEG ratio of perhaps 1.5 to 1 as a cutoff when determining whether to invest in a company. If the estimated future earnings growth is 15 percent, the highest acceptable PE would be 22.5 (1.5 times the projected growth).

Such an approach would support my recommendation that you never forecast a future high PE over 30—which is what you'd get if you stick with 20 percent as a maximum for your forecast of earnings growth.

For my money, I'll stick with the method for forecasting future PEs that I outlined in Chapter 10!

Uncertainty bands.   *Uncertainty bands* can help you assess just how erratic a company's growth can be and still be acceptable. In a word, if a company's zigging and zagging don't cut too wide a swath, you might be able to justify an expectation of sound growth.

Jay Berry, an NAIC member since 1960 and a conscientious contributor to the NAIC I-Club list (see Chapter 6)—and one of the "Web ops" who keeps that list running smoothly—came up with the idea of uncertainty bands. He suggests that you either visualize or actually draw lines on either side of your historical trendline that encompass all or most of the plotted points on either side of that line.

Then when you draw your projection out five years into the future, visualize or draw lines at the same distance from each side of that projection. Jay suggests that you assume the future value could be as far on either side of the projected value as those uncertainty bands imply (see Figure 13.6).

I recommend that you plot your forecast earnings where the lower band crosses the fifth year as in Figure 13.6. If you use that value as the FV (future value) to calculate the growth rate on your calculator and it's sufficient to give you your desired growth, then you can feel reasonably comfortable with your projection.

All in all, however, if the sales line is not reasonably smooth, I'd be inclined to look for another company anyway, because the kinds of things that can cause sales growth to be erratic are just the kinds of things that are likely to make the company an undesirable investment.

The business model.   There are two approaches you can use to estimate future earnings. The first, which I describe in Chapter 10 and I recommend that you start with, requires you to conservatively estimate future earnings growth and then calculate what earnings would be five years out if they were to grow at that rate. The second approach is the *business model.*

Used together, these approaches offer two perspectives, each helping to corroborate the result of the other. They give you a sort of financial depth perception that affords a more realistic view.

FIGURE 13.6   Uncertainty Bands

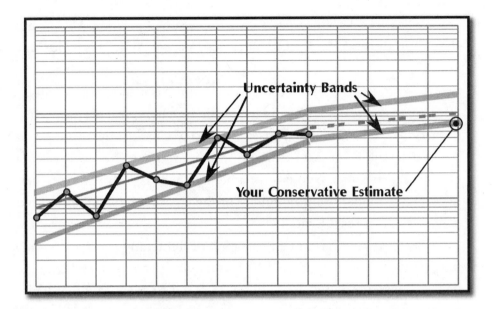

Users of the business model attempt to follow the company's income as it runs the gauntlet from the top to the bottom line—just as a company operates. That's why it's called the business model, which is synonymous with NAIC's *preferred procedure.*

I strongly recommend that you defer using the business model until you are comfortable with the basic method. Once you are comfortable with that, I just as strongly recommend that you go ahead and use the business model. It's an excellent way to understand how a business operates and to perceive the relationships among the elements that contribute to the company's earnings per share. (See Figure 13.7.)

Because a company's sales are usually more stable than its earnings, you can have a greater measure of confidence in your forecast of sales than of earnings. So we'll start with sales. We'll use ABC Company's figures for our example. The business model begins with default values for each of the elements of a company's income statement—values that you will use unless you have a compelling reason to change them.

1. **Forecast sales**—At our forecast growth rate of 13 percent, ABC Company should produce $1,395.5 million in sales in fiscal 2004. This is our starting point.

2. **Profit**—The next step is to estimate how much of those sales will be left after expenses are paid. Because the profit margin represents the percentage of sales that remain after expenses are paid, we look at the profit margin.

   The default value is the average profit margin we've already calculated. However, here's where your technamental analysis can prove very helpful. Look at the annual profit margins—or the chart on which they are plotted (Chapter 9, Figures 9.1 and 9.2).

   ABC Company has done a great job of tightening up its costs, causing the profit margins to trend up. When you look at a company whose margins have stabilized at a higher rate in the most recent years, you might want to raise your estimated future margin a little to reflect that improvement. ABC Company has achieved margins in excess of 30 percent for the last couple of years. So it would be reasonable to use last year's 30.3 percent as an estimate for the future and multiply the sales figure by that to arrive at a *pretax profit* of $422.8 million. Of course, if the margin has been declining, you probably will have already rejected the study for that reason.

3. **Taxes**—The next thing a business does is to pay taxes on its pretax profit. The default value for taxes is the amount of the taxes of the prior year. Unless you have reason to believe that Uncle Sam or his chums in the state capitals are going to make a serious change in the tax rates within the next five years, you can use the default value for taxes.

   Looking at the annual tax rates, we should stay with 35.1 percent from last year. So let's deduct 35.1 percent of the pretax profit, or $148.4 million, leaving a *net after taxes* of $274.4 million from which to deduct any further adjustments before allocating the remainder to the shares.

4. **Adjustments to income**—This is a catchall that allows you to include any items you can think of that might affect the bottom line after taxes. The

---

FIGURE 13.7   Applying the Business Model to Estimate Future Earnings

---

Tax Rate	(%)	31.7 %	32.6 %	32.3 %	32.2 %	34.8 %	36.6 %	37.1 %	37.1%	38.8 %	35.1%
Net Profit	($M)	29.9	39.5	51.8	64.0	69.8	79.2	94.1	106.5	124.7	149.1
Earnings	($)	.27	.36	.46	.56	.61	.69	.82	.94	1.11	1.32
Shares	(M)	110.4	112.4	113.5	115.3	114.4	115.2	115.8	111.2	112.0	112.6
Book Value		1.16	1.54	2.05	2.61	3.12	3.86	4.61	4.97	5.96	6.89
Pre-tax Margin	(%)	27.0 %	27.9 %	27.8 %	28.1 %	28.7 %	27.6 %	28.0 %	29.2 %	31.3 %	30.3%

Using trailing

Forecast Earnings	Business Model	5yr. Fcst.			5yr. Fcst.	Forecast Growth Model	Forecast Earnings
				Forecast Sales	1,395.5		per
	x Profit Margin	30.3 %	=	Pre-tax Profit	422.8	From growth at	**Share**
Complete this section only if Growth, above, is satisfactory	less Taxes @	35.1 %	=	Net after taxes	274.4	forecast EPS growth rate.	
	less Adjustments	--		= Net to shareholders	274.4		Lower of two
	+ Average Shares	112.6		= Business Model EPS	2.44	or 2.43 =	2.43

---

adjustment most frequently found would be preferred dividends. For companies that are paying preferred shareholders, their dividends are the most predictable such charge and would be the default value.

ABC Company has no preferred shareholders so the *net available to common shares* is still $274.4 million.

5. **Shares outstanding**—You should estimate the number of shares that will be outstanding five years in the future. The default value is the current number of shares.

Look at the last ten years for common shares outstanding, which you'll find in the data section of your computer program or on the worksheet. Has the company had a history of issuing shares on a regular basis and increasing its capitalization that way? Has your research revealed that the company has embarked on a share repurchase program, which tends to reduce the number of shares? You can look at Value Line's estimate (in the right column) or simply add more shares based on the company's history. (Don't reduce the number of shares because that would give you a less conservative earnings figure when you're finished.)

I saw no reason to change ABC Company's figure from the default value—the number of shares at the end of the last fiscal year—112.6.

6. **Earnings per share.** When you divide the net available to common shares by the forecast number of shares, you will come up with an estimate of future earnings per share (EPS) using the business model. ABC Company would be expected to produce $274.4 ÷ 112.6, or *$2.44, in earnings per share.*

As you can see, this estimate is almost the same as the one you calculated by simply extrapolating earnings growth. And this is the purpose of this exercise—to compare the result from the business model with the result arrived at using the basic method. I would generally prefer to use the lower of the two results—especially if there were a substantial difference between them.

Evaluating Risk

The process of estimating the high price is fairly cut-and-dried, but there are some options for estimating the low price you might want to think about.

Being extra cautious. Some investors wish to be extra conservative. They factor into their forecast low price all possibilities for losing money on the investment—a declining market, an industry slump, or the worst that they think could happen if the company is the inevitable one out of five that's a loser. These cautious investors arbitrarily reduce their estimate of the forecast low price to make sure that it falls below the current price. This way the risk index remain positive, reflecting their view that there is always some risk. That's okay to do if it gives you a greater sense of security.

Using the yield-supported low price. For a company that pays substantial dividends, you can use the alternative *yield-supported low price* to raise your estimate of the low price (see Figure 13.8).

Yield is the return on a stock that its dividend represents. It is calculated by dividing the annual dividend by the price of the stock. Obviously, the lower the stock's price, the higher the yield.

It's possible for the price of a stock to decline far enough that the investment becomes attractive to investors looking for income. If, for example, the stock of a large, well-established company falls to a price so low that the yield is very near the interest on a government bond, many investors would prefer to buy the stock than to buy a bond. Not only would they receive an income that would be competitive with that of the bond, but their investment would have the potential for some good appreciation when the stock's price resumed its growth. This low price could be construed to be a *resistance point* (to borrow a term from the technical analysts) because income investors would likely jump in and prevent the price from going lower.

This alternative method of arriving at a low price is useful only for companies whose dividend payout is substantial. The projected dividend payout is the product of the current yield and the forecast high PE. If it comes to 35 or more, it might be worth the trouble to calculate the yield-supported low price.

To do so, first look in your newspaper under "U.S. Securities" for the securities whose maturity date corresponds to your forecast date. Find the approximate yield for those securities.

Then calculate the yield-supported low price as follows:

Potential high price × Current yield ÷ (Competitive bond yield −1)

Here's an example:
Assume that the competitive bond yield is 6.4, the current yield is 1.4 percent, and the potential high price is 130.0

Yield-supported low price = 130 × 1.4 ÷ 5.4 = 33.70

If this value is higher than your forecast low price, you may substitute it for the forecast low instead.

Because you'll rarely be interested in large companies that pay high dividends, you won't have cause to use this option often, but it can give such companies a little help when you assess their rewards and risks.

These are but some samples of the lore and wisdom that you'll gather as you progress on your investment journey. Some of the ideas are good, and some of

FIGURE 13.8 Yield-Supported Low Price

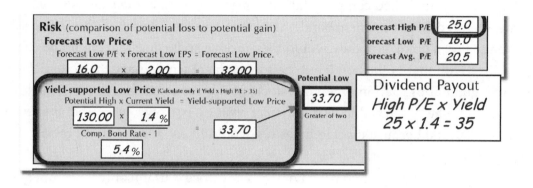

them aren't for you—just as it will be with other new things you'll hear along your way. Take them all with a grain of salt and test them with your common sense. That common sense is your most important asset on your road to becoming a successful investor. And as I said at the outset, the things that appear to be over your head are things you don't need to know!

Well, that's it from my point of view. You now know more than the average stockbroker about investing and about how businesses run. You should be able to deal with them with confidence. (If you doubt this, just ask them questions about what you've learned and see how they respond. You might be surprised.)

I hope that you've enjoyed reading this as much I've enjoyed writing it. Your pleasure will have only begun here and should extend to your future investment experience.

I've given you all I think you need to know to be a successful investor. The rest is simply a matter of getting in there and doing it—and not being intimidated by the things you don't need to know. Other things that you may find to be important to you will be important because your own curiosity draws you to them. And that can be fun too.

I wish you a happy and prosperous journey as you Take Stock and build your successful financial future.

APPENDIX A

Investing without a Computer

People who do not (yet) have access to a computer can be just as effective technamental investors as those who do. It just takes a little more time and effort. Investors have been working manually with great success since long before the computer came along, and well before the hand-held calculator showed up on the scene, for that matter. So if you don't yet own a computer, be of good cheer. You don't *need* one, although you may wind up *wanting* one before it's all over.

The manual chore consists of two tasks: preparing a worksheet and using it. The Technamental Stock Study Worksheet (TSSW), Figures A.1 and A.2, and NAIC's Stock Selection Guide (SSG), Figures A.3 and A.4, are the worksheets that you can choose from.

There are several differences between the TSSW and the SSG that may affect your preference:

- The TSSW provides space for all data items.
- The TSSW uses ten years of annual data for PE analysis. The SSG uses five.
- The TSSW uses four quarters and the trailing 12 months (TTM) for recent activity. The SSG uses a single quarter.

- The SSG provides space for debt, debt/capital, insider and institutional holdings, preferred stock, industry, and other information. The TSSW does not.

- The TSSW provides charts for the optional plotting of profit margins, return on equity, and PEs.

- The TSSW uses the term *business model*. This is the same as NAIC's *preferred procedure,* which NAIC suggests that you manually enter on the front of the SSG form.

- The TSSW is designed for use with a financial calculator for the computation of growth rates, return, and other such items. The SSG uses chart radials and nomographs for those calculations.

- The TSSW uses the risk index to compare risk with reward. The SSG uses the upside/downside ratio for that purpose.

- The TSSW provides for calculation of the buy price. The SSG does not.

You will find as you examine the examples of both forms that there are minor discrepancies between the two that result from the differences described above. I have used common values where I could in order to reduce the number of differences in the result, but the differences in the forms make it impossible to produce exactly the same results. The primary differences are in the average high and low PEs (I prefer to use ten years to analyze PE history; the SSG offers only five); the "yield-supported low price" versus the "price the dividend will support" on the SSG, which are calculated differently; and the total return. (The TSSW uses the actual period over which the appreciation is realized rather than a flat five years for the SSG. If you use the Investor's Toolkit software described in Appendix B to produce the SSG, the return is calculated in the same fashion as on the TSSW.) Again, this is not an exact science, so slight differences are not likely to seriously affect the result.

Many people have found the stock study process hard to learn, and volunteer educators have found it tough to teach when it shouldn't be. They traditionally cram the *whats* and *whys* in with the *hows,* and often with the more advanced judgment issues as well. The result is like trying to pour the contents of a wide-

FIGURE A.1 The Technamental Stock Study Worksheet (Front)

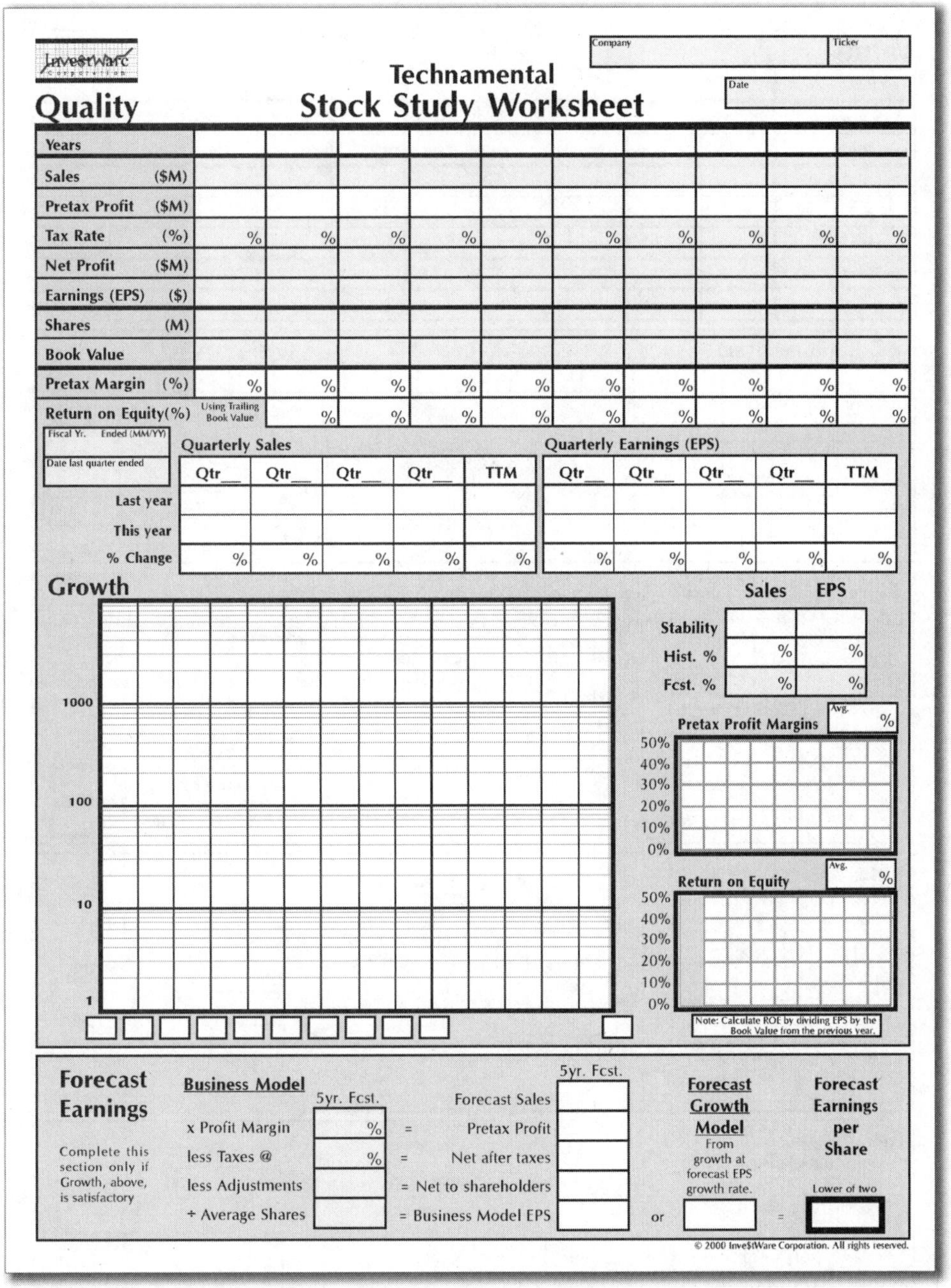
InvestWare Corporation

Company | Ticker | Date

Quality

Technamental Stock Study Worksheet

Years										
Sales ($M)										
Pretax Profit ($M)										
Tax Rate (%)	%	%	%	%	%	%	%	%	%	%
Net Profit ($M)										
Earnings (EPS) ($)										
Shares (M)										
Book Value										
Pretax Margin (%)	%	%	%	%	%	%	%	%	%	%
Return on Equity(%)	Using Trailing Book Value	%	%	%	%	%	%	%	%	%

Fiscal Yr. Ended (MM/YY)

Date last quarter ended

Quarterly Sales	Qtr__	Qtr__	Qtr__	Qtr__	TTM
Last year					
This year					
% Change	%	%	%	%	%

Quarterly Earnings (EPS)	Qtr__	Qtr__	Qtr__	Qtr__	TTM
Last year					
This year					
% Change	%	%	%	%	%

Growth

1000
100
10
1

	Sales	EPS
Stability		
Hist. %	%	%
Fcst. %	%	%

Pretax Profit Margins — Avg. %

50% 40% 30% 20% 10% 0%

Return on Equity — Avg. %

50% 40% 30% 20% 10% 0%

Note: Calculate ROE by dividing EPS by the Book Value from the previous year.

Forecast Earnings

Complete this section only if Growth, above, is satisfactory

Business Model

	5yr. Fcst.			5yr. Fcst.
			Forecast Sales	
x Profit Margin	%	=	Pretax Profit	
less Taxes @	%	=	Net after taxes	
less Adjustments			= Net to shareholders	
÷ Average Shares			= Business Model EPS	

or

Forecast Growth Model — From growth at forecast EPS growth rate. =

Forecast Earnings per Share — Lower of two

FIGURE A.2   The Technamental Stock Study Worksheet (Back)

Value

Company		Ticker

Earnings										
High Price										
Low Price										
High P/E										
Low P/E										
Average P/E										
Dividends										
Years										

P/E Ratio Analysis

50
45
40
35
30
25
20
15
10
5
0

Avg. High PE   Avg. Low PE   **Current Price** ÷ **TTM EPS** = **Current PE**

Average of the Historical Average PEs (less outliers) = **Signature PE**

Current PE ÷ Signature PE = **Historical Value Ratio (HVR)**   %

Forecast High, Low, and Average PEs

Average half or majority of the lowest High PEs = **Forecast High PE**

Average half or majority of the lowest Low PEs = **Forecast Low PE**

Average of the Forecast High and Low PEs = **Forecast Avg. PE**

Reward (compound, annual return from appreciation and yield)

Potential High and Projected Average Price Latest Dividend: [ ] ÷ Current Price = **Current Yield**   %

Forecast High PE [ ] x Forecast High EPS [ ] = **Potential High** Price: [ ]

Forecast Avg. PE [ ] x Forecast High EPS [ ] = **Projected Avg.** Price: [ ]

Return through (M/Y 5th Fiscal Year ends): [/]   Months from now ÷ 12 = **Period:** [ ]

Appreciation   Yield

PV = Current Price; FV = Pot. High Price; N = Period; **i%** = [ ]% + [ ]% = **Total Return**   %

PV = Current Price; FV = Proj. Avg.Price; N = Period; **i%** = [ ]% + [ ]% = **Proj. Avg. Return**   %

Risk (comparison of potential loss to potential gain)

Forecast Low Price

Forecast Low PE x Forecast Low EPS = Forecast Low Price.

[ ] x [ ] = [ ]

Yield-supported Low Price (Calculate only if Yield x High P/E > 35)

Potential High x Current Yield = Yield-supported Low Price

[ ] x [ ]% = [ ]

Comp. Bond Rate − 1

[ ]%

Potential Low [ ]
Greater of two

Risk Index

Current Price — Pot. Low [ ]

Pot. High — Pot. Low [ ]

= **Risk Index**   %

Price Analysis

For desired **Total Return** (14.9%):

FV = Pot. High; **i%** = 14.9 − Yield; **N** = Period   PV = Price **for 14.9% Total Return:** [ ]

For desired **Risk Index** (25%):

3 x Potential Low = [ ] + Potential High = [ ] ÷ 4 = Price **for 25% Risk Index:** [ ]

Buy Price [ ]
Lower of two

FIGURE A.3 NAIC's Stock Selection Guide (Front)

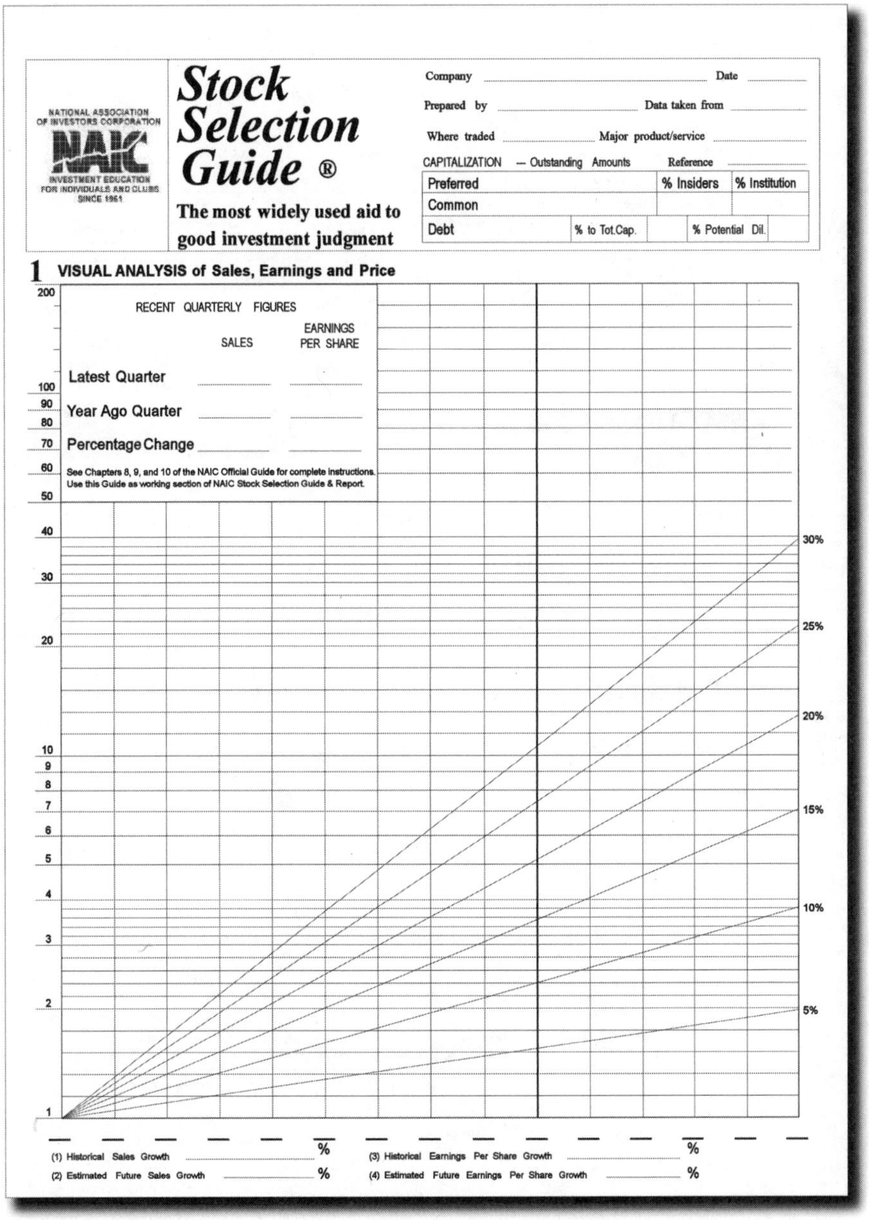
NATIONAL ASSOCIATION OF INVESTORS CORPORATION
NAIC
INVESTMENT EDUCATION FOR INDIVIDUALS AND CLUBS SINCE 1951

Stock Selection Guide ®

The most widely used aid to good investment judgment

Company ______ Date ______

Prepared by ______ Data taken from ______

Where traded ______ Major product/service ______

CAPITALIZATION — Outstanding Amounts Reference ______

Preferred		% Insiders	% Institution
Common			
Debt	% to Tot.Cap.	% Potential Dil.	

1 VISUAL ANALYSIS of Sales, Earnings and Price

RECENT QUARTERLY FIGURES

	SALES	EARNINGS PER SHARE
Latest Quarter		
Year Ago Quarter		
Percentage Change		

See Chapters 8, 9, and 10 of the NAIC Official Guide for complete instructions.
Use this Guide as working section of NAIC Stock Selection Guide & Report.

(1) Historical Sales Growth ______ %
(2) Estimated Future Sales Growth ______ %
(3) Historical Earnings Per Share Growth ______ %
(4) Estimated Future Earnings Per Share Growth ______ %

Source: The NAIC Stock Selection Guide is copyrighted property of the National Association of Investors Corporation, 711 W. Eleven Mile Road, Madison Heights, MI 48071. For a full explanation of the Guide, the reader should refer to the NAIC Official Guide.

FIGURE A.4   NAIC's Stock Selection Guide (Back)

2 EVALUATING MANAGEMENT   Company _____

									LAST 5 YEAR AVG.	TREND	
										UP	DOWN
A % Pre-tax Profit on Sales (Net Before Taxes ÷ Sales)											
B % Earned on Equity (E/S ÷ Book Value)											

3 PRICE-EARNINGS HISTORY as an indicator of the future

This shows how stock prices have fluctuated with earnings and dividends. It is a building block for translating earnings into future stock prices.

Year	PRESENT PRICE		C Earnings Per Share	HIGH THIS YEAR		F Dividend Per Share	LOW THIS YEAR	
	A PRICE HIGH	B PRICE LOW		D Price Earnings Ratio HIGH A÷C	E Price Earnings Ratio LOW B÷C		G % Payout F÷C X 100	H % High Yield F÷B X 100
1								
2								
3								
4								
5								
6 TOTAL								
7 AVERAGE								
8 AVERAGE PRICE EARNINGS RATIO			9 CURRENT PRICE EARNINGS RATIO					

4 EVALUATING RISK and REWARD over the next 5 years

Assuming one recession and one business boom every 5 years, calculations are made of how high and how low the stock might sell. The upside-downside ratio is the key to evaluating risk and reward.

A HIGH PRICE – NEXT 5 YEARS

Avg. High P/E _____ (3D7 as adj.)   X Estimate High Earnings/Share _____ = Forecast High Price $ _____ (4A1)

B LOW PRICE – NEXT 5 YEARS

(a) Avg. Low P/E _____ (3E7 as adj.)   X Estimated Low Earnings/Share _____ = $ _____

(b) Avg. Low Price of Last 5 Years = _____ (3B7)

(c) Recent Severe Market Low Price = _____

(d) Price Dividend Will Support   Present Divd _____ = _____ = _____
High Yield (H)

Selected Estimate Low Price _____ = $ _____ (4B1)

C ZONING

_____ (4A1) High Forecast Price Minus _____ (4B1) Low Forecast Price Equals _____ (C) Range. 1/3 of Range = _____ (4CD)

(4C2) Lower 1/3 = (4B1) _____ to _____ (Buy)

(4C3) Middle 1/3 = _____ to _____ (Maybe)

(4C4) Upper 1/3 = _____ to _____ (4A1). (Sell)

Present Market Price of _____ is in the _____ (4C5) _____ Range

D UP-SIDE DOWN-SIDE RATIO (Potential Gain vs. Risk of Loss)

High Price (4A1) _____ Minus Present Price _____

= _____ = _____ To 1

Present Price _____ Minus Low Price (4B1) _____ (4D)

E PRICE TARGET (Note: This shows the potential market price appreciation over the next five years in simple interest terms.)

High Price (4A1) _____

= (_____) X 100 = (_____) - 100 = _____ % Appreciation

Present Market Price _____ (4E)

5 5-YEAR POTENTIAL   This combines price appreciation with dividend yield to get an estimate of total return. It provides a standard for comparing income and growth stocks.

Note: Results are expressed as a simple rate; use the table below to convert to a compound rate.

A Present Full Year's Dividend $ _____

Present Price of Stock $ _____ = _____ X 100 = _____ (5A) Present Yield or % Returned on Purchase Price

B AVERAGE YIELD OVER NEXT 5 YEARS

Avg. Earnings Per Share Next 5 Years _____ X Avg. % Payout (3G7) = _____ = _____ % (5B)

Present Price $ _____

C ESTIMATED AVERAGE ANNUAL RETURN OVER NEXT FIVE YEARS

5 Year Appreciation Potential (4E) _____

_____ 5 = _____ %

Average Yield (5B) ... ... = _____ %

Average Total Annual Return Over the Next 5 Years (5C) = _____ %

Table to Convert From Simple to Compound Rate

Simple Rate 2 4 6 8 10 12 14 16 18 20 22 24 26 28 30 32 34 36 38 40

Compound Rate 2 4 6 8 10 12 14 16 18 20 22 24

mouthed pitcher into a narrow-necked bottle. It all pours out easily, but too little goes in where it's supposed to! It can be just as difficult for the savvy college professor as it is for the novice who's scared to death of arithmetic. I've seen both types shake their heads in bewilderment and frustration! Hopefully, we've covered that base to some extent already by exposing you to the *whats* and *whys*.

In addition to a pencil, an eraser, a financial calculator (see Chapter 7), and one of the worksheets, the only item you will need is the data. You may make copies of the Technamental Stock Study Worksheet and use it freely. The NAIC Stock Selection Guide has been reproduced for your perusal, but it is NAIC's copyrighted product. If you wish, you may obtain copies of that form from NAIC.

GATHERING DATA

For your technamental stock study, you will need to assemble and enter on your worksheet the following data for any company you study.

A minimum of five years, and optimally ten years of:

Sales/revenue	Book value
Tax rate	High and low prices
Net profit	Shares outstanding (optional)
Earnings per share (EPS)	Pretax profit (optional)

A minimum of five, and optimally eight quarters of:

Quarterly sales   Quarterly earnings
And the most recent dividend paid, if any

From the data above you (or your computer) will calculate:

Pretax profit for each year (if you don't already have the data)
Shares outstanding for each year (if you don't already have the data)
Pretax profit margins for each year (Pretax profit ÷ Sales)
Return on equity for each year (Earnings per share ÷ Beginning book value)
High and low PEs for each year (High/low prices ÷ Earnings per share)

After eliminating irrelevant data you (or your computer) will calculate:

Historical growth rates of sales and earnings   Average return on equity

Average profit margins   Current and signature PE

Historical value ratio (HVR) (Current PE ÷ signature PE)

From the historical data you will estimate:

Future growth rates of sales and earnings   Future high and low PEs

Future value of earnings   Future high and low prices

From these estimates, you (or your computer) will calculate, and you will evaluate:

Total return   Risk ratio

Average return   Reasonable price for the stock

Let's look at the two main sources of this data that don't require a computer:

1. **Value Line Survey**—The *Value Line Survey* is arguably the best single source of data, whether you'll be entering the data into a computer or manually completing worksheets. The basic survey includes about 1,700 companies; the expanded version adds another 1,800 or so. All the information you need to know about a company is to be found on a single page. The survey is updated quarterly in 13 sections so that the subscriber receives updates weekly. Unfortunately, an annual subscription is expensive, costing in excess of $500 per year. The good news is that most public libraries subscribe to the Survey, so you can usually get all of the information you need in a quick visit.

   If you contact Value Line and ask for a trial subscription, you can get all of the data for 13 weeks for about $65, and that's good enough to get you started.

2. **Standard & Poor's Stock Reports**—At one time, the Standard & Poor's Stock Reports were the most popular reports among NAIC investors. They contain nearly all the required data, but it's not laid out quite as intuitively as the data in the *Value Line Survey,* and the reports lack some minor information. The reports are available from your broker or directly from Standard & Poor's.

The next few pages include an example of each of these sources that is coordinated with the study of ABC Company in Chapters 7 through 10.

LAYING THE GROUNDWORK MANUALLY

When you break the stock study down into its simplest form, you really need to complete only eight exercises to prepare for it. These exercises are not even sophisticated enough to call math. They're simple arithmetic. Except for plotting data on a graph, each exercise is merely a matter of knowing where to find the data and what numbers to add, subtract, multiply, or divide. Of course, you'll need to know where on the forms to put the results so that you can analyze and evaluate the stock.

To make it simple for you, I've listed the eight items below, described them in detail, provided the formulas, and plugged in some sample data that has been keyed to the data sources so you can match the data and be sure of their proper locations. I've then provided numerical keys to show where on the forms the results of the calculations are supposed to go.

In Figure A.5 you will find a typical Value Line page. The data for our fictitious ABC Company will match up with the text. The required information is coded alphabetically so you will be able to see how the data are used in the calculations.

Here's where I strike the first blow for simplicity. Both excellent sources of data, the *Value Line Survey* and Standard & Poor's Stock Reports can be intimidating to a novice investor who looks at them for the first time. After all, how much can you absorb? But then again, how much do you need?

I've highlighted all of the information that you require. As you can see, the essential items represent only a small portion of the page. As you gain experience, your curiosity may lead you to explore some of the other information found on these pages, but don't be intimidated by the extent of the information here. Much of it may be interesting to you at some point, and some of it may be useful, but only the little that is highlighted is essential for now.

FIGURE A.5 Value Line Page for ABC Company

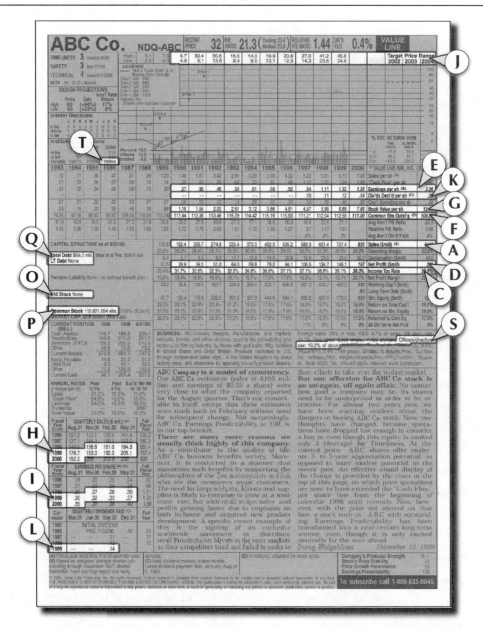

Note: B (Pretax profit) is not available. It must be calculated from net profit and tax rate.

In Figures A.6 and A.7 you will find ABC Company's Standard and Poor's Stock Report (called a *tear sheet*). Note that some of the data are different from the data in the *Value Line Survey*. For example, Value Line shows 37 cents in earnings for the fourth quarter of 1999 compared with S&P's 8 cents—a 29-cent difference. Usually when Value Line normalizes its earnings as it apparently does here, you'll find a footnote to that effect in the lower lefthand corner of the Value Line page, although there is no such footnote in this instance. (The footnote appeared in the following month.) Where there are differences, I have used the Value Line figures.

You can find a complete rundown on the differences between the data sources under Investors' Resources on the Inve$tWare Web site, <www.investware.com>. I didn't incorporate that table in this book because the information on it changes frequently. If you can access it, you're better off to get it hot off the Web.

The tables on pages 218 through 221 tell you how to prepare the worksheets. The first two pages describe the simple calculations that you will perform using the data shown in Figures A.5, A.6, and A.7. Pages 220 and 221 offer suggestions to help you plot the data on the charts.

Figures A.8 through A.11 show the front and back of the Technamental Stock Study Worksheet and NAIC's Stock Selection Guide, both prepared according to the instructions.

These steps represent all of the mechanical steps that you must take in advance. There will be some more calculations required as you apply the necessary judgments and generate the estimates and forecasts that you will use in the process of analyzing the data and evaluating the price of the company. They will be covered next.

As you can see, neither these calculations nor the ones to come require rocket science. For most people who read this, the calculations will be a piece of cake, but investors who have been away from a teacher and a blackboard for a while might need a little brushing up—and a little extra effort to plug these numbers into a calculator.

FIGURE A.6 S&P Stock Report for ABC Company (Front)

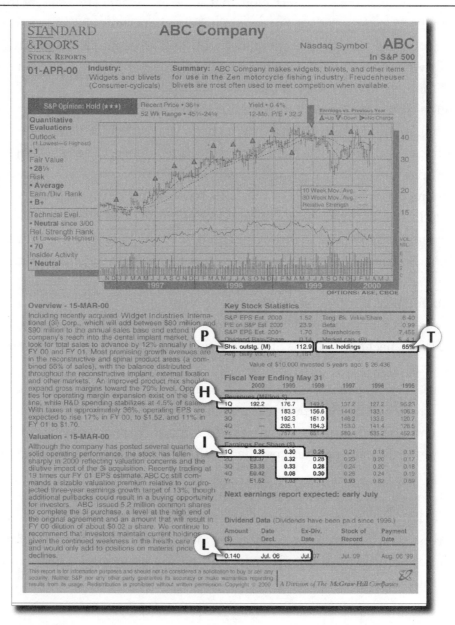

FIGURE A.7 S&P Stock Report for ABC Company (Back)

STANDARD & POOR'S STOCK REPORTS

ABC Company

01-APR-00

Business Summary - 15-MAR-00

ABC Company is the worlds largest producer of widgets and blivets, commonly used by Zen motorcyclists when they fish with golf balls.

In FY 99, the widgets outsold the blivets by a factor of nine to one and, although the unit price for blivets was ten times the average of widgets, they brought in barely enough to outdo the widget sales for the year.

The success of Freudenheuser blivets, produced by Widget Industries, International, was sufficient competition to induce the board of directors of ABC Company to make a tender offer of $998 per share which was accepted by Widgets Industries. Commencing on September 14th of this year, Widget Industries will be a wholly owned subsidiary of ABC Company.

Widgets in the motorcycling arena are a relatively new product, especially with Zen motorcyclists who are pleased with the blivets that they have used in the past but are having less success with the blivets in rounding up all of the fish that they require for the golf ball business.

Cycle seats that use the ABC widgets have met with a great deal of success, and, when the old blivets are introduced to the new users of those seats have found that users have had no trouble making the switch.

Widget support products, not including blivets, accounted for 33% of ABC's support business for FY 1999 and is expected to produce even higher revenues as they are introduced into the support market this year. Second quarter results are expected to be higher than first quarter results for the Spring season in FY 2000.

Blivet conduits, a product for which there has been no serious competition, will make up 13% of the dealer sales in FY 2000. A new conduit that charges up widgets as they are coming on line is expected to augment sales after the end of the second quarter and company officers have indicated that they have high hopes for this new entry into the Zen golf ball arena.

In December, 1999, the Board of Directors of ABC Company announced that they would offer management a stock option program beginning in the second quarter of FY 2000 in lieu of salary. Analysts have high hopes that this new business model will create new interest in both the widget and blivet industry as this industry leader moves further ahead.

Per Share Data ($) (Year Ended May 31)	1999	1998	1997	1996	1995	1994	1993	1992	1991	1990
Tangible Bk. Val.	6.40	5.41	4.74	4.42	3.59	3.12	2.61	2.05	1.54	1.16
Cash Flow	1.29	1.31	1.10	1.00	0.81	0.71	0.66	0.53	0.41	0.32
Earnings	1.03	1.11	0.94	0.82	0.69	0.61	0.56	0.46	0.36	0.27
Dividends	0.12	0.11	0.10	Nil	Nil	Nil	Nil	Nil	Nil	Nil
Payout Ratio	12%	10%	11%	Nil	Nil	Nil	Nil	Nil	Nil	Nil
Cal. Yrs.	1998	1997	1996	1995	1994	1993	1992	1991	1990	1989
Prices - High	41 1/8	27	20 5/8	19 7/8	14 1/4	16 1/2	30 1/2	32 3/8	9 5/8	7
- Low	23 5/8	14 1/4	12 1/2	13 1/8	9	8 3/8	13 3/4	8 1/8	4 7/8	4
P/E Ratio - High	40	24	22	24	21	27	54	70	27	26
- Low	23	13	13	16	13	14	25	18	14	15
Income Statement Analysis (Million $)										
Revs.	757	651	580	535	452	373	335	275	210	162
Oper. Inc.	256	204	178	158	133	114	102	78.0	59.5	47.6
Depr.	29.5	23.5	18.5	20.8	14.4	12.0	11.7	8.2	6.5	5.7
Int. Exp	Nil	0.3	0.7	1.1	1.0	0.6	0.9	0.8	0.5	0.4
Pretax Inc.	186	204	169	150	125	107	94.3	76.5	58.6	43.8
Eff. Tax Rate	34%	39%	37%	37%	37%	35%	32%	32%	33%	32%
Net Inc.	116	125	106	94.1	79.2	69.8	64.0	51.8	39.5	29.9
Balance Sheet & Other Fin. Data (Million $)										
Cash	129	117	123	137	90.0	141	93.6	74.6	50.7	42.9
Curr. Assets	682	571	464	463	392	342	271	210	152	115
Total Assets	1,068	849	628	598	539	418	354	279	211	155
Curr. Liab.	201	98.1	72.9	62.0	89.2	53.8	46.7	42.0	33.6	22.6
LT Debt	Nil	Nil	Nil	Nil	Nil	Nil	Nil	Nil	Nil	Nil
Common Eqty.	776	667	553	534	445	357	301	232	173	129
Total Cap.	866	750	555	536	447	361	304	234	174	130
Cap. Exp.	51.1	44.1	21.4	14.1	28.9	6.5	14.9	14.0	11.1	6.5
Cash Flow	146	148	125	115	93.6	81.9	75.6	60.0	46.0	35.6
Curr. Ratio	3.4	5.8	6.4	7.5	4.4	6.4	5.8	5.0	4.5	5.1
% LT Debt of Cap.	Nil	Nil	Nil	Nil	Nil	Nil	Nil	Nil	Nil	Nil
% Net Inc.of Revs.	15.4	19.1	18.3	17.6	17.5	18.7	19.1	18.9	18.8	18.4
% Ret. on Assets	12.1	16.9	17.4	16.5	16.5	18.1	20.0	21.1	21.5	21.8
% Ret. on Equity	16.1	20.4	19.6	19.2	19.8	21.3	23.8	25.5	26.0	26.3

Data as orig reptd.; bef. results of disc opers/spec. items. Per share data adj. for stk. divs. Bold denotes diluted EPS (FASB 128)-prior periods restated. E-Estimated. NA-Not Available. NM-Not Meaningful. NR-Not Ranked.

Office—Airport Industrial Park, P.O. Box 587, Warsaw, IN 46581-0587. **Tel**—(219) 267-6639. **Website**—http://www.biomet.com **Chrmn**—N. L. Noblitt. **Pres & CEO**—D. A. Miller. **SVP-Fin & CFO**—G. D. Hartman. **SVP & Secy**—D. P. Hann. **VP & Investor Contact**—Greg W. Sasso (219-372-1528). **Dirs**—J. L. Ferguson (Vice Chrmn), D. P. Hann, C. S. Harrison, M. R. Harroff, T. F. Kearns Jr., D. A. Miller, J. L. Miller, K. V. Miller, C. E. Niemier, N. L. Noblitt, M. T. Quayle, B. Scheuble, L. G. Tanner. **Transfer Agent**—Lake City Bank, Warsaw. **Incorporated**—in Indiana in 1977. **Empl**— 2,550. **S&P Analyst:** Robert M. Gold

Preparing a Stock Study Worksheet
Examples use ABC Company 1999 data
Letter codes are keyed to the Data in the Value Line and S&P examples
Item numbers are keyed to location in worksheets where results are used.

---

① Pretax Profit (PTP) (from net profit).

If Pretax profit is not available (*Value Line Survey*), calculate it from net profit and the tax rate. PTP is the profit made after paying all expenses management controls.

Calculation

$$\text{Pretax profit} = \frac{\text{Net profit}}{1 - \text{Tax rate}}$$

Example

Net Profit (D): 149.1
Tax Rate (C): 35.1% (=.351)

$$\frac{149.1}{1 - .351} = \frac{149.1}{.649} = 229.7$$

Hint: Don't forget to change the percent to a decimal by moving the decimal point two places to the left.

---

② Profit Margin (Pretax).

The SSG's "% Pretax Profit on Sales" shows the percent of sales dollars that remain after expenses (excluding taxes) have been paid.

Calculation

$$\text{Profit margin} = \frac{\text{Pretax profit}}{\text{Sales}}$$

Example

Pretax Profit (No. ① above): 229.7
Sales (A): 757.4

$$\frac{229.7}{757.4} = 30.3\%$$

---

③ Return on Equity.

ROE shows the percent of the shareholders' interest in the company that is represented by its profit—a measure of management effectiveness.

Calculation

$$\text{ROE} = \frac{\text{Earnings per share}}{\text{Book value}}$$

Note: The TSSW uses book value from the previous year. The SSG uses book value from the current year.

Example

EPS (E): 1.32
BV (G): TSSW: 5.96; SSG: 6.89

$$\text{TSSW:} \frac{1.32}{5.96} = 22.1\% \qquad \text{SSG:} \frac{1.32}{6.89} = 19.2\%$$

---

④ Percent Change.

The percentage of the original value that an increase or decrease in that value represents. Used to compare the most recent quarterly sales or earnings (or trailing 4 quarters) with the same period of the previous year.

Calculation

$$\% \text{ Change} = \left(\frac{\text{Latest Period}}{\text{Previous Period}} - 1 \right) \times 100$$

Example

1st Qtr. 2000 Sales (H): 192.2
1st Qtr. 1999 Sales (H): 176.7

$$\frac{192.2}{176.7} - 1 = .188 \times 100 = 18.8\%$$

TTM EPS (I): .32+.33+.37+.35 = 1.37
TTM Prev. year (I): .27+.28+.30+.30 = 1.15

$$\frac{1.37}{1.15} - 1 = .191 \times 100 = 19.1\%$$

(5) Averages.
The 5 and 10-year averages of profit margins and ROE can be useful for comparisons with peers in the industry and for determination of trends.

Calculation

$$\text{Average} = \frac{\textbf{Sum of data for desired periods}}{\textbf{Number of periods}}$$

Example
Profit Margins (2) (calculated values)
5-yr: 27.6+28+29.2+31.3+30.3 =146.4
10-yr: 27+27.9+27.8+28.1+28.7+27.6+
                   28+29.2+31.3+30.3 = 285.9

$$\textbf{5-yr Avg.} = \frac{146.4}{5} = 29.3\%$$

$$\textbf{10-yr Avg.} = \frac{285.9}{10} = 28.6\%$$

Note: With the SSG, the trend is derived from comparing the most recent year with the 5-year average. If the current year is above the 5-year average, the trend is up. **TSSW** users may also plot the data and visually analyze the trend.

(6) PE Multiples (Price-Earnings Ratios).
The PE or multiple is an expression of the relationship between the price that shareholders are willing to pay for a share of stock and the company's earnings per share. It is an important measure of investor confidence.

Calculations
Price-earnings Ratio (PE) = Price ÷ Earnings
Current PE = Current Price ÷ TTM EPS
Projected PE = Current Price ÷ (TTM EPS x [1 + Proj. growth]) (SSG only)
High PE = Highest Price ÷ EPS for year
(Historical) Low PE = Lowest Price ÷ EPS for year

Examples
Current Price: $32
TTM EPS (I): .32+.33+.37+.35 = 1.37
Proj. EPS Growth: 13%
High Price (J): 45.8
Low Price: (J): 24.6
EPS (E): 1.32

Current PE = 32 ÷ 1.37 = 23.4
Projected PE = 32 ÷ 1.55 = 20.7
High PE = 45.8 ÷ 1.32 = 34.7
Low PE = 24.6 ÷ 1.32 = 18.6

(7) Percent (Dividend) Payout. (SSG only)
The dividend is expressed as a percentage of earnings to signify the portion of earnings that is paid out to shareholders and not retained to common equity.

Calculation

$$\textbf{Dividend payout} = \frac{\textbf{Dividend}}{\textbf{EPS}} \textbf{ x 100}$$

Examples
Dividend (K): .12
EPS (E): 1.32

$$\textbf{Payout} = \frac{.12}{1.32} \textbf{ x 100} = 9.1\%$$

Note: The TSSW uses Yield x High PE to approximate dividend payout as a test for possible use of the *yield-supported low price.*

(8) Yield.
The dividend expressed as a percentage of the share price.

Calculations
Current yield = Current dividend ÷ Current price x 100
High yield = Dividend ÷ Low price x 100 (SSG only)

Examples
Current Dividend (K): .12
Low Price (J): 24.6

Current yield = .12 ÷ 32 x 100 = 0.4%
Note: **SSG** uses the latest declared dividend (L).
High yield   = .12 ÷ 24.6 x 100 = 0.5%

PLOTTING TIPS

Annual sales, earnings, and other values may be plotted on a growth chart to clearly show compounded growth. Growth at the same rate year after year will show up as a straight line. The following tips should be of help as you plot the points on your semilog growth chart.

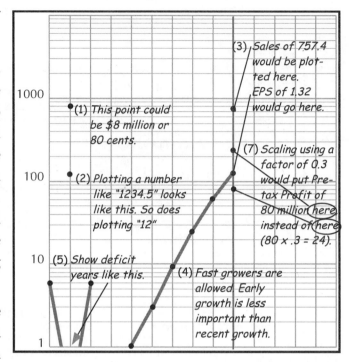

1. **"1" can mean one cent or one billion dollars.** Because you are interested only in relationships (one year to the next, or the slope of a sales growth line to that of an earnings growth line, and so on), the actual numbers are less important than the comparative slope of the lines. You may therefore choose any line that has a "1," "10," "100," or "1000" to represent one of something.

2. **Ignore all decimal points.** Use only two or three leftmost digits. It is impossible to depict much more detail than that. Low on the scale you will find it feasible to consider the first three digits, but most often the first two digits are all you will be able to plot sensibly.

3. **Start plotting sales for latest year on or below the "1000" line at year 10 and work backward.** This will ensure that you have room to plot future growth to the right and above the most recent data. The higher you can start (at "1000" or below), the more room you will have for the earlier data. (Use the "100" line on NAIC's Stock Selection Guide.)

   Next plot EPS, starting as close to the sales line as possible and preferably below if you have room. It's desirable to depict pretax profit (if you should decide to plot it), between sales and EPS to reflect the flow of business. By plotting the lines consistently in that order, you can see at a glance whether profit margins are increasing or decreasing, or whether earnings are growing at a faster or slower rate than sales. (See "Scale values" below for another means of placing your plotted data where you want it to go.)

4. **With fast growth, don't worry if you lose the early years.** The most significant data are the most recent data. If you are plotting the data for a particularly fast-growing company, you may not have room at the bottom of the graph as you work your way from right back to left. If the company is growing that quickly, you will lose little if you don't get to plot the earlier years.

5. **Connect the dots, bypassing but marking negative earnings data.** The slopes of the connecting lines tell you the growth rates from year to year. Differences in rates of growth will stand out clearly when you draw them.

6. **Use a Flair pen.** Don't bother with a sharp point. This is an inexact science and precision is not necessary. What is necessary is that the trends be easy to see.

7. **Scale values if you wish.** By scaling values, you can accommodate their appearance in the order you wish them to appear. If you would like your pretax profit line to fall just below the sales line, but pretax profit was $200 million in the last year while sales were $1 billion, it can be difficult to chart. However, you can multiply each value of pretax profit by the same constant—in this case let's make the constant 0.3—so that each number will fit nicely on the chart below the sales line, beginning on the right with 80. Most calculators permit the use of a constant: you can multiple a variety of numbers by a constant multiplier by entering the new multiplicand and hitting the = key. Thus, if you want to scale pretax profit numbers by 0.3, you enter 0.3 in your calculator, then hit the × key and the first pretax profit figure. When you press the = key, the answer will be your first number to plot. You then simply enter the second pretax profit number you want to scale and again hit the = key. The second number will be converted, and so on for all ten numbers. Try it. See if your calculator will do it for you and make scaling easy. Some will, some won't. At worst you can reenter the scale factor

FIGURE A.8 Technamental Stock Study Worksheet (Front) Prepared for Use

Technamental Stock Study Worksheet

Company ABC Company **Ticker** ABC

Quality — Technamental Stock Study Worksheet — **Date** 12/31/1999

Years		1990	1991	1992	1993	1994	1995	1996	1997	1998	1999
Ⓐ Sales	($M)	162.4	209.7	274.8	335.4	373.3	452.3	535.2	580.3	651.4	757.4
Ⓑ Pretax Profit ①(M)		43.8	58.6	76.5	94.4	107.1	124.9	149.6	169.3	203.8	229.7
Ⓒ Tax Rate	(%)	31.7%	32.6%	32.3%	32.2%	34.8%	36.6%	37.1%	37.1%	38.8%	35.1%
Ⓓ Net Profit	($M)	29.9	39.5	51.8	64.0	69.8	79.2	94.1	106.5	124.7	149.1
Ⓔ Earnings (EPS)	($)	.27	.36	.46	.56	.61	.69	.82	.94	1.11	1.32
Ⓕ Shares	(M)	110.4	112.4	113.5	115.3	114.4	115.2	115.8	111.2	112.0	112.6
Ⓖ Book Value		1.16	1.54	2.05	2.61	3.12	3.86	4.61	4.97	5.96	6.89
② Pretax Margin	(%)	27.0%	27.9%	27.8%	28.1%	28.7%	27.6%	28.0%	29.2%	31.3%	30.3%
③ Return on Equity(%)	Using Trailing Book Value		31.0%	29.9%	27.3%	23.4%	22.1%	21.2%	20.4%	22.3%	22.1%

Fiscal Yr. Ended (MM/YY) **1999 5/99**
Date last quarter ended **8/99**

Quarterly Sales Ⓗ — **Quarterly Earnings (EPS)** Ⓘ

	Qtr 2	Qtr 3	Qtr 4	Qtr 1	TTM	Qtr 2	Qtr 3	Qtr 4	Qtr 1	TTM
Last year	156.6	161.0	184.3	176.7	678.6	.27	.28	.30	.30	1.15
This year	183.3	192.3	205.1	192.2	772.9	.32	.33	.37	.35	1.37
④ % Change	17.1%	19.4%	11.3%	8.8%	13.9%	18.5%	17.9%	23.3%	16.7%	19.1%

Growth

	Sales	EPS
Stability		
Hist. %	%	%
Fcst. %	%	%

Pretax Profit Margins ⑤ Avg. 28.6 %

Return on Equity ⑤ Avg. 24.4 %

Note: Calculate ROE by dividing EPS by the Book Value from the previous year.

Forecast Earnings

Complete this section only if Growth, above, is satisfactory

Business Model

	5yr. Fcst.			5yr. Fcst.
x Profit Margin	%	=	Forecast Sales	
less Taxes @	%	=	Pretax Profit	
less Adjustments		=	Net after taxes	
+ Average Shares		=	Net to shareholders	
			= Business Model EPS	

Forecast Growth Model
From growth at forecast EPS growth rate.

or

Forecast Earnings per Share
Lower of two

=

FIGURE A.9 Technamental Stock Study Worksheet (Back) Prepared for Use

Value

| Company | ABC Company | Ticker | ABC |

E Earnings	.27	.36	.46	.56	.61	.69	.82	.94	1.11	1.32
J High Price	9.7	32.4	30.5	16.5	14.3	19.9	20.6	27.0	41.2	45.8
Low Price	4.9	8.1	13.8	8.4	9.0	13.1	12.5	14.3	23.6	24.6
6 High P/E	35.9	90.0	66.3	29.5	23.4	28.8	25.1	28.7	37.1	34.7
Low P/E	18.1	22.5	30.0	15.0	14.8	19.0	15.2	15.2	21.3	18.6
Average P/E	27.0	56.3	48.2	22.3	19.1	23.9	20.2	22.0	29.2	26.7
K Dividends	-	-	-	-	-	-	-	.10	.11	.12
Years	1990	1991	1992	1993	1994	1995	1996	1997	1998	1999

P/E Ratio Analysis

Avg. High PE **5**	Avg. Low PE	**Current Price** ÷	**TTM EPS** **6**	=	**Current PE**
30.4	17.2	32.00	1.37		23.4

Average of the Historical Average PEs (less outliers) = **Signature PE**

Current PE ÷ Signature PE = **Historical Value Ratio (HVR)**   %

Forecast High, Low, and Average PEs
Average half or majority of the lowest High PEs = **Forecast High PE**
Average half or majority of the lowest Low PEs = **Forecast Low PE**
Average of the Forecast High and Low PEs = **Forecast Avg. PE**

Reward (compound, annual return from appreciation and yield)

Potential High and Projected Average Price   Latest Dividend: **K** .12   + Current Price = **Current Yield** **8**   0.4 %

Forecast High PE [   ] x Forecast High EPS [   ] = **Potential High** Price: [   ]

Forecast Avg. PE [   ] x Forecast High EPS [   ] = **Projected Avg.** Price: [   ]

Return through (M/Y 5th Fiscal Year ends): [/   ]   Months from now ÷ 12 = **Period:** [   ]

	Appreciation	Yield		
PV = Current Price; **FV** = Pot. High Price; **N** = Period; **i%** =	[ ] % +	[ ] % =	**Total Return**	[ ] %
PV = Current Price; **FV** = Proj. Avg.Price; **N** = Period; **i%** =	[ ] % +	[ ] % =	**Proj. Avg. Return**	[ ] %

Risk (comparison of potential loss to potential gain)

Forecast Low Price
Forecast Low PE x Forecast Low EPS = Forecast Low Price.
[   ] x [   ] = [   ]

Risk Index
Current Price − Pot. Low

Yield-supported Low Price (Calculate only if Yield x High P/E > 35)
Potential High x Current Yield = Yield-supported Low Price
[   ] x [   ] % = [   ]

Comp. Bond Rate − 1
[   ] %

Potential Low [   ]   Greater of two

Pot. High − Pot. Low   [   ]

Risk Index [   ] %

Price Analysis

For desired **Total Return** (14.9%):
   FV = Pot. High; **i%** = 14.9 − Yield; **N** = Period   **PV** = Price **for 14.9% Total Return:** [   ]
For desired **Risk Index** (25%):

3 x Potential Low = [   ] + Potential High [   ] ÷ 4 = Price **for 25% Risk Index:** [   ]

Buy Price [   ]   Lower of two

FIGURE A.10 NAIC's Stock Selection Guide (Front) Prepared for Use

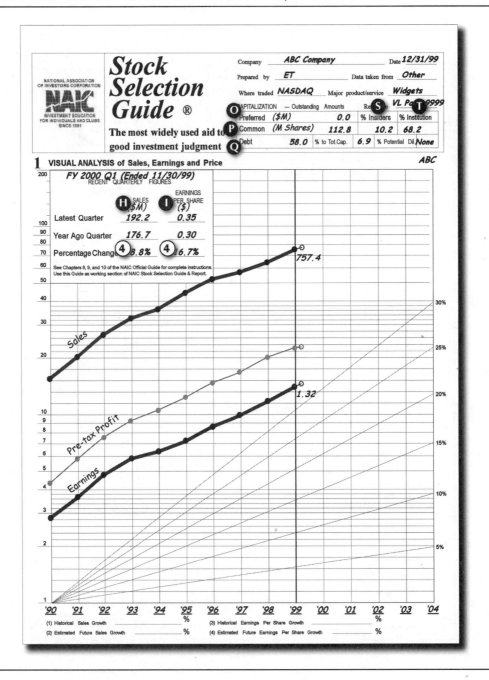

FIGURE A.11   NAIC's Stock Selection Guide (Back) Prepared for Use

2   EVALUATING   MANAGEMENT   Company *ABC Company*   *(ABC)*   02/29/00

		1990	1991	1992	1993	1994	1995	1996	1997	1998	1999	LAST 5 YEAR AVG.	TREND UP	DOWN
A	% Pre-tax Profit on Sales (Net Before Taxes ÷ Sales)	27.0	27.9	27.8	28.1	28.7	27.6	28.0	29.2	31.3	30.3	29.3	UP	
B	% Earned on Equity (E/S ÷ Book Value)	23.6	22.7	22.4	21.5	19.6	17.9	17.8	18.9	18.6	19.2	18.5	UP	

3   PRICE-EARNINGS HISTORY as an indicator of the future

This shows how stock prices have fluctuated with earnings and dividends. It is a building block for translating earnings into future stock prices.

PRESENT PRICE 32,000   HIGH THIS YEAR 45,800   LOW THIS YEAR 24,600

	Year	A PRICE HIGH	B PRICE LOW	Earnings Per Share	D Price Earnings Ratio HIGH A ÷ C	E Price Earnings Ratio LOW B ÷ C	Dividend Per Share	% Payout F ÷ C X 100	% High Yield F ÷ B X 100
1	1995	19.9	13.1	0.69	28.8	19.0	0.000	0.0	0.0
2	1996	20.6	12.5	0.82	25.1	15.2	0.000	0.0	0.0
3	1997	27.0	14.3	0.94	28.7	15.2	0.100	10.6	0.7
4	1998	41.2	23.6	1.11	37.1	21.3	0.110	9.9	0.5
5	1999	45.8	24.6	1.32	34.7	18.6	0.120	9.1	0.5
6	TOTAL		88.1		154.4	89.3		29.6	
7	AVERAGE		17.6		30.9	17.9			
8	AVERAGE PRICE EARNINGS RATIO 24.4				9 CURRENT PRICE EARNINGS RATIO 23.4				

Current P/E Based on Last 4 qtr. EPS [1.37]

4   EVALUATING   RISK and REWARD   over the next 5 years

Assuming one recession and one business boom every 5 years, calculations are made of how high and how low the stock might sell. The upside-downside ratio is the key to evaluating risk and reward.

A HIGH PRICE -- NEXT 5 YEARS
   Avg. High P/E _____ (3D7 as adj.)   X Estimate High Earnings/Share _____ = Forecast High Price $ _____ (4A1)

B LOW PRICE -- NEXT 5 YEARS
   (a) Avg. Low P/E _____ (3E7 as adj.)   X Estimated Low Earnings/Share _____ = $ _____
   (b) Avg. Low Price of Last 5 Years = _____ (3B7)
   (c) Recent Severe Market Low Price = _____ .14
   (d) Price Dividend Will Support Present Divd / High Yield (H) = _____ = _____
   Selected Estimate Low Price _____ = $ _____ (4B1)

C ZONING
   _____ High Forecast Price Minus _____ Low Forecast Price Equals _____ Range. 1/3 of Range = _____
   (4A1)   (4B1)   (C)   (4CD)
      (4C2) Lower 1/3 = (4B1) _____ to _____ (Buy)
      (4C3) Middle 1/3 = _____ to _____ (Maybe)
      (4C4) Upper 1/3 = _____ to _____ (4A1). (Sell)
   Present Market Price of _____ is in the _____ (4C5) _____ Range

D UP-SIDE DOWN-SIDE RATIO (Potential Gain vs. Risk of Loss)
   High Price (4A1) _____ Minus Present Price _____
   Present Price _____ Minus Low Price (4B1) _____ = _____ = _____ To 1 (4D)

E PRICE TARGET (Note: This shows the potential market price appreciation over the next five years in simple interest terms.)
   High Price (4A1) _____ = (_____) X 100 = (_____) - 100 = _____ % Appreciation
   Present Market Price _____   (4E)

5   5-YEAR POTENTIAL   This combines appreciation with dividend yield to get an estimate of total return. It provides a standard for comparing income and growth stocks.

A Present Full Year's Dividend $ .14   Note: Results are expressed as a single %; use the table below to convert to a compound rate.
   Present Price of Stock $ 32.00 = _____ X 100 = 0.4 Present Yield or % Returned on Purchase Price (5A)

B AVERAGE YIELD OVER NEXT 5 YEARS
   Avg. Earnings Per Share Next 5 Years _____ X Avg. % Payout (3G7) _____ = _____ = _____ % (5B)
   Present Price $ _____

C ESTIMATED AVERAGE ANNUAL RETURN OVER NEXT FIVE YEARS
   5 Year Appreciation Potential (4E)
      5. _____ = _____ %
   Average Yield (5B) _____ = _____ %
   Average Total Annual Return Over the Next 5 Years (5C) _____ = _____ %

   Table to Convert From Simple to Compound Rate
   Simple Rate 2 4 6 8 10 12 14 16 18 20 22 24 26 28 30 32 34 36 38 40
   Compound Rate 2 4 6 8 10 12 14 16 18 20 22 24

© 1996. National Association of Investors Corporation; 711 West Thirteen Mile Road, Madison Hgts., Michigan 48071

each time. The new placement on the graph may well be worth it. The computer scales values automatically in most of the technamental software.

In addition to plotting on the growth chart data whose growth you are interested in analyzing, you should plot some data on the linear charts provided. Such charts are available on the Inve$tWare Technamental Stock Study Worksheet for plotting profit margins, return on equity, and historical high and low PEs.

Plotting on linear charts is reasonably straightforward. The first line on each represents the first of ten years. The right margin represents the last fiscal year reported. Simply plot a point on each year of the grid that corresponds to the value for that year, then connect the dots as before. In cases where the data go off the chart, they should be treated as in the chart labeled PE Analysis on page 223.

It's helpful to draw lines across each of the linear charts to represent the averages so that you can see how the values behaved relative to those averages.

When you are finished with this exercise and have filled out the necessary spaces on your Technamental Stock Study Worksheet or NAIC Stock Selection Guide to prepare them for your analysis, you're ready to go on to the next task, using the stock study worksheets.

Once again, on pages 227 through 231, I've included a set of keys to guide you in applying the judgments, doing the calculations, and putting the results where they belong on the form. On page 227 is a summary of the 15 items that require you to make an estimate or decision. I've included a page reference for each item so you can review what's necessary for making each decision. The items are keyed to the worksheets as well, using the codes J1 through J15.

On pages 228 through 231, coded from C1 through C14, you'll find the calculations that are required to complete the study.

Figures A.12 through A.15, the completed worksheets showing you where the results should be recorded, constitute the remainder of this appendix.

This appendix should be a suitable reference for you if you are doing your stock studies by hand. I feel pretty sure, though, that if you don't already have a computer, you'll probably be grateful for this new justification for buying one. You certainly must value your time highly enough to see how cost effective it can be to automate your investment activities.

Completing the *Technamental* Analysis
Required Calculations
Item numbers are keyed to worksheets where results are used

Judgment Items. Calculations required to complete a stock study require certain judgments to provide some of the components of those calculations. These are discussed in detail in the text. The following is an index of judgment items that are depicted in the accompanying illustrations along with reference pages where these items are discussed in some detail.

(J1)	Eliminate sales outliers	Chapter 7,	page 94
(J2)	Eliminate earnings outliers	Chapter 7,	page 94
(J3)	Eliminate outliers in high/low PEs	Chapter 10,	page 131
(J4)	Estimate future high PE	Chapter 10,	page 137
(J5)	Estimate future low PE	Chapter 10,	page 137
(J6)	Estimate future sales growth	Chapter 10,	page 139
(J7)	Estimate future earnings growth	Chapter 10,	page 139
(J8)	Select low earnings estimate	Chapter 10,	page 145
(J9)	Select low price	Chapter 10,	page 147
(J10)	Estimate future profit margin	Chapter 13,	page 200
(J11)	Estimate future tax rate	Chapter 13,	page 200
(J12)	Estimate future adjustments	Chapter 13,	page 200
(J13)	Estimate future shares outstanding	Chapter 13,	page 201
(J14)	Estimate future dividend % payout	Chapter 13,	page 202
(J15)	Select high earnings estimate	Chapter 13,	page 202

Using the Stock Study Worksheets

Calculations. The calculations below are pretty simple. They are done automatically by the computer, but you can do them all quite easily by hand.

C1 Future Sales. Once you have estimated a growth rate for sales, you can estimate sales five years from the last reported fiscal year by growing the sales figure for the last fiscal year at your estimated growth rate.

Calculation

> **PV: Sales at end of last fiscal year (or TTM)**
> **i%: Forecast growth rate J6**
> **N: 5 (or, if using TTM sales, years and quarters remaining to 5th FY)**

Example

> **Future Sales = PV: 757.4; i%: 13; N: 5; FV = $1,395.5**
> **or: Future Sales = PV: 772.9; i%: 13; N: 4.75; FV = $1,381.2**

C2 Future EPS. In the same fashion, estimate future earnings using your estimate earnings growth rate.

Calculation

> **PV: EPS at end of last fiscal year (or TTM)**
> **i%: Forecast Growth Rate **
> **N: 5 (or, if using TTM EPS, years and quarters remaining to 5th FY)**

Example

> **Future EPS = PV: 1.32; i%: 13; N: 5; FV = $2.43**
> **or: Future EPS = PV: 1.37; i%: 13; N: 4.75; FV = $2.45**

C3 Historical Value Ratio (HVR). Compare the current PE with the signature PE (the historical (10 year) average PE). (On the SSG, relative value uses the 5 year average PE. Projected relative value uses the projected PE instead of the current PE).

Calculation

> **HVR = Current (trailing) PE ⑥ ÷ Average (10 year) PE ⑤**

Example

> **HVR = 23.4 ÷ 23.8 = 98.3%**
> (SSG: Relative value = 23.4 ÷ 24.4 = 95.9%; Projected relative value = 84.7)

C4 Business Model Forecast Earnings. Calculate earnings five years from the last fiscal year using estimates of expenses and shares outstanding.

Calculation

> $$\frac{([1 - \text{Est. tax rate}] \times \text{Forecast sales} \times \text{Est. profit margin}) - \text{Est. adjustments}}{\text{Est. shares outstanding}}$$

Example

> **Forecast EPS = ([1 − .351] x 1395.5 x .303) ÷ 112.6 = $2.44**
> *Can be done in a single, continuous series of calculator entries.*

Forecast High Price. Estimate highest likely price five years from the end of the last full fiscal year reported.

Calculation

Forecast High Price = Forecast high PE x Forecast high EPS

Example

Forecast high price = 27.1 x 2.43 = $65.85

 Forecast Average Price. Estimate price if sold at the average PE five years from last fiscal year.

Calculation

Forecast average price = Forecast average PE x Forecast high EPS

Example

Forecast average price = 21.4 x 2.43 = $52.00

 Forecast Low Price. Estimate of lowest possible price five years from last fiscal year if company produces lowest earnings.

Calculation

Forecast low PE x Forecast low EPS

Example

Forecast low price = 15.7 x 1.37 = $21.51

 Yield-Supported Low Price. The yield-supported low price is low enough that investors will buy the stock primarily for the dividend income. It's similar to NAIC's "Price Dividend will Support."

Calculation (useful only when Yield x High P/E is greater than 35)

$$\text{Yield-supported low price} = \frac{\text{Forecast high price x Current yield}}{\text{Competitive bond yield - 1}}$$

Example

Yield-supported low price = 65.85 x 0.4 ÷ 5.4 = 4.88

(C9) **Price Zoning.** On the NAIC's SSG only, "Buy," "Maybe," and "Sell" zones identify a rough estimate of the status of the current price.

Calculation

Range between forecast high and low prices divided in thirds
"Buy" = Lowest third; "Maybe" = Middle third; "Sell" = Highest third.
Note: It's more useful to Divide into fourths, with "Buy" and "Sell" being the lowest and highest fourths. This always puts the "Buy" range at a 3:1 upside/downside ratio or better (See C10 - Risk Index).

Example

"Buy" = 21.5 – 36.3; "Maybe" = 36.3 – 51.1; "Sell" = 51.1 – 65.9
Better: "Buy" = 21.5 – 32.6; "Maybe" = 32.6 – 54.8; "Sell" = 54.8 – 65.9

C10 **Risk Index.** Risk of loss is expressed as a percentage of the spread between the highest potential price and the lowest. A risk index of twenty-five percent or lower is optimum.

Upside-Downside Ratio (NAIC's SSG only). The upside-downside ratio is the ratio of the dollars to be gained if the stock is sold at the high PE to the dollars to be lost if it is sold at the low PE. Three to one or higher is optimum. (The ratio can range between zero and infinity.)

Calculation

$$\text{Risk index} = \frac{\text{Current price} - \text{Forecast low price}}{\text{Forecast high price} - \text{Forecast low price}} \times 100$$

$$\text{Upside-downside ratio} = \frac{\text{Forecast high price} - \text{Current price}}{\text{Current price} - \text{Forecast low price}}$$

Example

$$\text{Risk index} = \frac{32 - 21.51}{65.85 - 21.51} = \frac{10.49}{44.34} \times 100 = 23.7\%$$

$$\text{Upside-downside ratio} = \frac{65.9 - 32}{32 - 21.5} = \frac{33.9}{10.5} = 3.2$$

C11 **Period for forecast.** Calculate the time between the current month and five years from the end of the most recent fiscal year.

Calculation

(Assuming your data is not more than a year old):

$$\text{Forecast period} = 4 + \frac{\text{Months remaining in current fiscal year}}{12}$$

Example
Period = Dec to May

$$\text{Forecast Period} = 4 + \frac{5}{12} = 4.4$$

C12 **Potential Appreciation.** Estimate compounded growth (or decline) of the stock price between the date of the current price and five years from the end of the most recent fiscal year.

Calculation

PV: Current price   N: Period for forecast **C11**
FV: Forecast high price   Solve for i%

Example
Potential appreciation = PV: 32; FV: 65.85; N: 4.4; i% = 17.8%

C13 **Return.** Calculate the compounded annual return, including both dividends and appreciation, if the stock were purchased at price date and sold five years from the end of the most recent full fiscal year. Total return assumes sale at the forecast high price. **Average return** assumes sale at the forecast average price.

Calculation
Return = Forecast potential yield + Forecast potential appreciation

Example

Total return   = 0.4 + 17.8 = 18.2%
Average return = 0.4 + 11.7 = 12.1%

C14   **Buy Price** (Technamental Stock Study Worksheet only). The buy price is the price at which the risk index would be no more than 25% and the total return would be no less than 14.9%.

Calculation

Choose the lower of two figures:
Price for 25% risk index or Price for 14.9% return.

Price for 25% risk index = $\dfrac{\text{(Forecast low price x 3) + Forecast high price}}{4}$

Price for 14.9% Return:
FV: Forecast High Price; i%: 14.9 - Current yield; N: Forecast Period
Solve for PV

Example

Price for 14.9% return = FV: 65.85; i%: 14.5; N: 4.4; PV = $36.29
Price for 25% Risk Index = ([21.51 x 3] + 65.85) ÷ 4 = 130.38 ÷ 4 = $32.60

Place order at $32.60.

FIGURE A.12 Completed Technamental Stock Study Worksheet (Front)

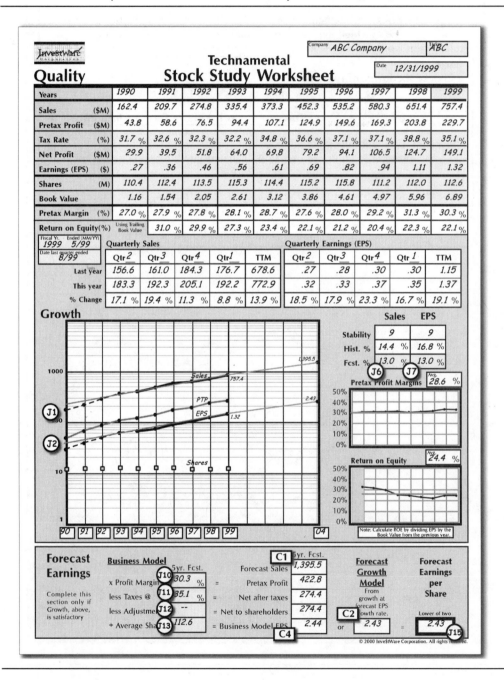

FIGURE A.13   Completed Technamental Stock Study Worksheet (Back)

Value

| Company ABC Company | Ticker ABC |

Earnings	.27	.36	.46	.56	.61	.69	.82	.94	1.11	1.32
High Price	9.7	32.4	30.5	16.5	14.3	19.9	20.6	27.0	41.2	45.8
Low Price	4.9	8.1	13.8	8.4	9.0	13.1	12.5	14.3	23.6	24.6
High P/E (J3)	35.9	90.0	66.3	29.5	23.4	28.8	25.1	28.7	37.1	34.7
Low P/E	18.1	22.5	30.0	15.0	14.8	19.0	15.2	15.2	21.3	18.6
Average P/E	27.0	56.3	48.2	22.3	19.1	23.9	20.2	22.0	29.2	26.7
Dividends	-	-	-	-	-	-	-	.10	.11	.12
Years	1990	1991	1992	1993	1994	1995	1996	1997	1998	1999

P/E Ratio Analysis

Avg. High PE	Avg. Low PE		Current Price	÷	TTM EPS	=	Current PE
30.4	17.2		32.00	÷	1.37	=	23.4

Average of the Historical Average PEs (less outliers) = **Signature PE**   23.8

Current PE ÷ Signature PE = **Historical Value Ratio (HVR)**   98.3%   C3

Forecast High, Low, and Average PEs

Average half or majority of the lowest High PEs = **Forecast High PE**   27.1

Average half or majority of the lowest Low PEs = **Forecast Low PE**   15.7

Average of the Forecast High and Low PEs = **Forecast Avg. PE**   21.4

Reward (compound, annual return from appreciation and yield)

Potential High and Projected Average Price   Latest Dividend: .12   ÷ Current Price Current Yield   0.4 %   C5

Forecast High PE (J4)   27.1   x Forecast High EPS   2.43   = **Potential High** Price: 65.85   C6

Forecast Avg. PE   21.4   x Forecast High EPS   2.43   = **Projected Avg.** Price: 52.00

Return through (M/Y 5th Fiscal Year ends): 5/04   Months from now ÷ 12 = **Period:**   4.4   C11

Appreciation Yield

PV = Current Price; FV = Pot. High Price; N = Period; i% = 17.8 % + 0.4 % = **Total Return**   18.2%   C13   (C12)

PV = Current Price; FV = Proj. Avg.Price; N = Period; i% = 11.7 % + 0.4 % = **Proj. Avg. Return**   12.1 %

Risk (comparison of potential loss to potential gain)

Forecast Low Price

Forecast Low PE x (J8) Forecast Low EPS = Forecast Low   C7

(J5)   15.7   x   1.37   =   21.51

Potential Low

21.51   (J9)

Yield-supported Low Price (Calculate only if Yield x High P/E > 35)

Potential High x Current Yield = Yield-supported Low Price

C8   65.85   x   0.4 %   Comp. Bond Rate - 1   =   4.88

5.4 %

Risk Index

Current Price − Pot. Low

10.49

Pot. High − Pot. Low

44.34

= **Risk Index**   23.7 %   C10

Price Analysis

For desired **Total Return** (14.9%):

FV = Pot. High; i% = 14.9 − Yield; N = Period   PV = **Price for 14.9% Total Return:**   36.29   **Buy Price** C14

For desired **Risk Index** (25%):

3 x Potential Low = 64.53 + Potential High = 130.38 ÷ 4 = **Price for 25% Risk Index:**   32.60   32.60   Lower of two

FIGURE A.14   Completed Stock Selection Guide (Front)

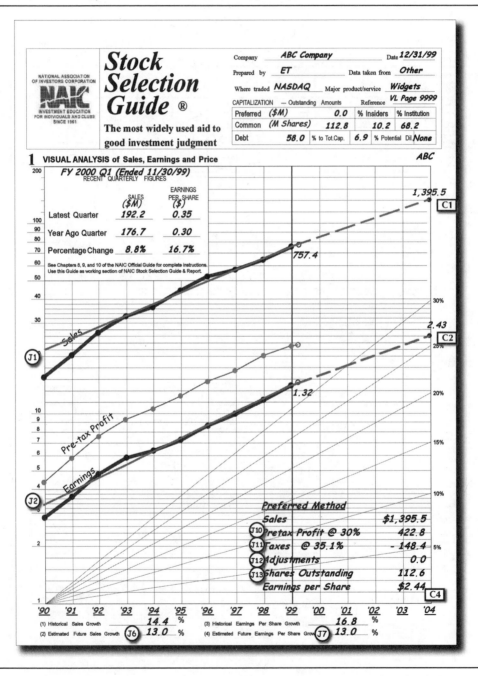

FIGURE A.15   Completed Stock Selection Guide (Back)

2 EVALUATING   MANAGEMENT   Company *ABC Company*   *(ABC)*   *12/31/99*

	1990	1991	1992	1993	1994	1995	1996	1997	1998	1999	LAST 5 YEAR AVG	TREND UP	TREND DOWN
A % Pre-tax Profit on Sales (Net Before Taxes ÷ Sales)	27.0	27.9	27.8	28.1	28.7	27.6	28.0	29.2	31.3	30.3	29.3	UP	
B % Earned on Equity (E/S ÷ Book Value)	23.6	22.7	22.4	21.5	19.6	17.9	17.8	18.9	18.6	19.2	18.5	UP	

3 PRICE-EARNINGS HISTORY **as an indicator of the future**

This shows how stock prices have fluctuated with earnings and dividends. It is a building block for translating earnings into future stock prices.

PRESENT PRICE ___*32.000*___ HIGH THIS YEAR ___*45.800*___ LOW THIS YEAR ___*24.600*___

	Year	A PRICE HIGH	B PRICE LOW	C Earnings Per Share	D Price Earnings Ratio HIGH A ÷ C	E Price Earnings Ratio LOW B ÷ C	F Dividend Per Share	G % Payout F ÷ C X 100	H % High Yield F ÷ B X 100
1	*1995*	19.9	13.1	0.69	28.8	19.0	0.000	0.0	0.0
2	*1996*	20.6	12.5	0.82	25.1	15.2	0.000	0.0	0.0
3	*1997*	27.0	14.3	0.94	28.7	15.2	0.100	10.6	0.7
4	*1998*	41.2	23.6	1.11	37.1	21.3	0.110	9.9	0.5
5	*1999*	45.8	24.6	1.32	34.7	18.6	0.120	9.1	0.5
6	TOTAL		88.1		154.4	89.3		29.6	
7	AVERAGE		17.6		30.9	17.9		9.9	
8	AVERAGE PRICE EARNINGS RATIO			24.4	9 CURRENT PRICE EARNINGS RATIO			23.4	

Proj. P/E [20.67] Based on Next 4 qtr. EPS [1.55]   *Current P/E Based on Last 4 qtr. EPS [1.37]*

4 EVALUATING   RISK and REWARD   over the next 5 years

Assuming one recession and one business boom every 5 years, calculations are made of how high and how low the stock might sell. The upside-downside ratio is the key to evaluating risk and reward.

A HIGH PRICE – NEXT 5 YEARS
Avg. High P/E ~~30.9~~ **27.1** (3D7 as adj.) X Estimate High Earnings/Share ___*2.43*___ = Forecast High Price $ ___*65.9*___ (4A1)

B LOW PRICE – NEXT 5 YEARS
(a) Avg. Low P/E ~~17.9~~ **15.7** (3E7 as adj.) X Estimated Low Earnings/Share ~~*1.32*~~ *1.37* = $ ___*21.5*___
(b) Avg. Low Price of Last 5 Years = ___*17.6*___ (3B7)
(c) Recent Severe Market Low Price = ___*23.6*___
(d) Price Dividend Will Support $\frac{Present\ Divd.}{High\ Yield}$ (H) = $\frac{0.140}{0.007}$ = ___*20.0*___
Selected Estimate Low Price = $ ___*21.5*___ (4B1)

C ZONING
___*65.9*___ (4A1) High Forecast Price Minus ___*21.7*___ (4B1) Low Forecast Price Equals ___*44.4*___ (C) Range. 1/3 of Range = ___*14.8*___ (4CD)

(4C2) Lower 1/3 = (4B1) *21.5* to *36.3* (Buy)
(4C3) Middle 1/3 = *36.3* to *51.1* (Maybe)
(4C4) Upper 1/3 = *51.1* to *65.9* (4A1) (Sell)

Present Market Price of ___*32.00*___ is in the **Buy** (4C5) Range

D UP-SIDE DOWN-SIDE RATIO (Potential Gain vs. Risk of Loss)
$\frac{High\ Price\ (4A1)\ 65.9\ \ Minus\ Present\ Price\ \ 32.00}{Present\ Price\ \ 32.00\ \ Minus\ Low\ Price\ (4B1)\ \ 21.5}$ = $\frac{33.9}{10.5}$ = $\frac{3.2}{(4D)}$ To 1

E PRICE TARGET (Note: This shows the potential market price appreciation over the next five years in simple interest terms.)
$\frac{High\ Price\ (4A1)\ \ 65.9}{Present\ Market\ Price\ \ 32.00}$ = (*2.059*) X 100 = (*205.9*) - 100 = *105.9* (4E) % Appreciation

Relative Value: 95.9% Proj. Relative Value: 84.7%

5 5-YEAR POTENTIAL   This combines price appreciation with dividend yield to get an estimate of total return. It provides a standard for comparing income and growth stocks.

Note: Results are expressed as a simple rate; use the table below to convert to a compound rate.

A Present Full Year's Dividend $ ___*0.140*___ = *0.004* X 100 = *0.4* (5A) Present Yield or % Returned on Purchase Price
Present Price of Stock $ ___*32.000*___

B AVERAGE YIELD OVER NEXT 5 YEARS
Avg. Earnings Per Share Next 5 Years *1.90* X Avg. % Payout (3G7) *9.9* = = *0.6* % (5B)
Present Price $ ___*32.00*___

C ESTIMATED AVERAGE ANNUAL RETURN OVER NEXT FIVE YEARS
5 Year Appreciation Potential (4E) *105.9* / 5 = *21.2* %
Average Yield (5B) = *0.6* %
Average Total Annual Return Over the Next 5 Years (5C) = *21.8* %

Table to Convert From Simple to Compound Rate

Simple Rate 2 4 6 8 10 12 14 16 18 20 **22** 24 26 30 32 34 36 38 40
Compound Rate 2 4 6 8 10 12 14 16 18 20 22 24 *(approx. 15.9%)*

© 1996. National Association of Investors Corporation; 711 West Thirteen Mile Road, Madison Hgts., Michigan 48071

Note: using a financial calculator and a 4.4 year period would produce 18.2% total return.

Resources for the Computer User

Here I'd like to recommend resources that will best serve your needs as you pursue your new investing skills using a computer. I feel good about recommending these resources because I have been involved in developing each of them.

I'll talk about the resources in the order in which the functions they will help you with appear in this book. This is the chronological order in which you will use them. You will find resources for prospecting and data, stock analysis, portfolio management, and portfolio tracking (recordkeeping).

PROSPECTING AND DATA

Stock Investor PRO. The American Association of Individual Investors (AAII), based in Chicago, was founded by its chairman, Jim Cloonan, Ph.D., in 1972, and is capably run by its charismatic president, John Markese, Ph.D. AAII aims to bring unbiased education to its members, regardless of the methodology. The long-term, fundamental, buy-and-hold methodology that NAIC teaches and the technamental derivative that I espouse are but one type of the many disciplines that AAII serves up to its membership.

AAII's screening product, Stock Investor PRO, is a superb screening tool that provides more information than you could possibly use for more than 9,000 publicly traded stocks.

Stock Investor PRO's interface is well thought-out and easy for a novice to master. And adequate help is available. The program includes a series of screens that deliver some excellent prospects for study.

The filters in the Inve$tWare Quality screen that I contributed allow you to list only companies having the following attributes:

- At least five years of public trading
- Most recent 12-months' sales of at least $100 million
- Sales that have been growing steadily for the past five years at a rate better than our benchmark (from a minimum of 7 percent for large companies to at least 12 percent for smaller companies)
- Earnings that have been growing steadily at a rate of at least 15 percent per year for at least the past five years, with a consensus among analysts that growth will continue at that rate
- Profit margins that are as good as or better than the average for the industry and that have not been trending down
- Return on equity that has been as good as or better than the average for the industry

As you can see, this covers the quality bases pretty well. However, more than a cursory screening is required to satisfy you that not only the quality issues but also the value issues are well in hand. In other words, don't even think of substituting Stock Investor PRO's screening process for your own rigorous study of a company before you spend a single penny on its stock!

You can do a quick defensive analysis of your portfolio each month when you receive the updated data because the percent changes in sales, earnings, and profits between the current quarter and the same quarter in the previous year are already calculated for you in Stock Investor Pro.

AAII also offers a less expensive product called Stock Investor. Stick with the higher-priced Stock Investor PRO. It's well worth the difference in price for two reasons. First, you will never want for information if you have the senior version, and you'll never grow out of it. Second, the PRO version ships with data for more than 9,000 companies in a format that can be imported into the analytical software that I describe next. Once you have developed your list of companies to study, you can export a list of those companies' ticker symbols. You can then use that list to automatically import the required data into the analytical software.

Stock Investor PRO includes both the screening database and the data for import and is shipped monthly on a CD-ROM. You can obtain a single month's compact disk—a full-blown version of the product complete with all of the data described in the next section—as a trial subscription for $55 at <www.investware .com/sipro.shtml>. You can go to the same site to check the prices or sign up for a full subscription. The data for Stock Investor PRO is provided by Market Guide, Inc., a division of Multex Corporation.

Other electronic data sources. If you're not ready to pay the price for Stock Investor PRO, the second best electronic source of data is Inve$tWare's Web site, <www.investware.com>. There you can download the data for import for an annual subscription fee, a monthly charge, or a modest charge per company without any subscription commitment.

STOCK ANALYSIS

Technamental investing has been practiced in one fashion or another for five decades, but it boasts only a few software products that deliver all or most of what the practitioner needs. Until recently, the only products available for this purpose were those developed for NAIC or marketed to its membership.

The compact disk included with this book will allow you to get a jump start on your analysis. It is based on the Technamental Stock Study Worksheet described in these pages, and it will allow you to enter the necessary data and see the results. Check out the information inside the back cover for a full description.

The CD will afford you the opportunity to make the necessary decisions and see the results of changing your mind, increasing or decreasing growth rates, and so on. It can serve you very well until you have become familiar with the methodology and want something a little more convenient—especially when it comes to using an electronic data source to save you keystrokes. When you arrive at that point, you'll be ready for one of the software products described below.

Take $tock and Take $tock PRO.   By the time this book is published, Inve$t-Ware expects to have a new version of its original software available. Take $tock, Version 4.0, will be the first technamental analysis product to emerge from beneath the NAIC umbrella to stand on its own.

The Take $tock program departs from the normal NAIC discipline in that it does not require the user to exercise judgment. The program makes decisions on the basis of the data; where there is an option, the software takes the most reasonable, conservative course.

When you enter the ticker symbol for the stock to be studied—and the current price if the program is not in a position to grab it from an open Internet connection—the program will access the necessary data and go through the complete technamental evaluation that this book describes.

The software provides a plain-language analysis of the growth of sales and earnings and the management's report card, making use of historical pricing and conservative earnings estimates to forecast a high and low price and to determine a reasonable price to pay for the stock. This evaluation is presented with enough detail to correlate with the material contained in this book and to help the user understand the basis for the evaluation. The charts provide the user with graphic justification for the analysis made in the textual report.

The downside of the Take $tock program is that it is always conservative. It is no more cautious than I recommend that a new investor should be, but there may come a time when you wish to make your own assessments. The PRO version of

Take $tock (not yet available as this book goes to press) will permit you to take charge of all of the judgment opportunities yourself.

NAIC's Investor's Toolkit and Investor's Toolkit PRO. The Investor's Toolkit, now in its fourth version, is NAIC's "official" stock analysis product and has been NAIC's best-selling product for the decade it's been around.

The beginning Toolkit includes three of the basic NAIC forms: the Stock Checklist, the Stock Selection Guide, and the Stock Comparison Guide. Caution flags tell the user when decisions may have exceeded reason. The depth of instruction, the context-sensitive help, and the documentation that accompanies the program have earned the Toolkit its place as the favorite of NAIC investors. And needless to say, all of these "training wheels" can be disabled when they're no longer needed.

The strong point of the Investor's Toolkit is its user interface, which is easy for the newcomer and equally comfortable for the power user. The Toolkit does everything that NAIC recommends for the stock selection process and follows NAIC protocols to the tee.

The Investor's Toolkit also has very powerful tools for coordinating your Internet activities: conducting research, pricing stocks, buying and selling using your online broker, updating data, and networking with fellow club members or other investment cronies.

The PRO version of the Investor's Toolkit contains everything that the beginning Toolkit has, plus all of the portfolio management tools required to make the most of your holdings.

You can buy the beginning Investor's Toolkit for a reasonable price, and when you become proficient and satisfied with it, you can simply pay for the portfolio management tools and own the PRO. That way there is less risk on the off chance that you are not happy with the program.

PORTFOLIO MANAGEMENT

Investor's Toolkit PRO includes NAIC's portfolio management tools. These include the PERT (Portfolio Evaluation and Review Technique), the Portfolio Trend Report, PERT Worksheets A and B, and the Challenger. The Challenger allows you to see the results of replacing one stock with another, taking into account the cost of taxes and commissions on the trades as well as the forecast return. These helpful tools draw their information from the data that you generate by doing the stock studies with the analysis tools. They help you to enhance your portfolio's performance by making implementation of your offensive and defensive strategies relatively painless.

PORTFOLIO TRACKING (RECORDKEEPING)

Portfolio tracking is satisfying because it tells you just how well you're doing, and it's required by Uncle Sam (who wants to know how well you're doing too).

Both Intuit's Quicken and Microsoft's MS Money are very popular and effective tools for tracking your progress, which is the fun part after you've done all of the tasks required to manage your portfolio. One of these programs is all you need if your activity is reasonably stable and infrequent and if you don't have a lot of reinvestment activity.

If you wish to do a more detailed job of recordkeeping—or need to because you are reinvesting dividends and must provide detailed records to the IRS—you may wish to use Quant IX Portfolio Record Keeper, an excellent program that was developed just for that purpose. Created at NAIC's request by Quant IX, a successful Milwaukee money management firm, this "official" software product was crafted especially for individual investors who want to watch closely the performance of their portfolios. It accomplishes all that you need for reporting to Uncle Sam, and that's not the half of it.

Almost any information you could want about the performance and makeup of your portfolio you can either find in an existing report or create a report that can tell you, and you can see your results graphically. The most recent version is state of the art. The novice can learn to get the most out of it practically over night.

With the software covered here, you should have all you need to take advantage of your computer to perform your investment chores easily, accurately, quickly, and painlessly—and even have a little fun while you do it. Everything you need to do to be a successful investor you can do with a computer in just a few hours a year!

RECOMMENDED READING

Starting and Running a Profitable Investment Club, Thomas E. O'Hara and Kenneth S. Janke, Sr., Random House, 1996. Written by the chairman of the board of NAIC, who is also one of its founders, and by its president and CEO, respectively, this is the definitive book about NAIC's long-standing method and is NAIC's "official guide."

Unfortunately, the book is not as clear as it should be, and it suffers some inconsistencies and blind spots. Nor does it seem to acknowledge that computers are the way of life today. However, the methods never change; this book is the "Bible" of NAIC-type investing.

One Up on Wall Street, Peter Lynch and John Rothchild, Simon and Schuster, 2000; and *Beating the Street,* Peter Lynch and John Rothchild, Fireside, 2000. Both of these books make up in inspiration what they lack in how-to guidance. There's no question about it: Peter Lynch believes that anyone can invest successfully. His generally excellent advice about what to do isn't quite specific enough to be used as a road map by the new investor. However, both books are excellent reads laced with down-to-earth common sense, and they should definitely be a part of every aspiring investor's library. The second chapter of the latter book is a testimonial to NAIC.

Lessons from the Legends of Wall Street: How Warren Buffett, Benjamin Graham, Phil Fisher, T. Row Price, and John Templeton Can Help You Grow Rich, Nikki Ross, CFP, Dearborn, 2000. This book is an excellent summation of the methods used by five of the world's all-time great investors. Nikki Ross has meticulously mined the gold from some of the richest veins in modern times—and has refined it in a way that makes it invaluable for all who want to invest intelligently. She's made required reading for the experienced understandable for the novice. You'll be able to clearly identify the common threads among these legends and see where the basis for technamental investing comes from.

Investor's Web Guide, Douglas Gerlach, Que, 1997; and *Complete Idiot's Guide to Online Investing,* Douglas Gerlach, MacMillan, 1999. Both of these books are excellent guides to the resources available on the World Wide Web. The latter does an excellent job of guiding the new investor down the sidewalks and alleys of Wall Street.

How to Read a Financial Report, 5th ed., John A. Tracy, CPA, John Wiley & Sons, 1999. This is the best book I've found that explains financial reports and the relationships between them. It reads like a children's primer and comes as close to talking about Lucy's Lemonade Stand as any book I've found in the financial press.

The Gorilla Game, Geoffrey Moore, Paul Johnson, and Tom Kippola, HarperCollins, 1998. This book offers some good insights into the world of technology. I recommend that investors stay away from the technology stocks until they have read and understood the premises that these authors propose and have decided to accept them.

The Roaring 2000s, Harry Dent, Touchstone, 1999. The book presents an optimistic view of this decade, offering a plausible explanation for what we've seen so far and an exciting vision of the changing world of American business and the global economy.

Net Profit, Peter Cohan, Jossey-Bass, 1999. Whatever combinations of education and experience Peter Cohan has accumulated certainly have played in concert to produce this book. Cohan clearly and intelligently dissects the wild and wooly world of Internet business. In this complex and misunderstood field, Cohan has done the impossible—stepping into the shoes of the investor, the e-commerce businessperson, and the non-e-commerce businessperson to make sense of this recondite world from the perspective of each—and in the process has produced a valuable resource for each. A must-read for anyone who thinks that the dot-coms are the key to the kingdom.

INDEX

USING THE CD-ROM

The CD-ROM that comes with this book is intended to be a fun companion to the text that will help you get the most out of it. Simply insert the CD into your drive and within 10 or 15 seconds it should launch on its own. From there, it is self-explanatory. (If it doesn't launch, select the CD-ROM drive in "My Computer" on your desktop, right-click on the icon, and then select "Auto Play" from the displayed menu.)

The software is divided into three significant parts: (1) a refresher quiz for each chapter, (2) a section to assist you in finding the necessary information on financial statements or the *Value Line Survey* page, and (3) a stock analysis section.

Take the test. Consisting of anywhere from five to a dozen questions for each chapter, you may select this option and quiz yourself about what you've read. This will reinforce the concepts and help you see what you might have missed. It's an interactive lesson that will tell you the right answer and explain it. I suggest that you take the short quiz after finishing each chapter.

Deal with data. This section will be of greatest value to you after you have studied Chapter 6, which discusses and defines in simple terms what data you will need to use for your stock analysis. The software will ask you to find the essential data wherever you can. The two most readily available sources are financial statements, which companies are generally pleased to provide, and the *Value Line Survey*, which you can obtain in most libraries. The software will let you know when you have produced the wrong or right answer and help you to locate the data if you don't know where to look.

Analyze a company. Starting with Chapter 7, you will take all the steps necessary to analyze a stock, using ABC Company, a fictional company whose data are very real. You may import the data for ABC Company—or enter the data yourself from a copy of a *Value Line Survey* that's provided—and follow along with the text.

When you have completed the study of ABC Company, you may then import the data for any of 30-odd other companies from whose data you can learn to apply the things you've learned. (These companies are included to show you good and bad investment candidates and not to suggest the purchase of these stocks. The data provided may be out of date and prices out of any reasonable range.) This will give you enough practical experience to be ready to do stock studies yourself. Experiment with different prices to see the effect on the result; for example, try the buy price for each.

You can also use this software to analyze stocks of your own choosing for which you have obtained the necessary data.

Investor's Toolkit demo. On this disk, you will also find a demo copy of NAIC's Investor's Toolkit software, which you can install and use for 30 days as a full-blown program before it restricts you from doing essential tasks like printing, saving, or importing and exporting data. If you like the demo and wish to order the software, you can do so at <www.investware.com>. I suggest you hold off installing the demo until you have become thoroughly familiar with the software associated with *Take Stock*. That way you'll be able to understand and get the most out of the Investor's Toolkit before it becomes restricted.

I hope you will enjoy using the software we've created for you and will see just how easy it is to make educated decisions about investing in common stocks on your own. It is also my wish that you will use the software to enrich both your learning and your bank account.